Using Psychoanalytic Techniques to Transform the Attachment Relationship to God

Using Psychoanalytic Techniques to Transform the Attachment Relationship to God demonstrates how clinicians can use Attachment-Informed Psychotherapy (AIP) to enhance clients' understanding of their relationship to God and significant others.

Geoff Goodman discusses four distinct attachment relationships to the God of personal spiritual experience and explains the implications for working with clients in psychotherapy. By asking how therapists can work through clients' attachment relationship to God as a displacement of their attachment relationships to parents, and how therapists can work through clients' attachment relationships to parents as a displacement of their attachment relationship to God, this book provides unique insight into the therapeutic process. Goodman's objective is to enable clinicians to transform these attachment relationships, restoring wholeness and unity—a crucial treatment goal of AIP.

This book will be a valuable resource for psychoanalysts, psychotherapists, marriage and family therapists, and pastoral counsellors in practice and in training.

Geoff Goodman is Professor of Psychiatry and Behavioral Sciences in the Emory University School of Medicine and Associate Professor of Psychology and Spiritual Care in the Emory University Candler School of Theology in Atlanta, Georgia, USA. He holds board certifications in clinical psychology and psychoanalysis from the American Board of Professional Psychology.

Using Psychoanalytic Techniques to Transform the Attachment Relationship to God

Our Refuge and Strength

Geoff Goodman

Routledge
Taylor & Francis Group

LONDON AND NEW YORK

Designed cover image: Kauernde Frau mit Kind in Schob, 1916, in Käthe Kollwitz and Fritz Boettger, Handzeichnungen in originalgetreuen Wiedergaben. Dresden: E. Richter, 1920. F. 741.943 K83H, Architecture and Art Library, University of Illinois at Urbana-Champaign

First published 2025
by Routledge
4 Park Square, Milton Park, Abingdon, Oxon OX14 4RN

and by Routledge
605 Third Avenue, New York, NY 10158

Routledge is an imprint of the Taylor & Francis Group, an informa business

British Library Cataloguing-in-Publication Data
A catalogue record for this book is available from the British Library

ISBN: 9781032913711 (hbk)
ISBN: 9781032913704 (pbk)
ISBN: 9781003562924 (ebk)

DOI: 10.4324/9781003562924

Typeset in Times New Roman
by Newgen Publishing UK

To Carlyn Chantal Dent Goodman
Once riding on Daddy's shoulders
Now climbing up the canyon boulders
Fly away, my butterfly
Fly to the tip-top of the sky

Contents

Acknowledgments

I have often read the conventional wisdom, "Don't make your hobby your job." By writing this book, I openly defied this advice. I have always been passionate about the integration of psychology and spirituality. My first journal article, written in graduate school, explored the meaning of empathy for Carl Rogers, Heinz Kohut, and Jesus. As a graduate student, I took as many courses related to psychology and spirituality as I could fit into my schedule. Yet I never pursued this interdisciplinary area as one of my research interests, perhaps due to my own ambivalence about the existence of a Higher Power. Now, having written this book, I can now claim that making my hobby my job has only inspired me to write more about the integration of psychology and spirituality. It has helped that my relationship with my Higher Power is now on firmer ground.

I want to thank my wife, Valeda Dent, who was present during this book's inception and who provided me with library books, journal articles, and PowerPoint reproduction of Figure 4.1, as well as her incisive editing skill. Her cheerleading was necessary for the writing process. Uli Guthrie edited the entire book and made me sound almost like a professional writer. Susannah Frearson and Saloni Singhania and Susan Dunsmore at Routledge took a chance on me and on this unusual subject matter, and I am grateful to them for valuing this work. My student, Chenyu Li, assisted me with sorting out some of the references. Emory University librarian Kim Collins and John Morgenstern assisted me with obtaining the rights to use the powerful book cover by Käthe Kollwitz.

Dean Jan Love at the Candler School of Theology at Emory University took a chance on hiring someone with no formal theology degree. I feel so grateful that she did, and I hope she feels the same way. My mentor at the Candler School of Theology, Ian McFarland, provided me with the encouragement I needed to complete this book. I also want to thank my Emory colleagues John Snarey, Wendy Jacobson, and Andy Miller for believing in me and listening to me pitch some of my ideas. First Presbyterian Church of Atlanta, including pastors Tony and Katie Sundermeier, Rob Sparks, and Barry Gaeddert, have provided me every week with spiritual resources and support.

I also want to thank the people whose work inspired the ideas contained in this book. As a graduate student at Columbia University in the fall of 1985, Larry Aber introduced me to attachment theory and research, which resulted in a lifelong love affair with studying the development of relationships of all kinds. The following semester, in Ann Belford Ulanov's Union Theological Seminary course, Religion and the Unconscious, I read the classic *Birth of the Living God* by Ana-Maria Rizzuto, which blew my mind. Rizzuto's book is where my psychological understanding of human relationships to God began. My book is merely an extension and application of her work. Pehr Granqvist, especially through his *Attachment in Religion and Spirituality*, has mentored me in applying attachment theory to the development of human relationships to God. I have appreciated our e-mail correspondence over the past couple of years. I also want to acknowledge Russell Siler Jones and Wayne Gustafson for their supervision in spiritually integrated psychotherapy, and James Griffith and Kenneth Pargament for their practical insights in using spiritual and religious patient material in psychotherapy sessions. I appreciate their distinctive approaches to working with patients who discuss spiritual issues, either explicitly or implicitly. I would be remiss if I neglected to acknowledge the significant influence of my instructors and supervisors during psychoanalytic training, as well as my personal psychoanalyst, all of whom helped me to become the certified psychoanalyst that I am today.

I am most grateful for the support that my institution has shown me since joining the Emory University faculty two years ago. The Emory University Center for Faculty Development and Excellence sent me on a writing retreat to complete this book.

I also want to express gratitude to Marvin Markowitz, Andy Phillips, and Juarlyn Gaiter for their personal support of me during the writing process. All my patients have taught me how to be a more effective therapist and a better version of myself.

Finally, I want to thank my 11-year-old daughter, Carlyn, to whom this book is dedicated, for making me stay forever young.

Note on the Text

I wrote this book, *Using Psychoanalytic Techniques to Transform the Attachment Relationship to God: Our Refuge and Strength,* while I was writing my other book, *Practical Applications of Transforming the Attachment Relationship to God: Using Attachment-Informed Psychotherapy.* Both books address humans' attachment relationships to God and their transformation by using Attachment-Informed Psychotherapy (AIP). While this book is more theoretically oriented, the second book is more practically oriented. I strongly recommend that the reader read both books to optimize their learning experience. Because theory and practice go hand in hand, these two books complement each other.

Chapter 1

Introduction

Intellectual Influences on This Book

In addition to the personal familial and spiritual experiences that have influenced my thinking, I want to underscore the major intellectual influences that helped me to write this book. In graduate school, I read the chapter by Main, Kaplan, and Cassidy (Main et al., 1985) seminal monograph chapter, "Security in Infancy, Childhood, and Adulthood: A Move to the Level of Representation." Main and her colleagues extended attachment theory beyond infancy. Until then, attachment theory had focused on infant behaviors in the presence of caregivers that ensure the infant's protection. Now, attachment theory extends to adulthood and the development of internalized mental representations of caregivers that provide a sense of security in place of seeking physical proximity and maintaining physical contact with caregivers. The breakthrough was the development of an instrument designed to assess these attachment-related mental representations, which she called the Adult Attachment Interview. Three years later, I read the classic by Ana-Maria Rizzuto (Rizzuto, 1979), *The Birth of the Living God*, which persuaded me that persons form mental images of God and that these God images consist of bits and pieces of parental mental representations. She also argued that even young children form images of God that often have virtually nothing to do with the God of the religion of their family. In her words, "No child arrives at 'the house of God' without his pet God under his arm" (p. 8). Rizzuto quoted from extensive interviews of four participants to show that perceptions of parents from early childhood comprise this pet God and that vestiges of this pet God persist into adulthood, regardless of the amount of religious training the person has had.

Despite this book's profound influence on my thinking, I found myself wondering whether this influence was bidirectional. In other words, could one's mental representation of God also influence parental images? Rizzuto did not seem to consider this possibility, preferring to examine the question from only one direction. Much later, as a professor in a clinical psychology doctoral program, I encountered Kirkpatrick's work (Kirkpatrick, 1999, 2005; Kirkpatrick & Shaver, 1990) and even later, Granqvist's work (Granqvist, 2020; Granqvist & Kirkpatrick, 2018) on understanding the correspondence and compensation between a person's

DOI: 10.4324/9781003562924-1

attachment relationship to God and their attachment relationship to their parents. It was intriguing to think of God as a secure base and safe haven for humans—key features of any human attachment relationship. According to Granqvist and Kirkpatrick (2018), the God representation can be an idealized parental representation or a compensation for an insecure parental representation. These authors also speculated that a person's attachment relationship to God "may aid in reparation of maladaptive IWMs [internal working models], for example, following loss of and/or experiences of having been insensitively cared for by other Afs [attachment figures]" (p. 932). Thus, a transformation in a person's attachment relationship to God (a focus of attachment-informed psychotherapy [AIP]; see Chapters 4–6) has the potential to facilitate a transformation in their attachment relationships to the emotionally significant others in their life, including parents and partners.

I enjoyed the book by Kenneth Pargament (Pargament, 2011), *Spiritually Integrated Psychotherapy*, because he was the first author I read who explicitly made room for the influence of spirituality on human relationships, even though he did not use the language of attachment theory. In my autobiographical narrative (see Goodman, 2025, Chapter 1), I indicated that my secure attachment relationship to God compensated over the years for my insecure attachment relationship to my mother; however, this past year, my secure attachment relationship to God seemingly influenced a shift in my attitude toward my mother; these attachment relationships—now both secure—correspond to each other rather than one compensating for the other.

My Perspective in Writing this Book

I want to make the reader aware of all the conscious biases and presuppositions that inevitably influenced the ideas and insights I write about in this book. On a macro level, in no particular order, race, ethnicity, culture, politics, gender, social class, and religious background shape some of these biases and presuppositions. On a micro level, my rural evangelical Christian upbringing, early childhood relationships to members of my family of origin, personality traits (both genetically inherited and developed over time in my environment), and attachment patterns also determine how I think about this subject matter and which conclusions I draw from my understanding of this field. I hope that the reader will forgive me for these limitations; however, I also view my perspective as worthy of consideration, not because I present the only right perspective but because I present a coherent perspective. There are other coherent perspectives that I would like to hear from on this topic.

Creating a Space for Spirituality in Human Motivation

Various authors (e.g., Goodman, 2014; Lichtenberg, 1989) have discussed the multiplicity of neurological systems motivating human behavior. Freud (1900, 1920) posited sexuality and aggression as the two primary behavioral systems of human motivation. John Bowlby (1982) later suggested that attachment—the emotional bond that forms between infants and their caregivers and observed when the infant experiences danger, pain, or separation—serves as a potent motivational system of behavior and as a template for subsequent intimate relationships, ultimately becoming a "primary mode of relatedness" (Slade, 1999, p. 588). Other motivational systems such as affiliation and dominance also exert their influence on human behavior. Can we also create a space for spirituality as a motivational system of behavior, its influence intertwined with the influence of other motivational systems?

This book argues that every human being experiences a yearning and a search for the sacred (Johnson & Boyatzis, 2006; Pargament, 2011). The sacred includes anything of ultimate importance, conveying a profound sense of transcendence, boundlessness, or the eternal. Humans often focus these qualities on a Higher Power or Supreme Being. Believing in Someone or Something greater than oneself is a natural human quality (Barrett, 2012), independent of whether a Someone or Something greater than oneself actually exists. Thus, according to Pargament (2011), "Everyone is a spiritual being" because "spirituality is, in short, a critical and distinctive dimension of human motivation" (p. 60). Jesus alludes to this universality of spirituality in humanity: "The kingdom of God is within you" (Luke 17:21; NIV, 1978). Thus, spirituality enters the therapy office, regardless of whether the therapist personally believes in spirituality.

Fortunately, even some nonreligious therapists have been shown to help their patients with spiritual struggles (Propst et al., 1992)—even outperforming some religiously inclined therapists—if they respect their patients' spirituality by practicing openness, sensitivity, and a willingness to learn about their patients' spiritual lives. If spirituality is a natural part of human existence, then both spiritual and nonspiritual therapists need to know how to address spirituality in psychotherapy. This book articulates one model for addressing spirituality in psychotherapy—Attachment-Informed Psychotherapy (AIP).

Relationship Between Spiritual and Attachment Motivational Systems

I discuss two of the many motivational systems of human behavior—attachment and spirituality—and demonstrate how they mutually influence each other during the course of life. The hallmarks of infant attachment behavior include seeking proximity and maintaining contact with a caregiver during experiences of danger, pain, or separation. When the caregiver is physically unavailable, the infant typically searches for the caregiver to reestablish contact (Ainsworth et al., 1978). Humans also search for the sacred in their lives—for many, a Higher Power to Whom they seek proximity and from Whom they seek comfort (Pargament, 2011).

Viewed from this angle, spirituality as a motivational system closely resembles attachment as a motivational system (see Chapter 4). This observation begs the question: what is the relationship between spirituality and attachment? Carter and Narramore (1979) articulate four models of integration between theology and psychology. Based on their models, four relationships between spirituality and attachment are possible: (1) spirituality and attachment are independently operating constructs that have nothing to do with each other; (2) spirituality subsumes attachment as a motivational system; (3) attachment subsumes spirituality as a motivational system; and (4) spirituality and attachment are distinct motivational systems that become intertwined over time, mutually influencing each other. Let me take each of these relationships in turn.

In the first scenario, spirituality and attachment operate on different planes of existence and therefore have no interaction. Each motivational system stays in its own lane. If a person has a spiritual problem, they go to the clergy; if a person has an attachment problem, they go to a mental health professional. As we have seen, however, seeking proximity and maintaining contact—hallmarks of attachment behavior—also characterize spiritual behavior. Granqvist (2020) summarizes the literature that demonstrates that persons use prayer—communication with a Higher Power—to seek proximity and maintain contact with that Higher Power. Meditation, attendance at places of worship, and communing with nature are prime examples of additional behaviors that tend to make persons feel closer to God. This scenario is therefore highly problematic because both spiritual and attachment behaviors phenomenologically and functionally seem to overlap during experiences of danger, pain, or separation.

In the second scenario, attachment is simply an expression of spirituality (see also May, 1982). When we attach to our caregivers and partners, our spiritual needs are thus gratified. This scenario is problematic, however, because some attachment relationships can cause significant emotional damage, such as intimate partner violence. Most of us would agree that seeking proximity and maintaining contact with a violent intimate partner would not be meeting the person's spiritual needs, whereas attachment could account for this relationship because the person's imagined alternative to violence—abandonment—represents a far worse outcome of being utterly alone.

In the third scenario, spirituality is simply an expression of attachment. In other words, seeking proximity to and maintaining contact with a Higher Power are merely gestures to gratify a person's attachment needs. This scenario is problematic, however, because many persons feel truly motivated to search for the sacred in their lives, which transcends any earthly motivation such as attachment. Reducing spirituality to a motivational system designed to provide protection to immature mammalian offspring (Bowlby, 1982) seems to trivialize spirituality and humans' natural yearning for the sacred. Identifying spirituality as an "irreducible aspect of human nature," Pargament (2011) writes, "Any psychology of human behavior remains incomplete without an appreciation for the motivation to know and connect to the sacred" (p. 343).

In the fourth scenario, spirituality and attachment exist independently of each other yet become intertwined over time, mutually influencing each other. In other words, both spirituality and attachment are equally respected as motivational systems of human behavior, and each has a voice in how the other expresses itself. In Chapter 3, I discuss how the quality of a person's attachment relationship to the caregivers during childhood and the quality of their attachment relationship to a Higher Power are related to each other. This discussion demonstrates exactly how these two motivational systems mutually influence each other.

I would add a corollary to this fourth, intertwined relationship between the spirituality and attachment motivational systems, which borrows from the second scenario of spirituality subsuming attachment. Perhaps infants express their inchoate spiritual needs to their caregivers, who are consistently responsive by providing comfort and security (or are inconsistently responsive or consistently unresponsive; see Chapter 2). Infants' spiritual needs for security and comfort are diverted to caregivers and become part of the attachment system, a distinct motivational system from spirituality. According to Pargament (2011), "Mother and father are the child's first divine-like figures" (p. 65).

Unfortunately, caregivers provide imperfect emotional responses to these spiritual needs presented by their infants, and these divine-like qualities become deflated as caregivers misattune to their infants. Detailed observations of mother-infant interactions at 3, 6, and 9 months revealed that infants and mothers are in "mismatched" states 70% of the time (Gianino & Tronick, 1985; Tronick et al., 1986), suggesting that infants have plenty of opportunities to feel rejected and inconsistently cared for even with the most empathic, emotionally attuned (Stern, 1985) mothers. Regardless of whether the attachment motivational system originates in the spiritual motivational system, by the time infants reach 12 months of age, they have developed an attachment relationship to their caregivers. From this point in development, the quality of these attachment relationships to the caregivers influences the quality of the attachment relationship to the sacred and vice versa. Psychotherapy can leverage these mutual influences in facilitating patients' greater emotional and spiritual well-being. For the spiritually grounded patient, perhaps the therapeutic goal would be to relinquish the fulfillment of attachment needs related to caregivers and other significant persons and reclaim these needs for the fulfillment of the person's spirituality. Jesus alludes to this detachment from significant others as central to becoming a disciple: "If anyone comes to me and does not hate father and mother, wife and children, brothers and sisters—yes, even their own life—such a person cannot be my disciple" (Luke 14:26; NIV, 1978).

In this scenario, I am assuming the primacy of the spiritual motivational system, with the attachment motivational system splitting off and following its own, secondary developmental trajectory. These two motivational systems, however, never function independently from each other. Romantic relationships also contain the search for the sacred, while spiritual relationships also contain the search for protection from danger. This book focuses on how attachment relationships to caregivers and to a Higher Power mutually influence each other rather than on how spiritual needs expressed within both romantic relationships and a relationship to a

Higher Power mutually influence each other. This idea, however, would make for its own intriguing book (e.g., May, 1982).

God Is an Attachment Figure

I view God as an attachment figure (see Chapter 3). My God might be the God of Christianity, but all three Western, so-called Abrahamic religions (i.e., Judaism, Christianity, Islam) worship a monotheistic God Who cares for creation, including human beings. In the sacred texts of these three religions, God is represented as a Caregiver. Attachment theory is more difficult to apply to pantheistic religions because, putting it simplistically, God is in everything, indeed, *is* everything; thus, forming an attachment relationship to a divine Being outside oneself is not necessarily possible. On the other hand, taking Hinduism and Buddhism as examples of popular Eastern religions, both Krishna (Dharma, 2020) and Buddha (Bodhi, 2005) are human beings worshipped as deities. Thus, even in some Eastern religions, the opportunity exists to establish and maintain an attachment relationship to a divine Being. The contents of this book, therefore, can apply to persons coming from a wide variety of religious and spiritual backgrounds despite its author's current location within the progressive Christian tradition.

Belief in a Higher Power Is Our Default Setting

The developmental psychologist Justin Barrett (2012) reviewed and summarized a treasure trove of compelling data suggesting that even young children are hard-wired to believe in an omnipotent, omniscient Being that supersedes even the powers of their own parents. For example, Barrett reported on research studies that feature the false-belief task, an experimental paradigm that reveals whether a child has achieved the cognitive milestone that the contents of others' minds do not necessarily correspond to the contents of one's own mind. Even after children discover the limitations of another person's beliefs (usually at age 4), they nevertheless recognize that God has no such limitations when asked what God knows about a situation that God was not physically present to observe. Thus, according to Barrett, belief in God is a natural process that transcends even culture and religious background (e.g., these experiments were replicated even with Yukatek Maya children living in rural villages in southeastern Mexico, who believe in many gods; Knight et al., 2004).

In his famous reply to the anonymous author of the atheistic essay, "Treatise of the Three Impostors" (Moses, Jesus, Mohammed), Voltaire (1769/1919) wrote, "If God did not exist, it would be necessary to invent Him" (p. 231). The thesis by Barrett (Barrett, 2012) that belief in a Higher Power is our default setting does not discount the possibility that no Higher Power exists. In Christian families in the West, it is "natural" for children to believe in the Easter bunny, when no such bunny exists. Voltaire was highlighting the profound need for persons to believe in a Higher Power, perhaps to cope with our awareness of our own mortality or to endure the painful emotions associated with suffering and loss—independent of this Higher Power's existence. If Voltaire's aphorism is true, then helping a person to restore their belief in a cosmic connection to the God of the universe to its default "factory" setting might motivate this person to trust that God is a "stronger and/or wiser" (Bowlby, 1988, p. 120) divine Being Who at least has the capacity to help them overcome their suffering and conflict.

The Problem of Atheism

Given the previous discussion that belief in God is a natural phenomenon and that, regardless of God's existence, we need God to help us cope with our mortality, suffering, and loss, then what do we do with the problem of atheism? An atheist, by definition, denies the existence of God and therefore denies an attachment relationship to God. If belief in God is hard-wired into our early maturational development (see empirical reviews by Granqvist, 2014; Richert & Granqvist, 2013), then how does a person resist this natural tendency to believe? The question of belief or lack of belief in God is not the same question as whether God exists or does not exist. As we shall see in Chapter 3, a person who has developed a secure attachment relationship to parents is likely also to have a secure attachment relationship to God; conversely, a person who has developed an insecure attachment relationship to parents is likely also to have an insecure attachment relationship to God (unless unbearable stressors are present). Research (see Granqvist, 2020) demonstrates that a person who has developed an insecure attachment relationship to parents is more likely to have a corresponding insecure attachment relationship to God or a nonexistent attachment relationship to God (see also Chapter 2). Thus, although an insecure attachment relationship to parents might be influencing one's choice to be an atheist, it could also be the case that God does not in fact exist. Thus, regardless of the verity of a belief in atheism, unconscious factors are undoubtedly influencing a belief in atheism.

The same is true of agnosticism and deism. As my autobiographical narrative illustrates (see Goodman, 2025, Chapter 1), my 22-year-long belief in agnosticism coincided with the collapse of my relationship to my father. I shifted from a belief in a personal relationship to God to grave doubts about this belief in a personal relationship, which paralleled what was going on between my father and me. Deism is the belief that God exists but occupies a remote space, separate from and uninvolved with creation. Although I know of no empirical studies concerning persons holding deistic beliefs, it is not a stretch to imagine that in such persons, anxious-avoidant attachment relationships to parents during childhood would predominate (see Chapter 2). Thus, early attachment relationships have the (often unconscious) power to motivate belief or lack of belief in God as well as characteristics of the very nature of God (e.g., remote and uninvolved vs. immanent in human affairs).

Spirituality in Psychotherapy

If spirituality is inherently a quintessential human experience, and if psychotherapy is a process of understanding human experience in relationship to a wiser person, then it follows that spirituality would fall under the purview of psychotherapy. Furthermore, spirituality must be present in psychotherapy, even if only implicitly. Therapists who refuse to recognize spirituality in their work do their patients a disservice and perhaps even impede their progress toward therapeutic goals. Research suggests that spiritual struggles and psychiatric symptoms are associated with each other (Exline & Rose, 2005; Fitchett et al., 2004; Pargament et al., 2005; Stauner et al., 2016; Yanni, 2003). Do spiritual struggles cause psychiatric symptoms or vice versa? They probably mutually influence each other. In one study, spiritual struggles, expressed as punishment from God, predicted anxiety and depression among patients experiencing terminal lung disease, even after controlling for non-religious coping ability (Burker et al., 2005). Prediction implies causation, but it is impossible to conclude with confidence that spiritual struggles cause psychiatric symptoms.

To demonstrate causation, researchers would need to randomly assign a large sample of persons to two groups, one of which is exposed to and develops spiritual struggles. Later, persons in both groups would complete measures of depression and anxiety. If spiritual struggles cause psychiatric symptoms, we would expect the group exposed to spiritual struggles to experience higher levels of depression and anxiety than the nonexposed group. Of course, such a study would not only be unethical but also impossible to conduct. How would a researcher induce spiritual struggles in participants? Thus, researchers must show how spiritual struggles predict rather than cause psychiatric symptoms.

One compelling research design that points in the direction of causation is known as a longitudinal design, where researchers assess a sample at an initial time point and then follow up with this sample years later to find out what happened to them. For example, researchers assessed first-year college students for levels of self-esteem, depression, and anxiety and then reassessed them in their third year for levels of spiritual struggles as well as these same symptoms. Even after adjusting for levels of self-esteem, depression, and anxiety from their first year, the third-year students with higher levels of spiritual struggles experienced higher levels of psychiatric symptoms (Bryant & Astin, 2008). In a study of an African American sample, researchers assessed levels of spiritual struggles and psychiatric symptoms at one time point and again two and a half years later. After adjusting for levels of psychiatric symptoms measured at the first assessment, the participants with higher levels of spiritual struggles were experiencing higher levels of psychiatric symptoms than the participants with lower levels of spiritual struggles two and a half years later (Park et al., 2018). After conducting an exhaustive literature review, Pargament and Exline (2022) conclude: "Spiritual struggles may lead to greater distress and disorientation" (p. 63). If spiritual struggles can lead to patient distress, why would therapists *not* address spirituality in therapy?

Psychiatric symptoms assessed at an initial time point can also predict spiritual struggles at a later time point. For example, in a sample of adolescents diagnosed with either cystic fibrosis or diabetes, depression predicted spiritual struggles in both groups two years later (Reynolds et al., 2014). Similarly, in a sample of African Americans who had experienced the death of a loved one to homicide, more severe grief reactions predicted spiritual struggles six months later (Neimeyer & Burke, 2011). All these studies suggest that spiritual struggles both influence and are influenced by psychiatric symptoms. The evidence is clear that the therapist's awareness of patients' spirituality and therapeutic interventions that address this spirituality falls within the purview of the conduct of psychotherapy.

If an explicit or implicit discussion of spirituality belongs in the therapeutic conversations between therapist and patient, then how can the therapist facilitate spiritual healing to patients who have experienced spiritual struggles? Pargament (2011) suggests three sacred qualities of the therapeutic relationship—grace, deep acceptance, and reassuring presence—that can help to heal these spiritual struggles, which, as we have seen, are also associated with psychiatric symptoms. Grace and deep acceptance suggest closely related interventions in the sense that the therapist demonstrates to the patient through careful listening, a nonjudgmental attitude, and nonreactivity an unconditional acceptance of the patient's entire being. Reassuring presence suggests that the therapist will not avert their gaze or withdraw their acceptance but instead bear witness to the patient's pain, even when being with the patient might be challenging.

Pargament (2011) points out that these three sacred qualities of the therapeutic relationship do not exclude the importance of gently confronting patients when needed. In fact, using these sacred qualities to intervene in a patient's life could be disorienting to a patient unfamiliar with them. For example, a patient diagnosed with histrionic personality disorder might interpret reflective listening, empathy, genuineness, and unconditional positive regard (Rogers, 1957) as invitations of seduction, while the patient diagnosed with narcissistic personality disorder might interpret these sacred qualities as condescending. A patient diagnosed with paranoid personality disorder might interpret them as a preparation for exploitation. Thus, the therapist must consider the patient's personality organization and adjust their interventions accordingly—even the sacred ones.

In Chapters 4, 5 and 6, I discuss the concept of providing a "gentle challenge" (Dozier, 2003, p. 254) to patients based on the quality of their attachment relationships, specifically, the type of attachment insecurity that they manifest. This gentle challenge might manifest itself in the level of therapist activity or boundary maintenance. Simply applying the sacred qualities of Pargament (Pargament, 2011) to patients indiscriminately would fail to produce the desired result. Considering sacred text, Jesus selected his intervention strategy based on the person he encountered rather than on a boilerplate array of sacred qualities. In the story of the Samaritan woman at the well (John 4:4–30; NIV, 1978), Jesus reveals that He is the Messiah to her without making any demands on her, whereas in the story of the rich young ruler (Matthew 19:16–24; Mark 10:17–25; Luke 18:18–25; NIV, 1978),

Jesus demands that this ruler sell all his possessions as a condition of discipleship. These are two different persons walking two different spiritual journeys, and Jesus responds to them according to their differences. Jesus treated no two persons alike (see also Goodman, 1991).

As mentioned earlier, research (Propst et al., 1992) suggests that it is unnecessary for a therapist to believe in a Higher Power or cultivate a spiritual life to conduct effective therapy. If the therapist treats the patient's spirituality with deep respect and curiosity, then healing can occur. In fact, spiritually integrated psychotherapy researchers have developed treatment manuals articulating therapeutic interventions that any spiritually respectful, curious therapist can use to treat their patients. For example, Solace for the Soul (Murray-Swank & Pargament, 2005), designed to treat sexually abused women, and Re-Creating Your Life (Cole & Pargament, 1998), designed to treat persons diagnosed with serious mental illness, explicitly incorporate spirituality into psychotherapy sessions. Still other therapists use existing brand-name treatment models such as psychodynamic therapy (PDT) or cognitive-behavioral therapy (CBT) to treat spiritually curious or spiritually grounded patients (see Goodman, 2025).

This book articulates one treatment model for addressing spirituality in psychotherapy—AIP. AIP assumes that both patients and therapists have mental images of a Higher Power and mental images of the relationship to a Higher Power. These mental images, or mental representations, profoundly influence a person's spiritual and psychological lives, including spiritual practices (or absence of practices) and psychiatric symptoms. Theologian Ann Belford Ulanov writes: "Our God-images are as idiosyncratically personal as is our handwriting, our breathing, or our walking" (Ulanov, 2001, p. 96). While these mental representations are as unique as snowflakes, we can nevertheless detect patterns of mental representations that certain groups of persons have in common. Just as all snowflakes are geometrically configured to have six sides, all persons who belong to a particular group share a certain "mode of primary relatedness" (Slade, 1999, p. 588) directly related to the specific quality of these persons' attachment relationships to their caregivers during childhood.

Studying these commonalities among early attachment relationships to caregivers, Ainsworth and her colleagues (1978) identified three attachment patterns (i.e., secure, anxious-resistant, anxious-avoidant) that seem to follow a developmental trajectory into adulthood (Waters et al., 2000). Main and Solomon (1986, 1990) later identified a fourth attachment pattern (i.e., disorganized/disoriented). Together, these four attachment patterns represent all the types of attachment relationships thus far identified throughout the world (Mesman et al., 2018; see Chapter 2). Although persons' mental representations of their attachment relationship to a Higher Power are unique, we can identify certain commonalities across these unique mental representations. Thus, we can implement intervention strategies that address the identifying characteristics of each of these groups rather than apply a set of boilerplate interventions to all patients or, on the other hand, make continual attempts to reinvent the wheel by creating a novel set of unique interventions for each patient (see Chapter 6).

These attachment patterns, developed in relationship to our caregivers during the earliest months of our lives, can increase or decrease our risk of developing psychopathology later in life. The quality of these early attachment relationships can expose us to or protect us from psychiatric symptoms. Specifically, secure attachment relationships can act as a buffer from adverse life events that might otherwise cause psychiatric symptoms (e.g., anxiety, depression), whereas insecure attachment relationships (i.e., anxious-resistant, anxious-avoidant, disorganized/ disoriented) can exacerbate our vulnerability to such symptoms (for a summary of findings, see Stovall-McClough & Dozier, 2018).

Furthermore, the quality of a person's early attachment relationships is also associated with the quality of their attachment relationship to a Higher Power. Either the type of attachment security or insecurity to the caregivers during childhood corresponds to the type of attachment security or insecurity to a Higher Power, or a Higher Power serves as a surrogate attachment figure, compensating for insecure attachment relationships to the caregivers during childhood (for a summary of findings, see Granqvist, 2020; Granqvist & Kirkpatrick, 2018). If the quality of a person's attachment relationships to the caregivers during childhood is related to both their psychiatric symptoms and the quality of their attachment relationship to a Higher Power, then it stands to reason that the quality of a person's attachment relationship to a Higher Power is also associated with their psychiatric symptoms. Preliminary evidence suggests the viability of this relationship (Granqvist, 2020; Granqvist & Kirkpatrick, 2018); however, the studies supporting this hypothesis used self-report assessments of attachment quality, which are known to suffer from poor construct validity (Roisman et al., 2007). Further research is obviously needed to establish the connection between the quality of a person's attachment relationship to a Higher Power and their psychiatric symptoms. From a therapeutic perspective, it also seems reasonable to hypothesize that targeting the quality of a person's attachment relationship to a Higher Power in psychotherapy might bring symptomatic relief to spiritually curious or spiritually grounded patients.

Psychotherapy for Spiritually Curious Persons

If human beings are maturationally hard-wired to believe in a Higher Power, and if awareness of mortality, suffering, loss, and insecure attachment relationships to parents sometimes interfere with a relationship to this Higher Power, then it follows that a potential treatment goal of psychotherapy would be to help a person to restore their default setting to a secure attachment relationship to the Higher Power of their understanding. Spiritually Integrated Psychotherapy (SIP; Pargament, 2011) is designed to do just that, but it does not leverage the explosion of knowledge about attachment theory and attachment relationships. Attachment researcher Arietta Slade (2018) explained it this way:

Therapists who are able to provide a secure and safe base for their patients, to remain emotionally present and compassionate while managing complex and potentially intense affects within a therapy session, are likely to be those who best facilitate their patients' development.

(p. 769)

Psychotherapy is not designed to last forever. When the work is completed, does the client simply mourn the therapist's loss and move on without this critical attachment relationship? A secure attachment relationship to God, however, would continue beyond a person's therapeutic relationship and potentially sustain the person through all kinds of suffering for which the therapist had previously provided comfort and security. Thus, a spiritually informed therapist, in addition to providing a "secure and safe base," would facilitate a secure attachment relationship to a Higher Power that would endure beyond the temporal limitations of psychotherapy. This work would naturally include making connections between a person's attachment relationships to parents and their attachment relationship to their Higher Power, as I did in my reflection on my autobiographical narrative (see Goodman, 2025, Chapter 1). Thus, there is a need for a spiritually integrated psychotherapy that capitalizes on the latest advances in attachment theory by applying them to this spiritual therapeutic context. This book is an attempt to present a model of spiritually integrated psychotherapy that incorporates the latest insights of attachment theory into its healing process.

In secular circles, AIP is designed to transform a person's attachment relationships to parents from insecure to secure, which presumably generalizes to other emotionally significant relationships in the person's life. In this treatment model, "Change in attachment status itself becomes the target of treatment" (Slade, 2018, p. 771). If we consider the relationship to God to be emotionally significant, then we would also expect this relationship to change from insecure to secure. Persons who were probably insecurely attached to parents during early childhood who become securely attached later in life due to the life-changing experience of a loving relationship or psychotherapy are later classified as "earned secure" (Hesse, 2018). In other words, these persons worked on themselves to overcome their early attachment insecurity with parents and have developed the capacity to form secure attachment relationships, and potentially, a secure attachment relationship to God. Can an insecurely attached person become securely attached later in life due to the life-changing experience of a loving relationship to God? The literature usually suggests only one direction of causality, with a secure attachment relationship to God as an outcome of the self-work required for the shift to occur from insecurity to security. AIP in a spiritual context acknowledges the bidirectionality of causality—that earning security in one attachment relationship can affect the security in another.

Basic Therapist Stance Toward Spiritually Integrated Psychotherapy

A therapist seeking to help a spiritually curious patient to establish a secure attachment relationship to a Higher Power and simultaneously to experience emotional and spiritual well-being must practice grace, deep acceptance, and reassuring presence during their sessions. Regardless of their spirituality, the therapist must first cultivate a spiritual curiosity, not only about the patient's spiritual beliefs, practices, and relationship to a Higher Power but also about the language that the patient uses to describe their spiritual experiences. The therapist must develop a conversational familiarity with this spiritual language, just as a person who takes a Portuguese course might immerse themselves in the culture and street life of São Paulo to develop a conversational familiarity with Portuguese. The patient observes the therapist's empathic effort and gradually trusts the therapist enough to open up about their authentic spirituality.

Second, the therapist must evaluate the patient's spirituality to determine whether it is benefiting or harming the patient. A stage actress who prays to her Higher Power before the curtain goes up to calm her nerves is benefiting from her spirituality, while a woman who refuses to allow her daughter to receive a smallpox vaccination because it is against God's will is not benefiting from her spirituality but instead is placing her daughter's life at risk. In this book, I place such moral dilemmas in the context of the attachment relationship to a Higher Power. What do a patient's spiritual practices say about the quality of their attachment relationships to the caregivers during childhood and to a Higher Power? How can the therapist help the patient to improve the quality of these attachment relationships? I am suggesting that these moral dilemmas work themselves out when a secure attachment relationship to a Higher Power is gradually restored.

Finally, therapists must turn on their "spiritual radars" (Pargament, 2011, p. 217). Whenever a patient begins to discuss any topic of ultimate importance, conveying a profound sense of transcendence, boundlessness, or the eternal, then the therapist's spiritual radar should be beeping, signaling that spirituality has entered the therapeutic relationship. The question is whether the therapist will capitalize on these opportunities to discuss the patient's spirituality. In my professional career, I have wasted many opportunities to notice spirituality with my patients. Like an old-fashioned merry-go-round, however, if I miss the brass ring, another one will always be waiting for me the next time around. In psychotherapy, chances to notice spirituality abound.

This book focuses on the therapeutic techniques that help patients improve the quality of their attachment relationships to the caregivers during childhood as well as to a Higher Power. I argue that these relationships are intertwined, such that working through attachment relationships to the caregivers during childhood influences the attachment relationship to the sacred and vice versa. The quality of the patient's attachment relationships has everything to do with the quality of their emotional and spiritual well-being. Therapists will expand their arsenal of therapeutic techniques to use with their spiritually curious and spiritually grounded patients in AIP. The therapeutic goal is to help patients to "develop images of God that accentuate the loving generosity of a personal God who not only gifts us with life but is intimately present as a support for the development of that life" (Au & Au, 2006, p. 127). For healing to occur, the patient must become aware of their spiritual and attachment needs and then develop the vulnerability to risk meeting these needs. The therapeutic relationship becomes the fulcrum of this change.

Structure of the Book

Section I Attachment Theory and Attachment to the Living God

Chapter 2 Getting Attached to Attachment Theory: A Brief Overview

I profile the work of three innovative pioneers of attachment theory—John Bowlby, Mary Ainsworth, and Mary Main. All three theorists placed attachment, separation, and loss at the center of their understanding of psychological development. Bowlby (1982) hypothesized that infants begin to form internal working models of their earliest attachment relationships with caregivers to assist them in making accurate predictions of their physical availability that could aid in their survival. Ainsworth and her colleagues (Ainsworth et al., 1978) documented individual differences in the patterns of attachment that infants form by 12 months of age through her assessment paradigm known as the Strange Situation. She also discovered qualitatively distinct caregiving behaviors associated with each of these individual differences in the patterns of attachment. Mary Main and her colleagues (Main et al., 1985) analyzed the discourse of adults recollecting their childhood attachment relationships with their parents, determining that these relationships are represented in the mind and are transmitted through caregiving behavior to offspring. The four attachment patterns are known as secure, anxious-resistant, anxious-avoidant, and disorganized/disoriented. I also discuss the methods used to assess attachment patterns in both childhood and adulthood. Finally, I review three instruments that purport to assess a person's attachment to God.

Chapter 3 Attachment to God: Four Attachment Relationship Patterns

In preparation for a discussion of attachment to the living God in the psychotherapy context, I present a summary of the nine interpersonal markers (Daniel, 2015) used to characterize the primary modes of relatedness associated with the four patterns of attachment across the lifespan. I summarize the work of Lee Kirkpatrick (2005) and Pehr Granqvist (2020), two attachment theorists and researchers who applied the insights of attachment theory to elucidate a person's attachment relationship to God. Extending the work of William James (1902), Kirkpatrick originally formulated the correspondence and compensation hypotheses to faith in a Higher Power. Individuals tend to continue professing beliefs in the God of their parents if their attachment relationships to their parents are secure (correspondence). On the other hand, individuals with insecure attachment relationships to their parents are more prone to having a conversion experience in adulthood, where they put their faith in a Higher Power to compensate for the deficiencies in their attachment relationships to their parents (compensation). Granqvist (2020) discussed these two pathways in the context of attachment relationships to parents discussed in Chapter 2. As the remainder of this book demonstrates, these qualitatively different attachment relationships to the Living God—the God of personal spiritual experience—have profound implications for the treatment of individuals in psychotherapy. How can we talk about a patient's attachment relationship to God as a displacement of his or her attachment relationships to parents? How can we talk about a patient's attachment relationships to parents as a displacement of their attachment relationship to God? Transforming these attachment relationships to restore wholeness and unity is a crucial treatment goal of Attachment-Informed Psychotherapy (AIP).

Section II Applying Attachment-Informed Psychotherapy to Transform the Attachment Relationship to God

Chapter 4 Attachment-Informed Psychotherapy: Addressing Attachment to God Through the Therapeutic Relationship

I explore Attachment-Informed Psychotherapy (AIP) depicting the psychology of therapeutic relationships, discussing this attachment relationship as a representation of a patient's attachment relationship to God. This model takes the caregiver-infant attachment relationship as a metaphor for both the therapist-patient and God-patient attachment relationships. I address the advantages and disadvantages of using such a metaphor. How does the attachment relationship formed in earliest infancy inform the therapist's theory and conduct of the patient's attachment relationship to the therapist and to God? How does this metaphor prevent us from examining other forces that shape the patient's attachment relationship to the therapist and to God? I explore the similarities and differences between these two relationships, for example, the fact that care and attention are contingent upon a payment of a fee in the therapist-patient attachment relationship, whereas the God-patient relationship is theoretically free of charge. Despite the differences, these two relationships are similar in the way in which the caregiver-therapist "marks," or labels, the infant-patient's emotional experiences as both experienced and understood by the caregiver-therapist and simultaneously not overwhelming to them. Can God serve a similar function in the patient's psychic economy outside the therapy office? It is this containment of emotional experiences—carrying the emotional burdens of the patient without collapsing, retaliating, or avoiding them—that gradually moves the infant-patient toward emotional development/emotional and spiritual health. Can the patient transfer this containment function to their Higher Power that will endure beyond the treatment? In other words, can the patient begin to rely on God as their refuge?

Chapter 5 The Therapist's Secure Base Provision and the Patient's Underlying Attachment Needs

In applying the findings of attachment theory to the therapist-patient relationship, how can the therapist provide a secure base to the patient from which the patient can explore their attachment relationship needs for others and for God without dismissing them or getting entangled in resentments from past disappointments? The therapist must behave as both an old, familial caregiver as well as a new, nonfamilial caregiver to promote transformation in the patient's attachment relationship to God. As a symbol of a familial caregiver, the therapist provides the patient with the opportunity to develop and transfer various facets of the familial caregiver relationship onto the therapist. This relationship to a familial caregiver often occurs in the understanding phase of treatment (Kohut, 1984). As a symbol of a nonfamilial caregiver, the therapist provides the patient with the opportunity to develop new expectations derived from the therapist's behavior that differ from the expectations developed from the familial caregiver's past behavior. These new expectations are also predicted to transfer and generalize to the patient's attachment relationship to God. The relationship to a nonfamilial caregiver often develops during the explanatory phase of treatment (Kohut, 1984). A therapist who behaves only like the old, familial caregiver deprives the patient of the opportunity to develop and transfer new expectations and new modes of regulating emotional experiences and relating to others and to God, while a therapist who behaves only like a new, nonfamilial caregiver deprives the patient of the opportunity of working through his or her relationship to the old, familial caregiver and to his or her Higher Power.

Chapter 6 Interaction Structures Formed by Therapist and Patient Secondary Attachment Strategies

I broadly outline my thoughts about four potential interaction structures (i.e., patterns of reciprocal interaction) that therapist-patient dyads can form, and I draw implications for the patient's transformation in his or her attachment relationship to God. Building on Chapter 5, I present a model for understanding how interaction structures develop out of the secondary attachment strategies of both members of the therapeutic dyad. Specifically, I propose a 2 x 2 typology in which the therapist's and the patient's secondary attachment strategies—deactivating and hyperactivating—form either complementary or noncomplementary interaction structures. I label the four interaction structures "sterile," "chaotic," "expressive," and "containing." I hypothesize that these four interaction structures are associated with four different treatment outcomes and have four different implications for the fate of the patient's attachment relationship to God. Psychotherapy process researchers could empirically test this hypothesis by assessing therapeutic dyads for their attachment histories and observing the resulting psychotherapy processes and outcomes in the relationships to others and to God. This four-category typology is not designed to capture the entire universe of relationships between therapists and patients but rather to underscore four broad interaction structures based on what psychotherapy research has begun to reveal to us.

Chapter 7 Final Thoughts on Transforming Attachment Relationships to God

I summarize the essential elements of attachment theory and how they form the foundation of Attachment-Informed Psychotherapy (AIP), which I use to work with my patients' spirituality in psychotherapy. Spiritually informed and spiritually curious patients who developed insecure attachment relationships to their caregivers during childhood must work toward an attachment status of "earned security," in which they can trust and rely on others, on themselves, and on a Higher Power. In addition, I summarize how to work with these patients using the four different attachment relationship models discussed in Section II and how to address the correspondence and compensation pathways to a patient's experience of their attachment relationship to God. Crucially, I suggest that therapists must follow their spiritual intuition in both listening and responding to the patient's verbal and nonverbal communications, especially their emotional expressions.

References

Ainsworth, M. D. S., Blehar, M. C., Waters, E., & Wall, S. (1978). *Patterns of attachment: A psychological study of the strange situation.* Erlbaum.

Au, W. W., & Au, N. C. (2006). *The discerning heart: Exploring the Christian path.* Paulist Press.

Barrett, J. L. (2012). *Born believers: The science of children's religious belief.* Free Press.

Bodhi, B. (Ed. & Trans.). (2005). *In the Buddha's words: An anthology of discourses from the Pali Canon.* Wisdom Publications.

Bowlby, J. (1982). *Attachment and loss*: Vol. 1. *Attachment* (2nd ed.). Basic Books.

Bowlby, J. (1988). *A secure base: Parent-child attachment and healthy human development.* Basic Books.

Bryant, A. N., & Astin, H. S. (2008). The correlates of spiritual struggle during the college years. *Journal of Higher Education, 79,* 1–27.

Burker, E. J., Evon, D. M., Sedway, J. A., & Egan, T. (2005). Religious and nonreligious coping in lung transplant candidates: Does adding God to the picture tell us more? *Journal of Behavioral Medicine, 28,* 513–526.

Carter, J. D., & Narramore, B. (1979). *The integration of psychology and theology: An introduction.* Zondervan.

Cole, B. S., & Pargament, K. I. (1998). Re-creating your life: A spiritual/psychotherapeutic intervention for people diagnosed with cancer. *Psycho-Oncology, 8,* 395–407.

Daniel, S. I. F. (2015). *Adult attachment patterns in a treatment context: Relationship and narrative.* Routledge.

Dharma, K. (2020). *Mahabharata: The greatest spiritual epic of all time.* Mandala Publishing.

Dozier, M. (2003). Attachment-based treatment for vulnerable children. *Attachment and Human Development, 5,* 253–257.

Exline J. J., & Rose, E. (2005). Religious and spiritual struggles. In R. F. Paloutzian & C. L. Park (Eds.), *Handbook of the psychology of religion and spirituality* (pp. 315–330). Guilford Press.

Fitchett, G., Murphy, P., Kim J., Gibbons, J. L., Cameron, J., & Davis. J. A. (2004). Religious struggle: Prevalence, correlates and mental health risks in diabetic, congestive heart failure, and oncology patients. *International Journal of Psychiatry in Medicine, 34,* 179–196.

Freud, S. (1900). The interpretation of dreams. In J. Strachey (Ed. and Trans.), *The standard edition of the complete psychological works of Sigmund Freud* (Vols. 4–5, pp. 1–625). Hogarth Press.

Freud, S. (1920). Beyond the pleasure principle. In J. Strachey (Ed. and Trans.), *The standard edition of the complete psychological works of Sigmund Freud* (Vol. 18, pp. 1–64). Hogarth Press.

Gianino, A., & Tronick, E. (1985). The mutual regulation model: The infant's self and interactive regulation and coping and defensive capacities. In T. Field, P. McCabe, & N. Schneiderman (Eds.), *Stress and coping* (pp. 1–39). Erlbaum.

Goodman, G. (1991). Feeling our way into empathy: Carl Rogers, Heinz Kohut, and Jesus. *Journal of Religion and Health, 30,* 191–205.

Goodman, G. (2014). *The internal world and attachment* (paperback ed.). Routledge.

Goodman, G. (2025). *Practical applications of transforming the attachment relationship to God: Using Attachment-Informed Psychotherapy.* Routledge.

Granqvist, P. (2014). Religion and cognitive, emotional, and social development. In V. Saroglou (Ed.), *Religion, personality, and social psychology* (pp. 283–312). Psychology Press.

Granqvist, P. (2020). *Attachment in religion and spirituality: A wider view.* Guilford Press.

Granqvist, P., & Kirkpatrick, L. A. (2018). Attachment and religious representations and behavior. In J. Cassidy & P. R. Shaver (Eds.), *Handbook of attachment: Theory, research, and clinical applications* (pp. 917–940). Guilford Press.

Hesse, E. (2018). The Adult Attachment Interview: Protocol, method of analysis, and selected empirical studies: 1985–2015. In J. Cassidy & P. R. Shaver (Eds.), *Handbook of attachment: Theory, research, and clinical applications* (pp. 553–597). Guilford Press.

James, W. (1902). *The varieties of religious experience: A study in human nature.* Longmans, Green, and Co.

Johnson, C. N., & Boyatzis, C. J. (2006). Cognitive-cultural foundations of spiritual development. In E. C. Roehlkepartain, P. E. King, L. Wagener, & P. L. Benson (Eds.), *The handbook of spiritual development in childhood and adolescence* (pp. 211–223). Sage.

Kirkpatrick, L. A. (1999). Attachment and religious representations and behavior. In J. Cassidy & P. R. Shaver (Eds.), *Handbook of attachment: Theory, research, and clinical applications* (pp. 803–822). Guilford Press.

Kirkpatrick, L. A. (2005). *Attachment, evolution, and the psychology of religion.* Guilford Press.

Kirkpatrick, L. A., & Shaver, P. R. (1990). Attachment theory and religion: Childhood attachments, religious beliefs, and conversion. *Journal for the Scientific Study of Religion, 29,* 315–334.

Knight, N., Sousa, P., Barrett, J. L., & Atran, S. (2004). Children's attributions of beliefs to humans and God: Cross-cultural evidence. *Cognitive Science, 28,* 117–126.

Kohut, H. (1984). *How does analysis cure?* University of Chicago Press.

Lichtenberg, J. D. (1989). *Psychoanalysis and motivation.* The Analytic Press.

Main, M., Kaplan, N., & Cassidy, J. (1985). Security in infancy, childhood, and adulthood: A move to the level of representation. In I. Bretherton & E. Waters (Eds.), *Growing points in attachment theory and research. Monographs of the Society for Research in Child Development, 50*(1–2, Serial No. 209) (pp. 66–104). Springer.

Main, M., & Solomon, J. (1986). Discovery of an insecure-disorganized/disoriented attachment pattern. In T. B. Brazelton & M. W. Yogman (Eds.), *Affective development in infancy* (pp. 95–124). Ablex.

Main, M., & Solomon, J. (1990). Procedures for identifying infants as disorganized/disoriented during the Ainsworth Strange Situation. In M. T. Greenberg, D. Cicchetti, & E. M. Cummings (Eds.), *Attachment in the preschool years: Theory, research, and intervention* (pp. 121–160). University of Chicago Press.

May, G. G. (1982). *Will and spirit: A contemplative psychology.* Harper & Row.

Mesman, J., van IJzendoorn, M. H., & Sagi-Schwartz, A. (2018). Cross-cultural patterns of attachment: Universal and contextual dimensions. In J. Cassidy & P. R. Shaver (Eds.), *Handbook of attachment: Theory, research, and clinical applications* (pp. 852–877). Guilford Press.

Murray-Swank, N. A., & Pargament, K. I. (2005). God, where are you?: Evaluating a spiritually-integrated intervention for sexual abuse. *Mental Health, Religion, and Culture, 8,* 191–204.

Neimeyer, R. A., & Burke, L. A. (2011). Complicated grief in the aftermath of homicide: Spiritual crisis and distress in an African American sample. *Religions, 2,* 145–164.

NIV (New International Version). (1978). *The holy Bible.* Zondervan.

Pargament, K. I. (2011). *Spiritually integrated psychotherapy: Understanding and addressing the sacred.* Guilford Press.

Pargament, K. I., & Exline, J. J. (2022). *Working with spiritual struggles in psychotherapy: From research to practice.* Guilford Press.

Pargament, K. I., Murray-Swank, N., Magyar, G. M., & Ano, G. (2005). Spiritual struggle: A phenomenon of interest to psychology and religion. In W. R. Miller & H. Delaney (Eds.), *Judeo-Christian perspectives on psychology: Human nature, motivation, and change* (pp. 245–268). American Psychological Association.

Park, C. L., Holt, C. L., Le, D., Christie, J., & Williams, B. R. (2018). Positive and negative religious coping styles as prospective predictors of well-being in African Americans. *Psychology of Religion and Spirituality, 10,* 318–326.

Propst, L. R., Ostrom, R., Watkins, P., Dean, T., & Mashburn, D. (1992). Comparative efficacy of religious and nonreligious-behavioral therapy for the treatment of clinical depression in religious individuals. *Journal of Consulting and Clinical Psychology, 60,* 94–103.

Reynolds, N., Mrug, S., Hensler, M., Guion, K., & Madan-Swain, A. (2014). Spiritual coping and adjustment in adolescents with chronic illness: A two-year prospective study. *Journal of Pediatric Psychology, 39,* 542–551.

Richert, R., & Granqvist, P. (2013). Religious and spiritual development in childhood. In R. F. Paloutzian & C. Park (Eds.), *Handbook of the psychology of religion and spirituality* (2nd ed., pp. 165–182). Guilford Press.

Rizzuto, A.-M. (1979). *The birth of the living God: A psychoanalytic study.* University of Chicago Press.

Rogers, C. R. (1957). The necessary and sufficient conditions of therapeutic personality change. *Journal of Consulting Psychology, 21,* 95–103.

Roisman, G. I., Holland, A., Fortuna, K., Fraley, R. C., Clausell, E., & Clarke, A. (2007). The adult attachment interview and self-reports of attachment style: An empirical rapprochement. *Journal of Personality and Social Psychology, 92*, 678–697.

Slade, A. (1999). Attachment theory and research: Implications for the theory and practice of individual psychotherapy with adults. In J. Cassidy & P. R. Shaver (Eds.), *Handbook of attachment: Theory, research, and clinical applications* (pp. 575–594). Guilford Press.

Slade, A. (2018). Attachment and adult psychotherapy: Theory, research, and practice. In J. Cassidy & P. R. Shaver (Eds.), *Handbook of attachment: Theory, research, and clinical applications* (pp. 759–779). Guilford Press.

Stauner, N., Exline, J. J., & Pargament, K. I. (2016). Religious and spiritual struggles as concerns for health and well-being. *Horizonte, 14*, 48–75.

Stern, D. N. (1985). *The interpersonal world of the infant: A view from psychoanalysis and developmental psychology.* Basic Books.

Stovall-McClough, K. C., & Dozier, M. (2018). Attachment states of mind and psychopathology in adulthood. In J. Cassidy & P. R. Shaver (Eds.), *Handbook of attachment: Theory, research, and clinical applications* (pp. 715–738). Guilford Press.

Tronick, E. Z., Cohn, J., & Shea, E. (1986). The transfer of affect between mothers and infants. In M. Yogman & T. B. Brazelton (Eds.), *Affective development in infancy* (pp. 11–25). Ablex.

Ulanov, A. B. (2001). *Finding space: Winnicott, God, and psychic reality.* Westminster John Knox Press.

Voltaire. (1919). *Voltaire in his letters: Being a selection from his correspondence* (S. G. Tallentyre, Trans.). Putnam. (Original work published 1769).

Waters, E., Merrick, S., Treboux, D., Crowell, J., & Albersheim, L. (2000). Attachment security in infancy and early adulthood: A twenty-year longitudinal study. *Child Development, 71*, 684–689.

Yanni, G. M. (2003). Religious and secular dyadic variables and their relation to parent–child relationships and college students' psychological adjustment. Unpublished doctoral dissertation, Bowling Green State University.

Section 1

Attachment Theory and Attachment to God

Chapter 2

Getting Attached to Attachment Theory

A Brief Overview

This book contends that a discernible pattern exists between a person's attachment relationships to their primary caregivers and their attachment relationship (or non-attachment relationship) to a Higher Power. I therefore outline the basics of attachment theory because these basics are necessary to understand the later chapters. We begin at the beginning: attachment theory has existed as a cohesive theory since its conception in the 1950s (Bowlby, 1958). John Bowlby, a British psychiatrist and psychoanalyst, pioneered this new understanding of psychology through his work with orphaned children during the London Blitz and in the aftermath of World War II. His theory, which has generated significant empirical research and clinical innovation, consists of a series of careful observations of infants' and children's behavior and placing these observations in the context of evolutionary theory and ethological studies. Perhaps attachment theory's reliance on observable rather than intrapsychic data accounts for the widespread appropriation of attachment concepts in the mental health fields.

Exercising caution in interpreting their empirical findings and not wanting to draw conclusions beyond where the data lead them, attachment theorists have been reluctant to make inferences regarding the contents of the infant's mind because these contents cannot be observed in the laboratory. On the other hand, object relations theorists, the school of thought predominating in London during Bowlby's time, were more eager to draw inferences; their own observations, though collected retrospectively in the consulting room and thus more ambiguous to interpret than laboratory data, have not deterred them. Hence, greater agreement is observed among attachment theorists than among object relations theorists.

I review here the work of three attachment theorists: John Bowlby, Mary Ainsworth, and Mary Main. Bowlby is relevant to object relations theory because, prior to formulating his attachment theory, he was an object relations-trained psychoanalyst (Karen, 1998) who distanced himself from his object relations supervisor, Melanie Klein, by disavowing drive theory—which postulated that all human motivation was governed by the instinctual forces of sex and aggression. Instead, Bowlby incorporated the insights of ethology, the study of animal behavior. Mary Ainsworth, Bowlby's Canadian student, was responsible for testing his theory empirically and documenting individual differences in infants' quality

DOI: 10.4324/9781003562924-3

of attachment to the caregiver as well as relating individual differences in care-giving to attachment quality. Two of the three patterns of attachment that she iden-tified were later associated with different forms of psychopathology. Mary Main, by identifying a fourth—disorganized/disoriented attachment pattern (Main & Solomon, 1990)—and redirecting attachment investigators to examine the mental representational components of attachment in addition to its behavioral correlates, heralded the empirical study of the cognitive/psychoanalytic aspect of Bowlby's theory, namely, internal working models.

John Bowlby

Bowlby (1973, 1980, 1982, 1988) reacted to Melanie Klein's emphases on drive theory and an unobserved infant fantasy life by creating his own theory of psycho-logical development. He borrowed from the studies of ethologists such as Harlow and Zimmerman (1959) and Lorenz (1935) to augment his understanding of early object relations theory (Klein, 1940). The result was an explicitly evolutionary theory of the infant's development of attachment to their caregiver. According to Bowlby, infants are genetically programmed with certain behaviors to ensure their survival. Infants use five instinctual classes of behavior—crying, smiling, sucking, following, and clinging—to foster their caregiver's attachment to them and vice versa. The first two classes of behavior—crying and smiling—function to elicit caregiving, whereas the other three classes of behavior—sucking, following, and clinging—function to seek proximity and maintain contact. These behaviors sug-gest an innate sociability to others that begins at birth (see Ainsworth et al., 1974).

Beginning at approximately nine months, these five classes of behavior eventu-ally become integrated as a behavioral system and are directed toward one person—the primary caregiver. For example, smiling becomes coordinated with following or sucking to activate and maximize the caregiver's protective and life-giving responses. In Bowlby's theory, infants make a direct impact on their caregivers immediately after birth, but this impact dramatically increases in efficiency with the coordination of the five classes of behavior. Initially reflexive and instinctual (as opposed to drive-related), these classes of behavior gradually become organ-ized templates using memories of previous interpersonal experiences to forecast caregiver behavior in response to the coordinated infant behavioral system.

This organization becomes activated in response to the primary caregiver—that one person historically most instrumental in caring for the infant's various needs. Bowlby (1982) applied in outline form the theory of imprinting of Lorenz (Lorenz, 1935), which was humorously demonstrated in video-recorded footage of Lorenz being mercilessly followed around by a brood of baby ducks. After an infant becomes attached to the primary caregiver, it is nearly impossible to reprogram the system (see Ainsworth et al., 1974). This sensitive period when the attachment is forming lasts until 18–24 months of age. Unique to the theory of Bowlby (Bowlby, 1982) is the supreme value placed on the organization, or pattern, of behaviors exhibited by an infant in the context of a danger posed by the environment, for example, the threat of a stranger.

While this behavioral system is becoming integrated, the increased locomotion of the infant activates a second behavioral system: exploration. When the attachment system becomes activated, the exploratory system becomes deactivated and vice versa (see George & Solomon, 1999; Solomon & George, 1996). The adaptive function of the attachment system is protection of the child from danger posed by predators or other unknown dangers in the environment. The degree to which the caregiver provides a *secure base* (Bowlby, 1982) from which the infant can explore the environment and a *safe haven* (Bowlby, 1982) to which the infant can return in times of perceived danger determines how securely attached the infant behaves toward the caregiver. The caregiver's responses to the infant's behaviors help to determine the infant's expectations of security, which create a sense of *felt security* (Sroufe & Waters, 1977), which deactivates the attachment system and permits activation of the exploratory system.

Episodic memories of these caregiver responses become consolidated into semantic memory, a more generalized, abstract memory that permits expectations to form. These initial expectations, constructed through the accumulation of early experiences of caregiver responses, form the foundation of the internal working model, the first mental representation of the infant in relation to the caregiver. The exploratory system also carries survival-promoting value by helping infants to develop the cognitive skills and obtain the worldly experiences necessary to survive someday on their own.

The internal working model, rather than gratifying an infant's needs during the caregiver's absence, represents a set of expectations that help the infant to predict the caregiver's behavior. Storing in memory how the caregiver behaves during moments when the attachment system is activated (e.g., when a stranger threatens a sense of security) assists infants in adapting their behavior to maximize feelings of security and insure survival. Typically, infants organize their attachment behaviors into two goals: proximity-seeking and contact-maintaining. The infant in our distant ancestry who failed to accomplish these tasks wandered off from the caregivers and risked being eaten by predators. As the infant develops, the goals of the attachment system evolve into a goal-corrected partnership (Bowlby, 1982), in which infant and caregiver negotiate with each other the caregiver's availability to the infant. This partnership is elastic to allow for increasing levels of physical and emotional independence in subsequent phases of development, but attachment security nevertheless remains a lifelong concern "from the cradle to the grave" (Bowlby, 1977, p. 203). Bowlby (1989) also related disturbances in attachment security to both child and adult psychopathology.

Bowlby (1973, 1980, 1982, 1988) also discussed defensive processes within the infant. Extended separations from the caregiver, which cause significant emotional pain, require the infant to exclude attachment-relevant information from awareness. Bowlby called this process "defensive exclusion." Thus, for Bowlby, the unconscious was not a "cauldron of seething excitations" (Freud, 1933, p. 73) but rather a repository for any painful aspects of interpersonal experience in external reality—rejection, separation, loss, death. The infant might develop an internal working model that accurately predicts caregiver rejection in response to proximity-seeking and contact-maintaining; however, the emotional pain associated with this inevitable outcome is defensively excluded. Under these conditions, in which the infant feels unwanted or unlovable—corresponding to the caregiver's emotional inconsistency or rejection—internal working models "reflect a complex interplay of multiple representations of self and other that are to some degree incompatible and difficult to integrate" (Solomon & George, 1999b, p. 6). The actual cognitive awareness of caregiver unavailability, as well as the infant emotions associated with this unavailability, appear to be excluded from consciousness, to be replaced by less negative appraisals of self and other.

In this theory, what are the origins of this emotional pain, and what functions does this emotional pain serve? We could speculate that this emotional pain results from an original expectation of the caregiver's emotional availability in conjunction with repeated violations of this expectation and consequent feelings of anger that nevertheless need to be hidden to prevent the infant from driving the caregiver even further away. Kernberg et al. (1989, pp. 137–141) discussed extreme separation anxiety as a form of pathological mourning of caregivers toward whom an infant has ambivalent feelings. If in Bowlby's theory the infant is programmed to form an accurate template of caregiver responsiveness (or its lack), then how does disappointment begin to develop? What is it about the infant mind that registers certain aspects of interpersonal experience in external reality as painful? Perhaps an innate internal working model already exists whose programmed expectations are repeatedly violated by interpersonal experiences in external reality, thus producing some form of mental anguish. Bowlby himself was not clear about these points. It is difficult to conceptualize this whole process of internalization without a theory of motivation (see Lichtenberg, 1989; Silverman, 1991, 1993, 2001).

The closest relatives to defensive exclusion in object relations theory are repression and splitting; however, defensive exclusion is used to ward off external reality, not instinctual impulses. In this sense, it is also closely related to the defense mechanisms of Freud (Freud, 1924): disavowal and denial. Defensive exclusion also operates throughout the lifespan. By recovering the episodic memories related to these experiences and by disrupting the semantic, "scripted" memories associated with repetitive caregiver behavior (see Chapters 4–6), psychotherapy can assist the individual in regaining access to these painful aspects of interpersonal experience excluded from consciousness.

Bowlby's theory implies that infants are accurate interpreters of external reality and only later distort their perceptions of external reality, which in turn produces psychopathology. Thus, according to this theory, newborn infants are the only "normal" humans, having no need for defensive processes. It is the inevitability of painful interpersonal experiences in external reality that activates defensive exclusion and results in psychopathology. Contrast these romantic ideas about the infant's mentation to the sobering ideas of psychoanalytic theory, which holds that an infant's mind is considered to be "polymorphously perverse" (Freud, 1905, p. 191) and consumed by hatred, greed, and envy (Klein, 1957). I have attempted to reconcile these contrasting ideas elsewhere (Goodman, 2014).

Mary Ainsworth

Whereas Bowlby primarily studied normative attachment processes in infant and child development, Mary Ainsworth (Ainsworth, 1967, 1979; Ainsworth et al., 1978) studied individual differences in the quality of infants' attachment to their caregivers. She conducted naturalistic observational studies of attachment patterns of Ugandan infants with their mothers and noticed individual differences in the ways in which the infants organized their attachment relationships. Ainsworth later moved to Baltimore, Maryland, and studied the interactions of 23 middle-income mothers and infants naturalistically in their homes. She recorded detailed descriptions of these interactions in 4-hour intervals conducted each month over the first 12 months. When the infants were 12 months old, she performed a laboratory procedure, which she called the "Strange Situation," designed to assess these individual differences in the organization of the attachment relationship (Ainsworth & Wittig, 1969).

In the Strange Situation, infant and caregiver participate in a series of eight 3-minute episodes that enact (1) the presence of caregiver and an observer, (2) the presence of caregiver, (3) the presence of caregiver and a stranger, (4) the separation from caregiver and presence of stranger, (5) the reunion with caregiver, (6) the second separation from caregiver, (7) the reunion with stranger, and (8) thesecond reunion with caregiver. On the basis of individual differences in the infants' organization of attachment behaviors in response to these anxiety-provoking episodes, particularly the reunion episodes, Ainsworth classified the infants into three categories: anxious-avoidant (type A), secure (type B), and anxious-resistant (type C). These different patterns of attachment organization were unanticipated and produced subsequent theoretical advances (Table 2.1).

Secure (B) infants cry when separated from the caregiver, vigorously seek proximity and physical contact with the caregiver upon reunion, and then quickly return to exploration. Anxious-avoidant (A) infants seldom cry when separated from the caregiver and avoid the caregiver upon reunion. Anxious-resistant (C) infants, on the other hand, display intense distress when separated and behave angrily and are inconsolable toward the caregiver upon reunion; they seek physical contact yet resist when the caregiver offers it (see Table 2.1). Main and Cassidy (1988) later validated a modified Strange Situation for 6-year-old children and found these same three attachment categories. Other assessment procedures for preschool and school-aged children yielded the same three patterns of attachment and are now

Table 2.1 Patterns of attachment organization at ages 12–18 months, 5–8 years, and adulthood

12–18 Months[a]	5–8 Years[b]	Adulthood[c]
(Strange Situation behavior)	(Attachment story completions)	(Adult Attachment Interview responses)
A (Anxious-Avoidant)	A (Casual)	Ds (Dismissing)
Not distressed during separation; conspicuous avoidance of proximity to or interaction with mother during reunion	Ordinary events; undoes separation or demonstrates casual disinterest in reunion	Attachment relationships are of little concern, value, or influence; dismissing of their significance
B (Secure)	B (Confident)	F (Secure-Autonomous)
Distressed during separation; actively seeks proximity and contact with mother during reunion	Danger and rescue themes; acknowledges separation and reunion, and relies on mother for protection	Attachment relationships are valued, influential on personality; childhood relationships with parents are readily recalled with ease
C (Anxious-Resistant)	C (Busy)	E (Preoccupied-Entangled)
Distressed even prior to separation; angry and inconsolable with mother during reunion	Caregiving themes; engages in delay tactics at reunion with busy activities that appear digressive	Attachment relationships are preoccupying; actively dependent on and entangled by relationships with parents
D (Disorganized-Disoriented)[d]	D (Frightened)	U (Unresolved)
Contradictory display of behavior patterns during reunion; misdirected, incomplete, mistimed movements; apprehension of mother; freezing	Either unresolved danger leading to chaos and disintegration, or inhibited and constricted in storytelling	Incomplete mourning process over loss of parent in childhood; also related to abuse and other traumatic events

Notes: [a]Adapted from Ainsworth et al. (1978). [b]Adapted from Solomon et al. (1995). [c]Adapted from Main et al. (1985). [d]Adapted from Main and Solomon (1990).

also used (e.g., Bretherton, Ridgeway, & Cassidy, 1990; Goodman et al., 1998; Solomon et al., 1995). Van IJzendoorn and Kroonenberg (1988) conducted a meta-analysis of 18 Strange Situation studies and concluded that the worldwide distribution of the three traditional patterns of attachment was as follows: 21% A, 65% B, and 14% C. This distribution—based on almost 2,000 Strange Situation attachment classifications—is almost identical to the distribution found in the original study by Ainsworth et al. (1978).

In every culture studied thus far, children "were observed to show attachment behavior in stressful circumstances and to have a preferential bond with one or more caregivers" (Mesman et al., 2018, p. 866). Socioeconomic hardship and other adverse circumstances seem to attenuate the percentage of attachment security in many cultures. In addition, the percentages of the type of attachment insecurity (i.e., anxious-avoidance or anxious-resistance) can vary by cultural milieu. For example, compared to US samples, Anglo-Saxon and European samples tend to feature higher percentages of anxious-avoidance and lower percentages of anxious-resistance, while Asian samples tend to feature higher percentages of anxious-resistance and lower percentages of anxious-avoidance (Mesman et al., 2018). Nevertheless, in every culture studied thus far, researchers have identified all four attachment patterns. Attachment is a universal phenomenon, not a cultural one. Culture seems to play a role, however, in the relative percentages of attachment insecurity. In Chapter 4, I discuss the roles that gender and race can play in Attachment-Informed Psychotherapy (AIP). For further reading on how social and economic social structures can influence persons' attachment relationship to a Higher Power, I refer the reader to a fascinating chapter in the book by Granqvist (2020) titled, "God Versus the Welfare State."

Ainsworth (Ainsworth, 1979; Ainsworth et al., 1978) also discovered that specific caregiver behaviors assessed during the first 12 months predicted each of the three original attachment patterns. Caregiver sensitivity, emotional availability, and responsiveness to infant cues, most importantly to attachment behaviors, predicted infant attachment security at 12 months. Caregiver rejection of attachment cues (i.e., consistent unresponsiveness) predicted infant avoidance, while caregiver inconsistency in responding to attachment cues (i.e., inconsistent responsiveness) predicted infant resistance (also known as ambivalence). Waters et al. (2000) established 64% stability of attachment patterns after 20 years and 70% stability among individuals with no major negative life events, while de Wolff and van IJzendoorn (1997) established through a meta-analysis of 66 studies that sensitivity moderately predicts attachment security (effect size $r = .24$). Thus, the overt manifestation of attachment patterns might change (Sroufe, 1979), but their underlying organization (Sroufe & Waters, 1977) becomes increasingly resistant to change as past interactional experiences become habitual, expected, and reliable forecasters of future caregiver behavior (Bowlby, 1980; Bretherton, 1985; Main et al., 1985). Psychotherapy, however, has the capacity to change these internal working models, or underlying attachment organization (e.g., Levy et al., 2006).

Mary Main

Mary Main (Main et al., 1985; Main & Solomon, 1986, 1990) extended attachment theory and research in two important ways: (1) she discovered a fourth pattern of attachment later shown to be related to the development of psychopathology (e.g., Carlson, 1998; Lyons-Ruth et al., 1997; Solomon & George, 1999a; van IJzendoorn et al., 1999), and (2) she undertook the task of assessing the quality of attachment patterns at the level of mental representation—the internal working model. Conducting their own studies of middle-income infants, Main and Solomon (1986) sought to discover attachment categories additional to Ainsworth's three original ones. To their surprise, they found "the striking *absence* of such new [coherent] categories of [attachment]" (p. 97, emphasis in original). Instead, they discovered a group of infants who, unlike their more coherently behaving avoidant, secure, and resistant counterparts, demonstrated no clear strategy for responding to the anxiety elicited upon reunion with the caregiver and hence defied classification into the traditional Ainsworth attachment categories. These infants appeared to lack both organization and coherence in their responses to separation and reunion distress. Main and Solomon thus called these infants "disorganized/disoriented" (D), and placed them in their own, admittedly amorphous, "category." The D attachment category is assigned in conjunction with a best-fitting attachment category within the original A-B-C attachment classification system. Thus, infants receive an organized attachment classification in conjunction with a D attachment classification. In these cases, the D attachment category is considered primary; the organized attachment category, secondary.

The authors noted the wide diversity of behaviors that exist within this new category. These behaviors typically seem out of context and inexplicable and fail to serve the purpose of maximizing the infant's feeling of attachment security toward the caregiver. Examples of D behavior include falling prone on the floor upon the caregiver's return, walking around aimlessly with a dazed expression in the caregiver's presence, and approaching the returning caregiver with a distressed cry and head sharply averted.

Because of the diversity of these observed behaviors, Main and Solomon (1990) later identified seven different indices of D attachment in infancy. They suggested that other subcategories might exist and have encouraged others to document potential candidates. In particular, they pointed out the need to identify "predictable and distinct sequelae" (p. 153) of any new subcategory, as well as a "specific and distinct history" (p. 153) to validate its authenticity. Indeed, the D attachment classification is associated with the caregiver's own history of abuse and general maltreatment (Carlson et al., 1989a, 1989b; Lyons-Ruth et al., 1989), caregiver's depression (Lyons-Ruth et al., 1990; Lyons-Ruth et al., 1997; Lyons-Ruth et al., 1986), caregiver's unresolved childhood trauma (Ainsworth & Eichberg, 1991), and caregiver's frightening behavior (Hesse & Main, 1999; Lyons-Ruth et al., 1999; Main & Hesse, 1990; Schuengel et al., 1999). One research group (Lyons-Ruth et al., 1993), assessing a high-risk sample of 12-month-olds and 18-month-olds, demonstrated that all infants assigned a C attachment classification were primarily classified as D, a finding suggesting significant overlap between these two attachment categories. Van IJzendoorn et al. (1999) conducted a meta-analysis of 80 Strange Situation studies, including more than 6,000 Strange Situation attachment classifications, and concluded that the incidence of the D attachment category among low-risk, middle-income families is approximately 15%.

Main et al. (1985) also directed their attention to uncovering additional clues to the psychic organization of attachment relationships. They extended the assessment of attachment beyond the observation of behavior in infancy to the analysis of discourse in later development. They discussed the potential implications of this shift:

> Our reconceptualization of individual differences in attachment organization as individual differences in the mental representation of the self in relation to attachment permits the investigation of attachment not only in infants but also in older children and adults and leads to a new focus on representation and language ... Individual differences in these internal working models will therefore be related not only to individual differences in patterns of nonverbal behavior but also to patterns of language and structures of mind.
>
> (p. 67)

According to Main and her colleagues, increasingly abstract assessments of language replace concrete behavioral observations as indices of the structure and function of internal working models beyond infancy. This methodological breakthrough permitted attachment researchers to test for the intergenerational transmission of internal working models.

Assessment of Internal Working Models

A summary of efforts at measuring the quality of internal working models is necessary. Internal working models were investigated at the behavioral level by Ainsworth et al. (1978) as well as at the mental representational level through story completions administered to children (e.g., Bretherton, Ridgeway, & Cassidy, 1990; Goodman et al., 1998; Solomon et al., 1995) and a semistructured interview administered to adolescents and adults (George et al., 1996; Main et al., 1985). The literature is currently divided over whether a person develops a generalized internal working model that consolidates the mental representations of their relationships with both caregivers or whether a person maintains relationship-specific internal working models. The Adult Attachment Interview (discussed below) yields only one attachment category, even though the interview questions probe for childhood memories related to all caregivers.

Several authors (Bretherton & Mulholland, 2008; Daniel, 2015; Main, 2000) have suggested that everyone possesses both generalized and relationship-specific internal working models and that these two types of internal working models are activated depending on both the person's generalized attachment quality as well as the circumstances surrounding the interpersonal interaction. First, insecurely attached persons are more likely to use generalized internal working models than securely attached persons because securely attached persons' internal working models are more flexible and open to a variety of relationship-specific interpersonal experiences. By contrast, insecurely attached persons' internal working models are less flexible. Thus, an anxious-avoidantly attached person will respond to most others with a reserved interpersonal style, whereas a securely attached person will titrate their responsiveness depending on the immediate interpersonal encounter. Second, stressful or threatening conditions are more likely to activate procedural memories that access generalized internal working models. Thus, a person stressed out at work might come home and isolate from their partner, which might reflect an anxious-avoidant internal working model, even though under more relaxed conditions, the person might experience a secure attachment relationship to their partner. Can attachment to God depend on the person's generalized internal working model as well as a relationship-specific internal working model? Empirical assessment of attachment to God could help answer this question (see below).

Interview Assessments of Attachment

Attachment Story-Completion Task (ASCT)

In this representational spirit, Inge Bretherton et al. (Bretherton et al., 1989; Bretherton, Prentiss, & Ridgeway, 1990; Bretherton, Ridgeway, & Cassidy, 1990) developed the Attachment Story-Completion Task (ASCT), a semistructured interview totaling 30 minutes that consists of five story stems designed to gain access into the internal working models of prepubertal children. This instrument was designed specifically from an attachment perspective: "We attempted to access the internal working models of attachment of 3-year-olds through a story-completion task, acted out with small family figures" (Bretherton, Ridgeway, & Cassidy, 1990, p. 284). C. George (personal communication, October 29, 1997) suggested that beginning in the preschool years, children typically no longer have caregiver-specific internal working models but, rather, more consolidated models of attachment security. Story completions are thus coded according to organization and content, not according to responses to a specific caregiver doll. Given the latest thinking regarding generalized versus relationship-specific internal working models (see above), it might be enlightening to conduct the ASCT with only one parental doll (either mother or father), alternating the parent one month apart, to determine what percentage of children at this age rely on generalized internal working models and under what circumstances.

In this assessment procedure (coding guidelines by George & Solomon, 2000), a family of dolls is used to tell the beginning of a series of five stories designed specifically to activate the child's attachment system and to elicit responses from the child regarding the child's interactions with the primary caregiver in five

Table 2.2 The Attachment Story-Completion Task: story stems and descriptions

Story stem	Story description
Birthday (practice)	Mother announces to family a birthday party
Spilled Juice	Child spills juice at dinner; mother points it out to child
Hurt Knee	Family is walking in park; child climbs rock and hurts knee
Monster in the Bedroom	Mother sends child to bed; child goes to bed and is scared by a monster
Departure	Mother leaves on an overnight trip; child stays with grandmother
Reunion	Mother returns from trip

attachment-relevant situations: confrontation (spilled-juice story), pain (hurt-knee story), fear (monster-in-the-bedroom story), separation (departure story), and reunion (reunion story). The child is expected to complete the stories begun by the interviewer and is permitted to stop the procedure at any time (see Table 2.2).

The child and interviewer are video-recorded together. The child is first introduced to the doll family and then asked to name the dolls and to make up stories about them. The child is encouraged to express themselves through both words and dramatic actions to complete each story. The interview begins with a practice story (birthday story) to warm up the child to the task. The interviewer starts each story, then prompts the child to finish it by saying, "Show me what happens now." Nondirective prompts such as, "What happens next?" or "Where are they going?" are used to facilitate the storytelling. In addition, a standard inquiry accompanies each story in the form of, "What do they do about [the story's central feature]?" to determine how the child resolves the story. For example, in the hurt-knee story, the interviewer asks, "What do they do about the hurt knee?" Standard inquiries are always made at the end of every story to clarify the child's story resolutions or lack of resolutions. Verbal and behavioral contents of the interviews are transcribed to ensure accurate coding of the quality of the child's internal working model of attachment security. On the basis of the ratings of these stories, the child is assigned an attachment category (A-B-C-D) analogous to the infant and adult classification systems (see Table 2.1).

Attachment quality assessed using this method was shown to be associated with contemporaneous child attachment behavior as well as previous assessments of attachment. The following statistically significant effect sizes of the associations with other, previously validated attachment measures are nevertheless attenuated by both the temporal instability of attachment classification related to significant life events and the differences in assessment methodology (e.g., behavioral vs. narrative modes of expression). In a sample consisting of 29 middle-income, Caucasian children aged 37 months, Bretherton et al. (Bretherton et al., 1989; Bretherton, Prentiss, & Ridgeway, 1990; Bretherton, Ridgeway, &

Cassidy, 1990) reported that attachment security assessed by the ASCT was significantly correlated with a modified Strange Situation (Main & Cassidy, 1988) at 37 months ($r = .49$, $p < .01$), the Attachment Q-Sort (Waters & Deane, 1985) at 37 months ($r = .26$, $p < .05$), and at 25 months ($r = .61$, $p < .001$), and the Strange Situation (Ainsworth et al., 1978) at 18 months ($r = .33$, $p < .05$), as well as with other constructs previously known to be significantly related to attachment. Using this coding system in a low-income, African American sample of 3- to 5-year-olds ($r = .30$, $p < .01$), Goodman et al. (1998) reported that mothers' sensitivity to their children, assessed during unstructured play, was associated with their children's attachment security.

Solomon et al. (1995) used a four-category (A-B-C-D) classification system. Forty-two middle-income children, ages 5–8, were administered the modified Strange Situation of Main and Cassidy (1988) (originally validated on 50 middle-income 6-year-olds) along with the ASCT. Correspondence between the two procedures was high (Cohen's kappa = .74, $t(40) = 8.23$, $p < .001$). Disorganized story completions predicted aggressive behavior in nonpsychiatric samples of middle-income (Solomon et al., 1995) and low-income (Hubbs-Tait et al., 1996) prepubertal children. Thus, George and Solomon (2000; see also Solomon et al., 1995) developed a valid and reliable coding system for the ASCT, which was used to code the child's stories. By use of the MacArthur Story-Stem Battery (Bretherton, Ridgeway, & Cassidy, 1990), whose 12 story stems include four ASCT story stems, children's perceptions of their mothers were shown to relate to the children's moral development (Buchsbaum & Emde, 1990), distinguish maltreated from nonmaltreated disadvantaged children (Buchsbaum et al., 1992), and relate to the mothers' psychological distress and children's behavior problems (Oppenheim et al., 1997; Warren et al., 1996).

Two initial subtypes of attachment disorganization were identified in a middle-income classroom population (Solomon et al., 1995). The authors reported that 21% of their sample of 5- to 8-year-olds demonstrated "frightened" behavior in their doll play: "Catastrophe, sometimes multiple catastrophes, often arise without warning; dangerous people or events are vanquished, only to surface again and again. Objects float and have magical, malignant powers; punishments are abusive and unrelenting" (p. 454). A smaller group of children in this frightened category told "markedly constricted" (p. 454) stories in which the children themselves, when telling their stories, "appear inhibited and frightened" (p. 454). The authors suggested, that unlike the destructive children, these children often perceive the caregiver as fragile and unable to tolerate their fear and rage. Attempts at disowning rage could thus produce severe inhibition of both action and thought, sometimes manifested as a refusal to participate. Goodman and Pfeffer (1998) proposed four new subcategories of the D attachment category in a prepubertal psychiatric inpatient population and related them to specific clinical symptomatology. They observed that aggression typified the story completions classified as D and that the direction of this aggression—whether projected, introjected, denied, or displaced—could serve as a means of differentiating subcategories of D. Green et al. (2001) took a different approach, using a different version of the ASCT to identify attachment subcategories of D on the basis of duration of disorganization within each story completion, whether pervasive, episodic, or bizarre.

British attachment researcher Shmueli-Goetz et al. (2008) developed an interview to assess school-aged children's internal working models. This assessment instrument, modeled after the Adult Attachment Interview, has been heralded as superior to the ASCT; it solicits information about attachment relationships with caregivers in a more straightforward manner that more intensely activates the child's attachment needs than does the ASCT and relies on the analysis of the structure of discourse rather than the thematic story content (Slade, 2001). Recent coding guidelines developed for the ASCT (George & Solomon, 2000), however, were also designed to analyze the structure of discourse. Furthermore, we do not know the extent to which school-aged children would share deeply personal feelings and experiences about their parents with a total stranger, if they did not know whether this stranger would protect their confidentiality and withhold the highly sensitive information from their parents. Regarding interviewing school-aged children, Ainsworth (1989) remarked:

> Metacognitive ability is not sufficiently developed in children under about the age of 12 to enable them to reflect about relationships in an interview and actually to put into words subtle feelings and attitudes that have been implicit since a much younger age.
>
> (p. 714)

Extensive validation and reliability testing of this instrument are needed to match the published work validating the ASCT.

Adult Attachment Interview (AAI)

George et al. (1996) developed the Adult Attachment Interview (AAI) to assess internal working models in adulthood. The AAI is an audio-recorded, semistructured 60-minute interview consisting of 20 questions designed to assess the internal working model that a person has formed in relation to their caregivers. The goal of the interview is to " 'surprise the unconscious' with respect to attachment, through repeated, insistent probing upon the same topic" (George et al., 1985, p. 6). Questions stimulate childhood memories of caregivers (typically, mother and father) in such attachment-relevant situations as separation, injury, illness, fear, and punishment. Five adjectives to describe the childhood relationship (ages 5–12) to each caregiver are also elicited. Interviewees are then asked to support these adjectives with actual childhood memories. Memories of significant losses, abuse, and traumatic events are also elicited. Interviewees are then asked to reflect on the reasons for their caregivers' behavior and the effects that their relationships to their caregivers have had on the development of their own personality and current relationships.

Main and Goldwyn (1994) designed a coding system that yields attachment clas-sifications analogous to the infant classification system (A-B-C-D; see Table 2.1). The coding system relies on verbatim transcription of the AAI. Like the ASCT, in coding the AAI, the structure of discourse, not thematic content, is the single most important determinant. A person is assigned an attachment classification based on continuous scores assigned on a series of 9-point rating scales divided into three groups: (1) inferred parental behavior during childhood (loving, rejecting, role-reversing/involving, neglecting, and pressuring to achieve), (2) patterned or organ-ized states of mind (coherence of transcript, idealization of parent, insistence on lack of recall, involved/involving anger, passivity of discourse, fear of loss, dis-missing derogation, metacognitive monitoring, overall coherence of mind), and (3) unresolved (disorganized/disoriented) states of mind (unresolved experiences of loss through death, unresolved abusive experiences).

The secure/autonomous (freely valuing and objective; F) category is assigned to persons who appear free to explore their thoughts and feelings during the course of the interview. Those persons appear relaxed and open, and their rendering of their relationships to their parents is coherent and organized. Secure persons usually score high on the coherence scales and low on the idealization, lack of recall, anger, and derogation scales.

The dismissing (Ds) category is assigned to persons who "limit the influence of attachment relationships and experiences in thought, in feeling, or in daily life" (Main & Goldwyn, 1994, p. 126). These interviewees provide little information about their childhoods; they offer semantic memories of idealized caregivers com-bined with episodic memories of rejection. Dismissing persons usually score high on the rejection, idealization, lack of recall, and derogation scales (depending on subclassification) and low on the loving, role-reversing, coherence, and anger scales.

The preoccupied/entangled (confused and unobjective; E) category is assigned to persons who appear embroiled in past experiences with parents. Their inter-views appear scattered and confusing, dominated by passive and vague memories. Persons in this category portray themselves as either fearful and overwhelmed, or angry, conflicted, and lacking insight. The extensive focus on parents appears tan-gential, rambling, and ultimately unconvincing. Preoccupied persons usually score high on the role-reversing and anger scales and low on the loving, rejecting, ideal-ization, lack of recall, derogation, and coherence scales.

The unresolved (disorganized/disoriented; U) category, in conjunction with one of the other three organized categories, is assigned as a primary classification to persons who appear unresolved about significant losses, abuse, or other traumatic events. Although qualitatively different from each other, significant loss and sig-nificant abuse nevertheless seem to produce the same effects on discourse when a person talks about the traumatic event. Unresolved persons exhibit "lapses in the monitoring of reasoning or discourse" (Main & Goldwyn, 1994, p. 148) when dis-cussing traumatic events, meaning that they might begin to talk as if the lost person were still alive or as if the abuse were occurring in the present. Unresolved persons score at least moderately high (anchor point greater than or equal to 5) on the unresolved scale and high, moderate, or low on the other scales, although three studies demonstrated a high degree of overlap between the U and E categories in psychiatric samples (Adam et al., 1996; Fonagy et al., 1996; Pianta, Egeland, et al., 1996).

The cannot-classify (CC) category is assigned to persons who cannot be classified within the original Ds-F-E attachment classification system. Their interviews appear to contain the marked presence of two different internal working models— either two insecure models (Ds and E) or a secure and insecure model (F and Ds; F and E). Seldom observed in low-risk samples (incidence of 7–10%; Hesse, 1996), the CC attachment category is reserved for persons in whom no single attachment pattern predominates. A person might be primarily identified as U but nevertheless receive a secondary attachment classification of CC if the interview contains the marked presence of two of the three original (Ds-F-E) attachment categories (e.g., U/CC/E1/Ds2). According to Main and Goldwyn (1994), the CC attachment category "should be assigned conservatively unless the judge has had extensive experience with high-risk samples" (p. 150). The cannot-classify attachment category is also available within the infant and school-age attachment classification systems, for example, when an infant manifests one attachment pattern during the first reunion episode and a different one during the second or "an incompatible mix of A and C characteristics" (Main & Goldwyn, 1994, p. 149) during the same reunion episode.

Interviewees are also assigned subcategories that capture subtle differences in the narrative that characterizes a particular attachment category. Main and Goldwyn (1994) described five secure subcategories (F1, F2, F3, F4, F5), four dismissing subcategories (Ds1, Ds2, Ds3, Ds4), and three preoccupied subcategories (E1, E2, E3). Most of these subcategories represent distinctions on a continuum ranging from extreme dismissing to extreme preoccupied. For example, the F5 subcategory comprises persons who have moderately high scores on the involving and anger scales, suggesting preoccupied features, but who otherwise fit the secure attachment classification profile. In the Ds1 subcategory, persons completely dismiss attachment experiences and relationships; there is no need to devalue attachment (Ds2) when attachment is denied. Because the labels assigned to the four attachment categories differ depending on a person's age (see Table 2.1), I will attempt to circumvent this confusion henceforth by using the infant attachment labels to refer to both infant and adult attachment categories in this book.

Administering the AAI on a low-risk, middle-income sample of mothers whose 6-year-old children had been administered the Strange Situation at 12 months of age, Main et al. (1985) were the first investigators to demonstrate retrospectively that the quality of caregivers' internal working models is highly associated with the quality of their children's patterns of attachment assessed five years earlier. Secure caregivers tended to have secure children; anxious-avoidant caregivers, anxious-avoidant children; and anxious-resistant caregivers, anxious-resistant children. The evidence supporting an association between an disorganized/disoriented internal working model in caregivers and a disorganized/disoriented attachment in their children is more equivocal (Ainsworth & Eichberg, 1991; Manassis et al., 1994; Solomon & George, 1999a).

Later investigators replicated the compelling findings of Main et al. (1985) retrospectively (Ainsworth & Eichberg, 1991; Grossmann et al., 1988), concurrently (Zeanah et al., 1993), and prospectively (Benoit & Parker, 1994; Fonagy et al., 1991; Ward & Carlson, 1995). Cross-generational concordances of AAI classification were reported between mothers and adult daughters (Benoit & Parker, 1994) and mothers and adolescents (Rosenstein & Horowitz, 1996). Test-retest reliabilities of 78% ($K = .63$) and 90% ($K = .79$) were reported by Bakermans-Kranenburg and van IJzendoorn (1993) and Benoit and Parker (1994), respectively. Ward and Carlson (1995) found no association between AAI classification and mother's age, education, or an assessment of expressive vocabulary ability. Bakermans-Kranenburg and van IJzendoorn (1993) reported that AAI classification is independent of verbal and performance intelligence, nonattachment memory, and social desirability and that it manifests high stability across time and interviewers (see Bakermans-Kranenburg & van IJzendoorn, 1993, and van IJzendoorn, 1995, for meta-analyses, including additional AAI validity and reliability information). Van IJzendoorn and Bakermans-Kranenburg (1996) conducted a meta-analysis of 33 AAI studies, including more than 2,000 AAI attachment classifications, and concluded that the worldwide distribution of the three traditional internal working models was as follows: 24% anxious-avoidant, 58% secure, and 18% anxious-resistant. Furthermore, approximately 19% were also assigned to the U attachment category. This distribution is almost identical to the distribution of the infant patterns of attachment (van IJzendoorn & Kroonenberg, 1988; van IJzendoorn et al., 1999).

Attachment researchers established not only developmental continuity of internal working models through intergenerational transmission but also the association between different categories of internal working models and concurrent psychopathology, specifically affective disorders (Dozier et al., 1991; Rosenstein & Horowitz, 1996), anxiety disorders (Fonagy et al., 1996; Manassis et al., 1994), depression (Cole-Detke & Kobak, 1996; Dozier, 1990; Fonagy et al., 1996; Kobak et al., 1991), dissociative disorders (Carlson, 1998; Liotti, 1999), dysfunctional anger (Kobak et al., 1993; Kobak et al., 1991; Kobak & Sceery, 1988), eating disorders (Cole-Detke & Kobak, 1996; Fonagy et al., 1996), substance abuse (Allen et al., 1996; Rosenstein & Horowitz, 1996), suicidal behavior (Adam et al., 1996), thought disorders (Dozier, 1990; Dozier et al., 1991), borderline personality disorder (Fonagy et al., 1996; Patrick et al., 1994; Rosenstein & Horowitz, 1996), antisocial, narcissistic, and paranoid symptomatology (Allen et al., 1996; Rosenstein & Horowitz, 1996), and other personality traits (Pianta, Egeland, et al., 1996; Rosenstein & Horowitz, 1996).

Clinician-researchers have also used the AAI to assess change in the quality of internal working models during therapy (e.g., Levy et al., 2006). The AAI also provides rich clinical information for case studies (Goodman, 2014; Granqvist, 2020, p. 266; Steele & Steele, 2008). Clinicians can also use this information to formulate a treatment plan and conduct psychotherapy (for additional information, see Chapter 3).

Adult Attachment Projective (AAP)

George and her colleagues (George & West, 2012; George et al., 1997, 1999) have developed the Adult Attachment Projective (AAP), another valid and reliable method of assessing attachment in adults that yields the same four attachment classifications as the AAI. The advantages of briefer administration and coding procedures as well as lower associated administrative and coding costs make the AAP an attractive alternative to both the labor-intensive AAI and the invalid self-report instruments. The AAP exploits the methodology of other adult projective instruments such as the Thematic Apperception Test. Interviewees are presented with eight ambiguously drawn, attachment-relevant pictures and are asked to make up a story about what is happening in each picture, what led up to the scene, what the characters are thinking and feeling, and what might happen next. Attachment classifications are based on applying to the verbatim transcription of interviewees' responses a coding system developed by the authors. Interrater reliability was high (Cohen's $K = .73$, $p < .0001$), and the convergence between the AAP and AAI was moderate, both between secure and insecure categories (Cohen's $K = .50$, $p < .01$) and among all four attachment categories (Cohen's $K = .59$, $p < .0001$; George et al., 1999). The AAP has the potential to become increasingly used in place of both the AAI and the self-report instruments used in adult attachment research.

Assessments of the Parental Internal Working Model of the Child

The attachment literature has produced numerous theoretical and empirical studies investigating parents' internal working models of their children (Aber et al., 1999; Benoit, Parker, et al., 1997; Benoit, Zeanah, et al., 1997; Bretherton et al., 1989; Cox et al., 1992; Cramer et al., 1990; George & Solomon, 1989, 1996; Pianta, Marvin, et al., 1996; Slade et al., 1999; Slade & Cohen, 1996; Solomon & George, 1996; Zeanah & Anders, 1987; Zeanah & Benoit, 1995; Zeanah et al., 1994; see George & Solomon, 1999, for a review of the literature). The instruments used to assess parent-to-child internal working models were developed by three different research groups: (1) Aber, Slade, and their colleagues, (2) George and Solomon, and (3) Zeanah, Benoit, and their colleagues.

The Parent Development Interview (PDI)

Aber et al. (1985) constructed the Parent Development Interview (PDI), which consists of 45 questions designed to assess parents' attachment representations of their relationships to their children. The interview yields three rating scales: recognition of joy and pleasure in the relationship and coherence of representation, recognition of anger in the relationship, and recognition of guilt and separation distress in the relationship (Slade et al., 1993). Both Aber et al. (1999) and Slade et al. (1999) reported specifically on mothers' relationships to toddlers. Mothers previously classified as secure on the AAI were rated highest on the joy-pleasure/coherence rating scale of parenting, and mothers rating highest on this rating scale also engaged in less negative and more positive behavioral interaction as observed during two one-hour, home observations at both 15 and 21 months. In addition, scores on all three rating scales at 15 months predicted scores at 28 months, suggesting that assessment of these constructs was reliable. Unfortunately, toddlers' quality of attachment was not measured.

On the basis of this approach, I (Goodman, 2005) reported on the Parent-to-Child Internal Working Model Q-Set, a 100-item instrument constructed to yield the quality of the prototypical parent's internal working model of their child at age 5. The first 60 items were designed specifically to assess the security of internal working models; the second 40 items were designed to measure a separate theoretical construct. A group of highly respected judges representing the attachment construct were selected to sort the items according to the prototypical parent. Attachment judges were asked to sort the items for a secure, coherent, freely valuing parental internal working model of a 5-year-old child. Judges' prototypical Q-sorts were averaged to yield a composite prototypical Q-sort of the quality of the prototypical parent's internal working model.

The Caregiving Interview

Seeking to define an approach that captures the parent's perspective of "providing protection" (George & Solomon, 1999, p. 651) to the child as the key ingredient in fostering a child's attachment security, George and Solomon (1989) developed the Caregiving Interview assessing two dimensions of the parent's model of caregiving—secure base and competence. Both secure base and competence in parents were positively correlated with the secure attachment dimension and negatively correlated with the controlling attachment dimension in their children at age 6. Secure base was also negatively correlated with the avoidant attachment dimension. Home observations were not associated with the two dimensions of caregiving. A later study (George & Solomon, 1996), added three other dimensions of caregiving—rejection, uncertainty, and helplessness. Rejection was positively correlated with the avoidant attachment dimension: uncertainty, positively correlated with the resistant/ambivalent attachment dimension; and helplessness, positively correlated with the controlling attachment dimension in children at age 6. In addition, the quality of parents' AAI-assessed internal working models was associated with their dimensions of caregiving and their children's attachment dimensions.

The Working Model of the Child Interview (WMCI)

Zeanah and his colleagues (Benoit, Parker, et al., 1997; Benoit, Zeanah, et al., 1997; Zeanah & Benoit, 1995; Zeanah et al., 1994) constructed the Working Model of the Child Interview (WMCI) to assess parents' internal working models of their children. A categorical coding system analogous to the one used to code the Strange Situation

(Ainsworth et al., 1978) was also developed. In this coding system, a secure attachment corresponds with a balanced internal working model of the child; an avoidant attachment, with a disengaged model; and a resistant/ambivalent attachment, with a distorted model. The WMCI classifications—assessed both during the third trimester of pregnancy and when the infant was 12 months old—were significantly associated with attachment classifications in infants at age 12 months. The WMCI classifications assessed during pregnancy also predicted WMCI classifications when the infant was 12 months old, suggesting that measurement of these constructs was reliable (Benoit, Parker, et al., 1997; Zeanah & Benoit, 1995; Zeanah et al., 1994).

In addition, WMCI classifications were able to distinguish clinically referred from nonreferred infants and toddlers, with mothers of clinically referred infants and toddlers more likely having distorted or disengaged internal working models of their children (Benoit, Zeanah, et al., 1997; Zeanah & Benoit, 1995). Unfortunately, in this clinical study, mothers' and children's attachment quality was not assessed, and behavioral observations of the mothers were not made. Taken together, however, all three coding systems of the parental internal working model of the relationship to the child establish associations among parents' quality of internal working models of their own parents, parents' quality of internal working models of their children, the quality of their behavioral interaction with their children, and finally, their children's quality of internal working models.

Self-Report Attachment Measures

Researchers, working mostly from a social psychology perspective, have attempted to develop self-report instruments that yield assessments of internal working models of adult attachment (Bartholomew & Horowitz, 1991; Brennan et al., 1998; Collins & Read, 1990; Hazan & Shaver, 1987; Hindy & Schwarz, 1994; Simpson, 1990; Sperling & Berman, 1991; West et al., 1987). Despite their consistency with each other (Sperling et al., 1996), self-report instruments nevertheless demonstrate little convergent validity with the AAI—the gold standard of adult attachment assessment (Bartholomew & Shaver, 1998; Crowell & Treboux, 1995; Crowell et al., 1999; de Haas et al., 1994; Diamond et al., 1999; George & West, 1999; Main & Goldwyn, 1994). In fact, in a head-to-head matchup, the correlation between the AAI and self-report attachment measures was an abysmal $r = .09$ (Roisman et al., 2007). This lack of correspondence is not surprising because self-report instruments measure conscious processes, whereas the AAI "surprises"—and assesses—the unconscious (George et al., 1985, p. 6).

Administering a self-report instrument rather than conducting an extensive, clinically informed interview regarding attachment relationships would be like handing a new patient a packet of questionnaires to complete in lieu of an initial in-depth consultation and expecting to derive equally reliable results. One of these self-report developers, who was observed at an AAI training workshop, stated that he had given up on his instrument because it had no construct validity (M. West, personal communication, June 10, 1996). Most crucially, self-report instruments fail to detect the effects of defensive distortions on recall and narrative expression that reflect underlying distinctions in attachment organization (see also Dozier, 1990; Dozier et al., 1991; Dozier & Lee, 1995; Kobak & Sceery, 1988; Pianta, Egeland, et al., 1996; Shedler et al., 1993, 1994). Consistent with this explanation, Eagle (2006) has suggested that the concordance between self-report and narrative-based attachment items found by Westen and his colleagues (2006) reflects the fact that an informant other than the patient (in this study, the therapist) completed their attachment instrument. The potential for self-deception among anxious-avoidant persons is especially great because of their need to maintain a grandiose self that underlies this attachment organization (Goodman, 2014).

Self-report instruments that purport to measure adult attachment also tend to focus on the quality of interpersonal relationships rather than on specific relationships on which a person relies during attachment-activating situations. These instruments are also unlikely to activate the attachment system during their administration. The AAI, on the other hand, was designed specifically to activate the attachment system to yield an accurate assessment of the person's internal working model by asking the interviewee to recall specific attachment-activating childhood events to support their general impressions of childhood relationships with their caregivers. An insufficiently stressed attachment system can yield inaccurate attachment classifications (e.g., Fonagy et al., 1991; Goodman et al., 1999). Thus, it is easy to understand the discrepancy between self-report instruments and narrative-based instruments coded by outside informants such as the AAI.

Assessments of Attachment to God

Because this book concerns attachment to God, it is only natural that I would spend a brief amount of time reviewing the options available for assessing a person's attachment to God. What follows is a review of two self-report measures and one interview assessment.

Attachment to God Prototype Questionnaire

The Attachment to God Prototype Questionnaire (Kirkpatrick & Shaver, 1992) follows the design of the Romantic Love Attachment Style Prototype Questionnaire, one of the first self-report attachment measures by the second author (Hazan & Shaver, 1987). The dubious assumption behind the conceptualization of this instrument is that "romantic love and religion can be thought of as parallel" (Kirkpatrick & Shaver, 1992, p. 271). Thus, the authors took the three attachment prototypes representing the three romantic attachment patterns and reworded each of these to reference God as a parent instead of a romantic partner. The secure prototype thus reads as though God behaves almost like a human parent:

God is generally warm and responsive to me; He always seems to know when to be supportive and protective of me, and when to let me make my own mistakes.

My relationship with God is always comfortable, and I am very happy and satisfied with it.

(p. 270)

This questionnaire suffers from all the shortcomings that bedevil self-report attachment measures (see above).

Attachment to God Inventory (AGI)

The Attachment to God Inventory (AGI; Beck & McDonald, 2004) was modeled
after a more recently designed self-report attachment measure, the Experiences in
Close Relationships Scale (ECR; Brennan et al., 1998), updated by Fraley and his
colleagues (2000). The AGI is a 28-item questionnaire that rewords the ECR items,
with each item theoretically loading onto one of two ECR factors: anxiety and
avoidance. Here is an example of an item that loads onto the avoidance factor: "I
just don't feel a deep need to be close to God" (item 2; $r = .64$; p. 103). Like the
previous questionnaire, this questionnaire suffers from all the shortcomings that
bedevil self-report attachment measures.

Religious Attachment Interview (RAI)

The Religious Attachment Interview (RAI; Granqvist & Main, 2017) shows the
most promise as an assessment of attachment to God because it is modeled after
the AAI as an interview that elicits a narrative about the person's attachment relationship to God. A sophisticated coding system could unlock the secrets underlying this narrative to discover the person's attachment classification with respect
to their relationship to God. Aside from some preliminary results reported in
Granqvist (2020), the RAI has not yielded any published research. Unfortunately,
Mary Main died in early 2023, and Pehr Granqvist has written that the interview remains unvalidated, declaring its coding principles and scales to be "quite
crude" (Granqvist, personal communication, January 16, 2023). Thus, he is not
sharing the RAI publicly.

Without a valid, reliable assessment of attachment to God, it will be impossible
to assess changes in this attachment as a function of participation in the process of
psychotherapy. The field awaits an instrument that could provide empirical support
for deep change at the mental representational level of attachment organization of a
person's relationship to God. Attachment researchers could also use such an instrument to assess whether change in a person's attachment relationship to God can
predict changes in human attachment relationships, such as when a person enters
a 12-step program of recovery, thus transforming their attachment relationship to
God, which subsequently changes their attachment relationships to a partner or to
parents. Like Estragon and Vladimir in *Waiting for Godot* (Beckett, 2011), however, those of us deeply interested in investigating these empirical questions will
continue waiting for this instrument to arrive.

Adult Attachment to God Interview (AAGI)

In Chapter 6 of Goodman (2025), I introduce a modification of the AAI, which I called the Adult Attachment to God Interview (AAGI). Instead of asking the interviewee questions about their attachment relationships to their parents, the interviewer asks these same questions about their attachment relationship to God. A graduate student administered the AAGI to my patient to determine the quality of his attachment relationship to his Higher Power. No validity or reliability data are associated with the AAGI; I used it simply to enrich my discussion of this patient's treatment.

Conclusion

I have profiled the work of three innovative pioneers of attachment theory: John Bowlby, Mary Ainsworth, and Mary Main. All three theorists placed attachment, separation, and loss at the center of their understanding of psychological development. Bowlby (1982) hypothesized that infants normatively begin to form internal working models of their earliest attachment relationships with caregivers to assist them in making accurate predictions of their physical availability that could aid in their survival. Ainsworth et al. (1978) documented individual differences in the patterns of attachment that infants form by 12 months of age through her assessment paradigm known as the Strange Situation. She also discovered qualitatively distinct caregiving behaviors associated with each of these individual differences in the patterns of attachment. Main et al. (1985) analyzed the discourse of adults recollecting their childhood attachment relationships with their parents, determining that these relationships are represented in the mind and are transmitted through caregiving behavior to offspring. The four attachment patterns are known as secure, anxious-resistant, anxious-avoidant, and disorganized/disoriented. I also discuss the methods used to assess attachment patterns in both childhood and adulthood. Finally, I review three instruments that purport to assess a person's attachment to God.

References

Aber, J. L., Belsky, J., Slade, A., & Crnic, K. (1999). Stability and change in mothers' representations of their relationship with their toddlers. *Developmental Psychology, 35,* 1038–1047.

Aber, J. L., Slade, A., Berger, B., Bresgi, I., & Kaplan, M. (1985). The parent development interview. Unpublished manuscript. Columbia University, New York.

Adam, K. S., Sheldon-Keller, A. E., & West, M. (1996). Attachment organization and history of suicidal behavior in clinical adolescents. *Journal of Consulting and Clinical Psychology, 64,* 264–272.

Ainsworth, M. D. S. (1967). *Infancy in Uganda: Infant care and the growth of love.* Johns Hopkins University Press.

Ainsworth, M. D. S. (1979). Infant-mother attachment. *American Psychologist, 34,* 932–937.

Ainsworth, M. D. S. (1989). Attachments beyond infancy. *American Psychologist, 44,* 709–716.

Ainsworth, M. D. S., Bell, S. M., & Stayton, D. J. (1974). Infant-mother attachment and social development: "Socialization" as a product of reciprocal responsiveness to signals. In M. P. M. Richards (Ed.), *The integration of a child into a social world* (pp. 99–135). Cambridge University Press.

Ainsworth, M. D. S., Blehar, M. C., Waters, E., & Wall, S. (1978). *Patterns of attachment: A psychological study of the strange situation.* Erlbaum.

Ainsworth, M. D. S., & Eichberg, C. G. (1991). Effects on infant-mother attachment of mother's unresolved loss of an attachment figure, or other traumatic experience. In C. M. Parkes, J. Stevenson-Hinde, & P. Marris (Eds.), *Attachment across the life cycle* (pp. 160–183). Tavistock/Routledge.

Ainsworth, M. D. S., & Wittig, B. A. (1969). Attachment and exploratory behavior of one-year-olds in a strange situation. In B. M. Foss (Ed.), *Determinants of infant behaviour IV* (pp. 111–136). Methuen.

Allen, J. P., Hauser, S. T., & Borman-Spurrell, E. (1996). Attachment theory as a framework for understanding sequelae of severe adolescent psychopathology: An 11-year follow-up study. *Journal of Consulting and Clinical Psychology, 64,* 254–263.

Bakermans-Kranenburg, M. J., & van IJzendoorn, M. H. (1993). A psychometric study of the adult attachment interview: Reliability and discriminant validity. *Developmental Psychology, 29,* 870–879.

Bartholomew, K., & Horowitz, L. M. (1991). Attachment styles among young adults: A test of a four-category model. *Journal of Personality and Social Psychology, 61,* 226–244.

Bartholomew, K., & Shaver, P. R. (1998). Methods of assessing adult attachment: Do they converge? In J. A. Simpson & W. S. Rholes (Eds.), *Attachment theory and close relationships* (pp. 25–45). Guilford Press.

Beck, R., & McDonald, A. (2004). Attachment to God: The attachment to God inventory, tests of working model correspondence, and an exploration of faith group differences. *Journal of Psychology and Theology, 32,* 92–103.

Beckett, S. (2011). *Waiting for Godot.* Grove Press.

Benoit, D., & Parker, K. C. H. (1994). Stability and transmission of attachment across three generations. *Child Development, 65,* 1444–1456.

Benoit, D., Parker, K. C. H., & Zeanah, C. H. (1997). Mothers' representations of their infants assessed prenatally: Stability and association with infants' attachment classifications. *Journal of Child Psychology and Psychiatry and Allied Disciplines, 38,* 307–313.

Benoit, D., Zeanah, C. H., Parker, K. C. H., Nicholson, E., & Coolbear, J. (1997). "Working model of the child interview": Infant clinical status related to maternal perceptions. *Infant Mental Health Journal, 18,* 107–121.

Bowlby, J. (1958). The nature of the child's tie to his mother. *International Journal of Psycho-Analysis, 39,* 350–373.

Bowlby, J. (1973). *Attachment and loss:* Vol. 2. *Separation: Anxiety and anger.* Basic Books.

Bowlby, J. (1977). The making and breaking of affectional bonds. I. Aetiology and psychopathology in the light of attachment theory. *British Journal of Psychiatry, 130,* 201–210.

Bowlby, J. (1980). *Attachment and loss:* Vol. 3. *Loss,* sadness and depression. Basic Books.

Bowlby, J. (1982). *Attachment and loss:* Vol. 1. *Attachment* (2nd ed.). Basic Books.

Bowlby, J. (1988). *A secure base: Parent-child attachment and healthy human development.* Basic Books.

Bowlby, J. (1989). The role of attachment in personality development and psychopathology. In S. I. Greenspan & G. H. Pollock (Eds.), *The course of life*: Vol. 1. *Infancy* (pp. 229–270). International University Press.

Brennan, K. A., Clark, C. L., & Shaver, P. R. (1998). Self-report measurement of adult attachment: An integrative overview. In J. A. Simpson & W. S. Rholes (Eds.), *Attachment theory and close relationships* (pp. 46–76). Guilford Press.

Bretherton, I. (1985). Attachment theory: Retrospect and prospect. *Monographs of the Society for Research in Child Development, 50*(1–2), 3–35.

Bretherton, I., Biringen, Z., Ridgeway, D., Maslin, C., & Sherman, M. (1989). Attachment: The parental perspective. *Infant Mental Health Journal, 10*, 203–221.

Bretherton, I., & Munholland, K. A. (2008). Internal working models in attachment relationships: Elaborating a central construct in attachment theory. In J. Cassidy & P. R. Shaver (Eds.), *Handbook of attachment: Theory, research, and clinical applications* (2nd ed., pp. 102–127). Guilford Press.

Bretherton, I., Prentiss, C., & Ridgeway, D. (1990). Family relationships as represented in a story-completion task at thirty-seven and fifty-four months of age. *New Directions for Child Development, 48*, 85–105.

Bretherton, I., Ridgeway, D., & Cassidy, J. (1990). Assessing internal working models of the attachment relationship: An attachment story completion task for 3-year-olds. In M. T. Greenberg, D. Cicchetti, & E. M. Cummings (Eds.), *Attachment in the preschool years: Theory, research, and intervention* (pp. 273–308). University of Chicago Press.

Buchsbaum, H. K., & Emde, R. N. (1990). Play narratives in 36-month-old children: Early moral development and family relationships. *Psychoanalytic Study of the Child, 45*, 129–155.

Buchsbaum, H. K., Toth, S. L., Clyman, R. B., Cicchetti, D., & Emde, R. N. (1992). The use of narrative story stem technique with maltreated children: Implications for theory and practice. *Development and Psychopathology, 4*, 603–625.

Carlson, E. A. (1998). A prospective longitudinal study of attachment disorganization/disorientation. *Child Development, 69*, 1107–1128.

Carlson, V., Cicchetti, D., Barnett, D., & Braunwald, K. (1989a). Disorganized/disoriented attachment relationships in maltreated infants. *Developmental Psychology, 25*, 525–531.

Carlson, V., Cicchetti, D., Barnett, D., & Braunwald, K. G. (1989b). Finding order in disorganization: Lessons from research on maltreated infants' attachments to their caregivers. In D. Cicchetti & V. Carlson (Eds.), *Child maltreatment: Theory and research on the causes and consequences of child abuse and neglect* (pp. 494–528). Cambridge University Press.

Cole-Detke, H., & Kobak, R. (1996). Attachment processes in eating disorder and depression. *Journal of Consulting and Clinical Psychology, 64*, 282–290.

Collins, N. L., & Read, S. J. (1990). Adult attachment, working models, and relationship quality in dating couples. *Journal of Personality and Social Psychology, 58*, 644–663.

Cox, M. J., Owen, M. T., Henderson, V. K., & Margand, N. A. (1992). Prediction of infant-father and infant-mother attachment. *Developmental Psychology, 28*, 474–483.

Cramer, B., Robert-Tissot, C., Stern, D. N., Serpa-Rusconi, S., De Muralt, M., Besson, G., Palacio-Espasa, F., Bachmann, J., Knauer, D., Berney, C., & D'Arcis, U. (1990). Outcome evaluation in brief mother-infant psychotherapy: A preliminary report. *Infant Mental Health Journal, 11*, 278–300.

Crowell, J. A., & Treboux, D. (1995). A review of adult attachment measures: Implications for theory and research. *Social Development, 4*, 294–327.

Crowell, J. A., Treboux, D., & Waters, E. (1999). The adult attachment interview and the relationship questionnaire: Relations to reports of mothers and partners. *Personal Relationships, 6*, 1–18.

Daniel, S. I. F. (2015). *Adult attachment patterns in a treatment context: Relationship and narrative*. Routledge.

de Haas, M. A., Bakermans-Kranenburg, M. J., & van IJzendoorn, M. H. (1994). The Adult Attachment Interview and questionnaires for attachment style, temperament, and memories of parental behavior. *Journal of Genetic Psychology, 155*, 471–486.

de Wolff, M., & van IJzendoorn, M. H. (1997). Sensitivity and attachment: A meta-analysis on parental antecedents of infant attachment. *Child Development, 68*, 571–591.

Diamond, D., Clarkin, J., Levine, H., Levy, K., Foelsch, P., & Yeomans, F. (1999). Borderline conditions and attachment: A preliminary report. *Psychoanalytic Inquiry, 19*, 831–884.

Dozier, M. (1990). Attachment organization and treatment use for adults with serious psychopathological disorders. *Development and Psychopathology, 2*, 47–60.

Dozier, M., & Lee, S. W. (1995). Discrepancies between self- and other-report of psychiatric symptomatology: Effects of dismissing attachment strategies. *Development and Psychopathology, 7*, 217–226.

Dozier, M., Stevenson, A. L., Lee, S. W., & Velligan, D. I. (1991). Attachment organization and familial overinvolvement for adults with serious psychopathological disorders. *Development and Psychopathology, 3*, 475–489.

Eagle, M. N. (2006). Attachment, psychotherapy, and assessment: A commentary. *Journal of Consulting and Clinical Psychology, 74*, 1086–1097.

Fonagy, P., Leigh, T., Steele, M., Steele, H., Kennedy, R., Mattoon, G., Target, M., & Gerber, A. (1996). The relation of attachment status, psychiatric classification, and response to psychotherapy. *Journal of Consulting and Clinical Psychology, 64*, 22–31.

Fonagy, P., Steele, H., & Steele, M. (1991). Maternal representations of attachment during pregnancy predict organization of infant-mother attachment at one year of age. *Child Development, 62*, 891–905.

Fraley, R. C., Waller, N. G., & Brennan, K. A. (2000). An item-response theory analysis of self-report measures of adult attachment. *Journal of Personality and Social Psychology, 78*, 350–365.

Freud, S. (1905). Three essays on the theory of sexuality. In J. Strachey (Ed. and Trans.), *The standard edition of the complete psychological works of Sigmund Freud* (Vol. 7, pp. 135–243). Hogarth Press.

Freud, S. (1924). The loss of reality in neurosis and psychosis. In J. Strachey (Ed. and Trans.), *The standard edition of the complete psychological works of Sigmund Freud* (Vol. 19, pp. 181–187). Hogarth Press.

Freud, S. (1933). New introductory lectures on psycho-analysis. In J. Strachey (Ed. and Trans.), *The standard edition of the complete psychological works of Sigmund Freud* (Vol. 22, pp. 1–182). Hogarth Press.

George, C., Kaplan, N., & Main, M. (1985). Adult attachment interview. Unpublished manuscript. University of California, Berkeley.

George, C., Kaplan, N., & Main, M. (1996). Adult attachment interview (3rd ed.). Unpublished manuscript. University of California, Berkeley.

George, C., & Solomon, J. (1989). Internal working models of caregiving and security of attachment at age six. *Infant Mental Health Journal, 10*, 222–237.

George, C., & Solomon, J. (1996). Representational models of relationships: Links between caregiving and attachment. *Infant Mental Health Journal, 17*, 198–216.

George, C., & Solomon, J. (1999). Attachment and caregiving: The caregiving behavioral system. In J. Cassidy & P. R. Shaver (Eds.), *Handbook of attachment: Theory, research, and clinical applications* (pp. 649–670). Guilford Press.

George, C., & Solomon, J. (2000). Six-year attachment doll play classification system (2nd ed.). Unpublished manuscript. Department of Psychology, Mills College.

George, C., & West, M. (1999). Developmental vs. social personality models of adult attachment and mental ill health. *British Journal of Medical Psychology, 72*, 285–303.

George, C., West, M., & Pettem, O. (1997). The adult attachment projective. Unpublished manuscript. Mills College.

George, C., West, M., & Pettem, O. (1999). The adult attachment projective: Disorganization of adult attachment at the level of representation. In J. Solomon & C. George (Eds.), *Attachment disorganization* (pp. 318–346). Guilford Press.

George, C., & West, M. L. (2012). *The adult attachment projective picture system: Attachment theory and assessment in adults.* Guilford Press.

Goodman, G. (2005). Empirical evidence supporting the conceptual relatedness of object representations and internal working models. *Journal of the American Psychoanalytic Association, 53*, 597–617.

Goodman, G. (2014). *The internal world and attachment.* Routledge.

Goodman, G. (2025). *Practical applications of transforming the attachment relationship to God: Using attachment-informed psychotherapy.* Routledge.

Goodman, G., Aber, J. L., Berlin, L., & Brooks-Gunn, J. (1998). The relations between maternal behaviors and urban preschool children's internal working models of attachment security. *Infant Mental Health Journal, 19*, 378–393.

Goodman, G., Hans, S. L., & Cox, S. M. (1999). Attachment behavior and its antecedents in offspring born to methadone-maintained women. *Journal of Clinical Child Psychology, 28*, 58–69.

Goodman, G., & Pfeffer, C. R. (1998). Attachment disorganization in prepubertal children with severe emotional disturbance. *Bulletin of the Menninger Clinic, 62*, 490–525.

Granqvist, P. (2020). *Attachment in religion and spirituality: A wider view.* Guilford Press.

Granqvist, P., & Main, M. (2017). The religious attachment interview: Coding and classification system. Unpublished manuscript. Stockholm University, Stockholm, Sweden/University of California, Berkeley.

Green, J., Goldwyn, R., Peters, S., & Stanley, C. (2001). Subtypes of attachment disorganisation in young school age children. Paper presented at the biennial meeting of the Society for Research in Child Development, Assessing attachment in middle childhood: New methods and early findings, Minneapolis, MN.

Grossmann, K., Fremmer-Bombik, E., Rudolph, J., & Grossmann, K. E. (1988). Maternal representations as related to patterns of infant-mother attachment and maternal care during the first year. In R. A. Hinde & J. Stevenson-Hinde (Eds.), *Relationships within families* (pp. 241–260). Oxford University Press.

Harlow, H. F., & Zimmerman, R. R. (1959). Affectional responses in the infant monkey. *Science, 130*, 421–432.

Hazan, C., & Shaver, P. R. (1987). Romantic love conceptualized as an attachment process. *Journal of Personality and Social Psychology, 52*, 511–524.

Hesse, E. (1996). Discourse, memory, and the adult attachment interview: A note with emphasis on the emerging cannot classify category. *Infant Mental Health Journal, 17*, 4–11.

Hesse, E., & Main, M. (1999). Second-generation effects of unresolved trauma in non-maltreating parents: Dissociated, frightened, and threatening parental behavior. *Psychoanalytic Inquiry, 19,* 481–540.

Hindy, C. G., & Schwarz, J. C. (1994). Anxious romantic attachment in adult relationships. In M. B. Sperling & W. H. Berman (Eds.), *Attachment in adults: Clinical and developmental perspectives* (pp. 179–203). Guilford Press.

Hubbs-Tait, L., Hughes, K. P., Culp, A. M., Osofsky, J. D., Hann, D. M., Eberhart-Wright, A., & Ware, L. M. (1996). Children of adolescent mothers: Attachment representation, maternal depression, and later behavior problems. *American Journal of Orthopsychiatry, 66,* 416–426.

Karen, R. (1998). *Becoming attached: First relationships and how they shape our capacity to love.* Oxford University Press.

Kernberg, O. F., Selzer, M. A., Koenigsberg, H. W., Carr, A. C., & Appelbaum, A. H. (1989). *Psychodynamic psychotherapy of borderline patients.* Basic Books.

Kirkpatrick, L. A., & Shaver, P. R. (1992). An attachment-theoretical approach to romantic love and religious belief. *Personality and Social Psychology Bulletin, 18,* 266–275.

Klein, M. (1940). Mourning and its relation to manic-depressive states. In R. E. Money-Kyrle (Ed.), *Love, guilt and reparation and other works, 1921–1945* (pp. 344–369). Delacorte Press.

Klein, M. (1957). Envy and gratitude: A study of unconscious sources. In R. E. Money-Kyrle (Ed.), *Envy and gratitude and other works, 1946–1963* (pp. 176–235). Delacorte Press.

Kobak, R. R., Cole, H. E., Ferenz-Gillies, R., Fleming, W. S., & Gamble, W. (1993). Attachment and emotion regulation during mother-teen problem solving: A control theory analysis. *Child Development, 64,* 231–245.

Kobak, R. R., & Sceery, A. (1988). Attachment in late adolescence: Working models, affect regulation, and representations of self and others. *Child Development, 59,* 135–146.

Kobak, R. R., Sudler, N., & Gamble, W. (1991). Attachment and depressive symptoms during adolescence: A developmental pathways analysis. *Development and Psychopathology, 3,* 461–474.

Levy, K. N., Meehan, K. B., Kelly, K. M., Reynoso, J. S., Weber, M., Clarkin, J. F., & Kernberg, O. F. (2006). Change in attachment patterns and reflective function in a randomized control trial of transference-focused psychotherapy for borderline personality disorder. *Journal of Consulting and Clinical Psychology, 74,* 1027–1040.

Lichtenberg, J. D. (1989). *Psychoanalysis and motivation.* The Analytic Press.

Liotti, G. (1999). Disorganization of attachment as a model for understanding dissociative psychopathology. In J. Solomon & C. George (Eds.), *Attachment disorganization* (pp. 291–317). Guilford Press.

Lorenz, K. (1935). Companionship in bird life: Fellow members of the species as releasers of social behavior. In C. H. Schiller (Ed. and Trans.), *Instinctive behavior: The development of a modern concept* (pp. 83–128). International Universities Press.

Lyons-Ruth, K., Alpern, L., & Repacholi, B. (1993). Disorganized infant attachment classification and maternal psychosocial problems as predictors of hostile-aggressive behavior in the preschool classroom. *Child Development, 64,* 572–585.

Lyons-Ruth, K., Bronfman, E., & Parsons, E. (1999). Maternal frightened, frightening, or atypical behavior and disorganized infant attachment patterns. *Monographs of the Society for Research in Child Development, 64*(3), 67–96.

Lyons-Ruth, K., Connell, D. B., Grunebaum, H., & Botein, S. (1990). Infants at social risk: Maternal depression and family support services as mediators of infant development and security of attachment. *Child Development, 61,* 85–98.

Lyons-Ruth, K., Connell, D. B., & Zoll, D. (1989). Patterns of maternal behavior among infants at risk for abuse: Relations with infant attachment behavior and infant development at 12 months of age. In D. Cicchetti & V. Carlson (Eds.), *Child maltreatment: Theory and research on the causes and consequences of child abuse and neglect* (pp. 464–493). Cambridge University Press.

Lyons-Ruth, K., Easterbrooks, M. A., & Cibelli, C. D. (1997). Infant attachment strategies, infant mental lag, and maternal depressive symptoms: Predictors of internalizing and externalizing problems at age 7. *Developmental Psychology, 33,* 681–692.

Lyons-Ruth, K., Zoll, D., Connell, D., & Grunebaum, H. U. (1986). The depressed mother and her one-year-old infant: Environment, interaction, attachment, and infant development. *New Directions for Child Development, 34,* 61–82.

Main, M. (2000). The organized categories of infant, child, and adult attachment: Flexible vs. inflexible attention under attachment-related stress. *Journal of the American Psychoanalytic Association, 48,* 1055–1096.

Main, M., & Cassidy, J. (1988). Categories of response to reunion with the parent at age 6: Predictable from infant attachment classifications and stable over a 1-month period. *Developmental Psychology, 24,* 415–426.

Main, M., & Goldwyn, R. (1994). Adult attachment scoring and classification systems (6th ed.). Unpublished manuscript. University College, London.

Main, M., & Hesse, E. (1990). Parents' unresolved traumatic experiences are related to infant disorganized attachment status: Is frightened and/or frightening parental behavior the linking mechanism? In M. T. Greenberg, D. Cicchetti, & E. M. Cummings (Eds.), *Attachment in the preschool years: Theory, research, and intervention* (pp. 161–182). University of Chicago Press.

Main, M., Kaplan, N., & Cassidy, J. (1985). Security in infancy, childhood, and adulthood: A move to the level of representation. *Monographs of the Society for Research in Child Development, 50*(1–2), 66–104.

Main, M., & Solomon, J. (1986). Discovery of an insecure-disorganized/disoriented attachment pattern. In T. B. Brazelton & M. W. Yogman (Eds.), *Affective development in infancy* (pp. 95–124). Ablex.

Main, M., & Solomon, J. (1990). Procedures for identifying infants as disorganized/disoriented during the Ainsworth Strange Situation. In M. T. Greenberg, D. Cicchetti, & E. M. Cummings (Eds.), *Attachment in the preschool years: Theory, research, and intervention* (pp. 121–160). University of Chicago Press.

Manassis, K., Bradley, S., Goldberg, S., Hood, J., & Swinson, R. P. (1994). Attachment in mothers with anxiety disorders and their children. *Journal of the American Academy of Child and Adolescent Psychiatry, 33,* 1106–1113.

Mesman, J., van IJzendoorn, M. H., & Sagi-Schwartz, A. (2018). Cross-cultural patterns of attachment: Universal and contextual dimensions. In J. Cassidy & P. R. Shaver (Eds.), *Handbook of attachment: Theory, research, and clinical applications* (pp. 852–877). Guilford Press.

NIV (New International Version). (1978). *The holy Bible.* Zondervan.

Oppenheim, D., Emde, R. N., & Warren, S. (1997). Children's narrative representations of mothers: Their development and associations with child and mother adaptation. *Child Development, 68,* 127–138.

Patrick, M., Hobson, R. P., Castle, D., Howard, R., & Maughan, B. (1994). Personality disorder and the mental representation of early social experience. *Development and Psychopathology, 6*, 375–388.

Pianta, R. C., Egeland, B., & Adam, E. K. (1996). Adult attachment classification and self-reported psychiatric symptomatology as assessed by the Minnesota Multiphasic Personality Inventory-2. *Journal of Consulting and Clinical Psychology, 64*, 273–281.

Pianta, R. C., Marvin, R. S., Britner, P. A., & Borowitz, K. C. (1996). Mothers' resolution of their children's diagnosis: Organized patterns of caregiving representations. *Infant Mental Health Journal, 17*, 239–256.

Roisman, G. I., Holland, A., Fortuna, K., Fraley, R. C., Clausell, E., & Clarke, A. (2007). The adult attachment interview and self-reports of attachment style: An empirical rapprochement. *Journal of Personality and Social Psychology, 92*, 678–697.

Rosenstein, D. S., & Horowitz, H. A. (1996). Adolescent attachment and psychopathology. *Journal of Consulting and Clinical Psychology, 64*, 244–253.

Schuengel, C., Bakermans-Kranenburg, M. J., & van IJzendoorn, M. H. (1999). Attachment and loss: Frightening maternal behavior linking unresolved loss and disorganized infant attachment. *Journal of Consulting and Clinical Psychology, 67*, 54–63.

Shedler, J., Mayman, M., & Manis, M. (1993). The illusion of mental health. *American Psychologist, 48*, 1117–1131.

Shedler, J., Mayman, M., & Manis, M. (1994). More illusions. *American Psychologist, 49*, 974–976.

Shmueli-Goetz, Y., Target, M., Fonagy, P., & Datta, A. (2008). The child attachment interview: A psychometric study of reliability and discriminant validity. *Developmental Psychology, 44*, 939–956.

Silverman, D. K. (1991). Attachment patterns and Freudian theory: An integrative proposal. *Psychoanalytic Psychology, 8*, 169–193.

Silverman, D. K. (1993). Attachment research: An approach to a developmental relational perspective. In N. Skolnick & S. Warshaw (Eds.), *Relational perspectives in psychoanalysis* (pp. 195–216). The Analytic Press.

Silverman, D. K. (2001). Sexuality and attachment: A passionate relationship or a marriage of convenience? *Psychoanalytic Quarterly, 70*, 325–358.

Simpson, J. A. (1990). Influence of attachment styles on romantic relationships. *Journal of Personality and Social Psychology, 59*, 971–980.

Slade, A. (2001). Discussant's remarks. Remarks made at the biennial meeting of the Society for Research in Child Development, Assessing attachment in middle childhood: New methods and early findings, Minneapolis, MN.

Slade, A., Aber, J. L., Cohen, L., Fiorello, J., Meyer, J., DeSear, P., & Waller, S. (1993). *Parent Development Interview coding system* (2nd ed.). Unpublished manuscript, City University of New York.

Slade, A., Belsky, J., Aber, J. L., & Phelps, J. L. (1999). Mothers' representations of their relationships with their toddlers: Links to adult attachment and observed mothering. *Developmental Psychology, 35*, 611–619.

Slade, A., & Cohen, L. J. (1996). The process of parenting and the remembrance of things past. *Infant Mental Health Journal, 17*, 217–238.

Solomon, J., & George, C. (1996). Defining the caregiving system: Toward a theory of caregiving. *Infant Mental Health Journal, 17*, 183–197.

Solomon, J., & George, C. (Eds.). (1999a). *Attachment disorganization*. Guilford Press.

Solomon, J., & George, C. (1999b). The place of disorganization in attachment theory: Linking classic observations with contemporary findings. In J. Solomon & C. George (Eds.), *Attachment disorganization* (pp. 3–32). Guilford Press.

Solomon, J., George, C., & De Jong, A. (1995). Children classified as controlling at age six: Evidence of disorganized representational strategies and aggression at home and at school. *Development and Psychopathology, 7*, 447–463.

Sperling, M. B., & Berman, W. H. (1991). An attachment classification of desperate love. *Journal of Personality Assessment, 56*, 45–55.

Sperling, M. B., Foelsch, P., & Grace, C. (1996). Measuring adult attachment: Are self-report instruments congruent? *Journal of Personality Assessment, 67*, 37–51.

Sroufe, L. A. (1979). The coherence of individual development: Early care attachment and subsequent developmental issues. *American Psychologist, 34*, 834–841.

Sroufe, L. A., & Waters, E. (1977). Attachment as an organizational construct. *Child Development, 48*, 1184–1199.

Steele, H., & Steele, M. (Eds.). (2008). *Clinical applications of the adult attachment interview*. Guilford Press.

van IJzendoorn, M. H. (1995). Adult attachment representations, parental responsiveness, and infant attachment: A meta-analysis on the predictive validity of the adult attachment interview. *Psychological Bulletin, 117*, 387–403.

van IJzendoorn, M. H., & Bakermans-Kranenburg, M. J. (1996). Attachment representations in mothers, fathers, adolescents, and clinical groups: A meta-analytic search for normative data. *Journal of Consulting and Clinical Psychology, 64*, 8–21.

van IJzendoorn, M. H., & Kroonenberg, P. M. (1988). Cross-cultural patterns of attachment: A meta-analysis of the Strange Situation. *Child Development, 59*, 147–156.

van IJzendoorn, M. H., Schuengel, C., & Bakermans-Kranenburg, M. J. (1999). Disorganized attachment in early childhood: Meta-analysis of precursors, concomitants, and sequelae. *Development and Psychopathology, 11*, 225–249.

Ward, M. J., & Carlson, E. A. (1995). Associations among adult attachment representations, maternal sensitivity, and infant-mother attachment in a sample of adolescent mothers. *Child Development, 66*, 69–79.

Warren, S. L., Oppenheim, D., & Emde, R. N. (1996). Can emotions and themes in children's play predict behavior problems? *Journal of the American Academy of Child and Adolescent Psychiatry, 35*, 1331–1337.

Waters, E., & Deane, K. E. (1985). Defining and assessing individual differences in attachment relationships: Q-methodology and the organization of behavior in infancy and early childhood. *Monographs of the Society for Research in Child Development, 50*(1–2, Serial No. 209), 41–65.

Waters, E., Merrick, S., Treboux, D., Crowell, J., & Albersheim, L. (2000). Attachment security in infancy and early adulthood: A twenty-year longitudinal study. *Child Development, 71*, 684–689.

West, M., Sheldon, A., & Reiffer, L. (1987). An approach to the delineation of adult attachment: Scale development and reliability. *Journal of Nervous and Mental Disease, 175*, 738–741.

Westen, D., Nakash, O., Thomas, C., & Bradley, R. (2006). Clinical assessment of attachment patterns and personality disorder in adolescents and adults. *Journal of Consulting and Clinical Psychology, 74*, 1065–1085.

Zeanah, C. H., & Anders, T. F. (1987). Subjectivity in parent-infant relationships: A discussion of internal working models. *Infant Mental Health Journal, 8*, 237–250.

Zeanah, C. H., & Benoit, D. (1995). Clinical applications of a parent perception interview in infant mental health. *Child and Adolescent Psychiatric Clinics of North America, 4*, 539–554.

Zeanah, C. H., Benoit, D., Barton, M., Regan, C., Hirshberg, L. M., & Lipsitt, L. P. (1993). Representations of attachment in mothers and their one-year-old infants. *Journal of the American Academy of Child and Adolescent Psychiatry, 32*, 278–286.

Zeanah, C. H., Benoit, D., Hirshberg, L., Barton, M. L., & Regan, C. (1994). Mothers' representations of their infants are concordant with infant attachment classification. *Developmental Issues in Psychiatry and Psychology, 1*, 1–14.

Chapter 3

Attachment to God

Four Attachment Relationship Patterns

Now that the reader is armed with a basic knowledge of attachment theory and assessment, I can finally contextualize this knowledge in a therapeutic setting by addressing four central issues.

First, the therapist must consider whether religion and spirituality are evolutionary adaptations built into our DNA or whether they are merely by-products of evolution. I suggest that religion and spirituality represent the default position in human experience because they provide a distinct survival-promoting advantage. I follow two lines of argument in favor of the evolutionary adaptation thesis by suggesting (1) that religion and spirituality are universal phenomena, and (2) that from very early in life, children reason that God exists. Support for this thesis is important because it means that every person who presents themselves for therapeutic intervention has a dormant spirituality that has the potential to be awakened. Thus, even the hardcore atheist is a spiritual being who is in denial of that part of their personality.

Second, based on our knowledge of the four attachment patterns discussed in Chapter 2, I suggest that we can individualize spiritual care with our patients. Each attachment pattern implies a "primary mode of relatedness" (Slade, 1999, p. 588) and emotion regulation, whose contours a therapist must consider when developing a treatment plan for working with a patient (see also Goodman, 2025, Chapters 2–6). Individualizing spiritual care is so important that I never work with a patient without first gathering information that contributes to my knowledge of a patient's attachment pattern.

Third, I discuss two attachment-informed pathways that account for the intergenerational transmission of religion and spirituality: the correspondence pathway and the compensation pathway (Granqvist, 2020; Kirkpatrick, 2005; Kirkpatrick & Shaver, 1990). Foreshadowed by the typology of "once-born" and "twice-born" characters of William James (1902, 80), the correspondence and compensation pathways use attachment theory to update James's typology. The therapist can use knowledge of these two pathways to surmise how a patient came to a spiritual (or nonspiritual) understanding and to what purposes the patient might be putting their spirituality (or nonspirituality) to use in maintaining their "psychic equilibrium," using the term in Rizzuto (1979, p. 88) to describe the dynamic balance of wishes

DOI: 10.4324/9781003562924-4

and defense mechanisms that occupy a person's mind. My own spiritual narrative outlined in Chapter 1 of Goodman (2025) provides an example of both correspondence and compensation pathways at work.

Fourth, I conclude the chapter by suggesting that Attachment-Informed Psychotherapy (AIP) can help the patient to achieve "earned security" (Hesse, 2018, p. 570; Main & Goldwyn, 1989) in the patient's attachment relationships to their parents during childhood through a process of generalizing from their secure attachment relationship to a Higher Power (Granqvist, 2020). This process can also work in reverse: the patient can achieve earned security in their attachment relationship to a Higher Power through a process of generalizing from their secure attachment relationships to their parents during childhood. Because of the correspondence pathway, however, the circumstances of this second process are typically associated with religious trauma (Griffith, 2010).

Belief in and Practice of Religion and Spirituality Are Humans' Default Positions

A therapist who is working with a patient who denies belief in a Higher Power and asserts that spirituality plays no role in their life must decide whether that patient's lack of belief is a legitimate expression of their authentic self or, alternatively, is a defensive protection against deeper fears related to divine judgment, abandonment, rejection, unworthiness, or loss. Even firm believers in a Higher Power experience moments of doubt. Pinned to a Roman cross, Jesus Himself cried out, "My God, my God, why have you forsaken me?" (Matthew 27:46; Mark 15:34; NIV, 1978). Jesus still seemed to believe in a Higher Power, however, even though he felt abandoned. Christian apologist C.S. Lewis (1961), stricken with grief over his wife's death, also seems to doubt his faith: "Go to Him when your need is desperate, when all other help is vain, and what do you find? A door slammed in your face, and a sound of bolting and double bolting on the inside. After that, silence" (p. 4). Some persons experienced their parents during childhood as distant, remote, and rejecting and thus attribute these same personality qualities to a Higher Power. Then there are those who experienced a religious trauma and have since turned away from a Higher Power, denying a divine existence. I am currently working in psychotherapy with an atheist who became disillusioned with his parents' Catholicism and stopped believing in a Higher Power sometime in college. It is not surprising that he experienced his parents (especially his father) as distant, remote, rejecting, and at times, scary. This patient seems to be saying, "God is just more of the same. Unlike my parents, I can choose not to believe in Him." In Chapter 1 of Goodman (2025), I highlighted my own turning-away from the God of my childhood, my turn toward agnosticism in adulthood, and my subsequent turn back to the default position of a relationship to a reconstituted God in later adulthood.

I am not arguing that God's existence can be proved or that God can be definitively known; I am arguing that all humans have a genetically determined predisposition to believe in a Higher Power; it follows that persons who deny the existence of this Higher Power are defying this predisposition and denying their own innate spirituality. Believing that all humans have an innate predisposition to spirituality that evolved over many thousands of years does not signify that God actually exists; it signifies only that belief in a Higher Power promoted survival in our ancestors and produced an evolutionary advantage over ancestors who did not have this belief. Belief in a Higher Power promoted survival and ultimately, enhanced opportunities for reproduction. This argument matters to us as therapists because our understanding of whether a patient has an innate spirituality affects how we work with them. If anyone needs a biblical reference to support the idea of an innate spirituality, one need look no further than Genesis 1:27: "So God created mankind in his own image, in the image of God he created them" (NIV, 1978). Bearing God's image implies possessing spirituality—the awareness of our participation in a larger narrative that might extend beyond our death. If we humans bear God's image, then we most certainly possess a spirituality intrinsic to our very nature—even if humanity's creation occurred through eons of evolution.

Are Religion and Spirituality Evolutionary Adaptations or By-products?

If spirituality is the default position in human experience, rooted in our DNA, then it stands to reason that possessing spirituality posed distinct evolutionary advantages over not possessing it. Without spending too much time on this subject, I will simply mention several advantages. First, spirituality can provide a safe haven (see Chapter 2), which permits humans to regulate their emotions, particularly anxiety and fear, enhancing their ability to think clearly in life-or-death situations. Second, spirituality can provide a secure base (see Chapter 2), which permits humans to take greater risks that could promote their survival. A caregiver's (or romantic partner's) provision of a safe haven and secure base is fallible, however, because humans are fallible. Conversely, God's love never fails (e.g., I Corinthians 13:8; NIV, 1978). Third, spirituality can provide a coherent set of moral norms that support a cooperative attitude toward others (e.g., "The Golden Rule"; Matthew 7:12; Luke 6:31; NIV, 1978). Like carpenter ants and honeybees, who succeed only by working together in harmonious community, humans promote their own survival by working together cooperatively rather than competitively. These same moral norms can also protect humans from engaging in behaviors that could threaten their survival, such as attempting to murder a community member, who survives and then murders you. Sociologist Robert Bellah and his colleagues (Bellah et al., 1985) argued that the American brand of rugged, individualistic capitalism worked so well in its earlier history because it was counterbalanced by a strong religious current that commanded its citizens to "Love your neighbor as yourself" (Leviticus 19:18; Matthew 22:39; Mark 12:31; NIV, 1978). With the decline of religion in the US, however, this counterbalance no longer exists so pervasively to curb the greed and self-centeredness animating the cutthroat capitalism that seems to dominate our current political and economic landscape. Wall Street mogul Gordon Gekko provided American culture with one of the most memorable lines in movie history: "Greed is good" (Stone, 1987). According to Bellah and his colleagues, without religion and spirituality to counterbalance the social Darwinism sanctioned by capitalism, the US is heading toward greater economic inequality and social fragmentation, aided by the prevailing attitude that greed is, in fact, good.

Almost 40 years later, nothing seems to be contradicting their thesis. In fact, coinciding with the worldwide decline of religion (Inglehart, 2020), we are observing an unparalleled concentration of the world's wealth in the hands of a few. According to *The Guardian* (2024, April 2), the world's 2,781 billionaires are

> collectively worth more than ever, with combined assets estimated at $14.2 trillion—a $2 trillion increase on 2023 and more than the GDP of every country except the US and China. Their collective wealth has risen by 120% in the past decade, at the same time as billions of people across the world have seen their living standards decrease in the face of inflation and the cost of living crisis.

Religion and spirituality are evolutionary adaptations designed to ensure individual survival through the mutual adherence to moral norms, fostering cooperation even in the context of competition for resources. Unfortunately, humans can repress their innate spirituality and ignore moral norms for short-term material gain. The idea that this obscene wealth proportionately improves the individual billionaire's evolutionary fitness is at best dubious.

Fourth, and related to the first point, spirituality can transform humans' knowledge of and anxiety surrounding our own impending death. As far as we can tell, humans are the only animal species who practices spirituality (which often includes the promise of life after death through resurrection or reincarnation), presumably because humans are the only animal species that demonstrates (1) an awareness of our own impending death, and (2) difficulty tolerating this awareness. Terror management theory (TMT; e.g., Pyszczynski et al., 1999) suggests that death anxiety—stimulated by awareness of death, or mortality salience—produces a connection to religion and culture that protects us from this overwhelming anxiety and permits us to survive by facilitating our ability to function successfully in the context of this somber awareness. This research group has conducted numerous experiments using subliminal priming techniques (e.g., exposing research participants to death imagery outside conscious awareness) to demonstrate increased affinity to religious symbolism. Presumably, death anxiety triggers a re-orientation to the spiritual realm, which provides comfort and a certain denial of the finality of death. For example, Jong et al. (2012) found that mortality salience (i.e., subliminal reminders of death) predicted implicit activation of supernatural concepts in both religious believers *and* atheists. There really are no atheists in foxholes. For all these reasons, spirituality poses an evolutionary advantage over a lack of spirituality. In summary, the universality of religious and spiritual phenomena reflects their necessity for human existence.

Some authors, such as Kirkpatrick (2005), take a different position, arguing that religion and spirituality are merely evolutionary by-products: "Many patterns of thought and behavior, particularly in our modern environment, are produced by mechanisms (or combinations of mechanisms) designed to do something else" (p. 233). According to Kirkpatrick, religion and spirituality are by-products of the attachment system, among other genuine evolutionary adaptations, designed to keep humans alive long enough to reproduce and pass along their genes to the next generation. The attachment system accomplishes this task by prioritizing proximity-seeking and contact-maintenance in relation to a "stronger and wiser" (Bowlby, 1988, p. 120) caregiver, who is suitably equipped to protect their off-spring. Religion and spirituality have co-opted this motivational system and applied it to a supernatural context. Recognizing the ultimate fallibility of caregivers to protect their offspring, humans apply their attachment systems to a perfectly strong, perfectly wise invisible Caregiver who is also presumably always available and never rejecting or inconsistently responsive or abusive. Kirkpatrick expresses these views succinctly:

> We do not have an evolved God module or psychological system whose adaptive function is to cause us to think about gods in this way. Instead, we have an evolved module or psychological system [i.e., the attachment system] whose evolutionary function is to promote survival of helpless offspring ... This mechanism is recruited in the context of thinking about gods and other religious figures and thus shapes religious ideas and behavior in particular ways.
>
> (p. 236)

I do not wish to dispute Kirkpatrick's assessment of the role of the attachment system in the development and maintenance of religion and spirituality in the human experience. Certainly, the attachment system does play a crucial role. On the other hand, Kirkpatrick seems to exclude the possibility that both statements are true: religion and spirituality are both an evolutionary adaptation to human beings' unique awareness of death *and* a by-product of other motivational systems such as the attachment system. Kirkpatrick's view thus seems unnecessarily limiting.

Finally, Kirkpatrick (2005) refutes the universality of religion and spirituality, pointing out that "many people are not in fact religious" (p. 217). He argues that if religion and spirituality were in fact an evolutionary adaptation, then all humans would manifest this adaptation, just as all humans manifest an attachment system. I find this argument problematic because it assumes that people who self-identify as nonreligious are in fact nonreligious. This surface-level categorization ignores the real possibility that nonreligious people are denying or ignoring a Higher Power for psychological reasons addressed throughout this book—namely, that people who have developed an anxious-avoidant attachment relationship to their parents during childhood are highly likely to transfer this relationship onto a Higher Power. Thus, just as anxious-avoidant infants snub the caregiver upon reunion in the Strange Situation (see Chapter 2), so too do anxious-avoidant adults often snub God—by ignoring God or denying God's existence altogether. Granqvist (2020, p. 142) cites numerous research studies—including three by Kirkpatrick himself (Kirkpatrick, 1998; Kirkpatrick & Shaver, 1992; Rowatt & Kirkpatrick, 2002)—that demonstrate a significant positive correlation between an anxious-avoidant attachment pattern and agnosticism or atheism. Thus, given this definitive finding, one could just as easily argue that anxious-avoidant persons ignore or deny religion and spirituality and disable this evolutionary adaptation, just as priests and nuns disable their sexual/reproductive systems in the service of their spirituality. Thus, the existence of atheism and agnosticism does not refute the argument that religion and spirituality are an evolutionary adaptation, not a by-product of other, domain-specific adaptations.

What does this argument have to do with a therapist and patient sitting in a consulting room? If religion and spirituality are an evolutionary adaptation and not a by-product, then they are an innate part of our psychology, just as the attachment system or the sexual/reproductive system is an innate part of our psychology. Thus, every patient comes into our consulting room with an innate spirituality, even if that innate spirituality is currently dormant, buried under many years of atheism or agnosticism (see Chapter 1). Prior to any formal religious training, "No child arrives at 'the house of God' without his pet God under his arm" (Rizzuto, 1979, p. 8). Belief in God is as inevitable as the eruption of one's baby teeth.

Does Developmental Psychology Research Support the Thesis that Humans Are Born Believers?

A second line of argument in favor of the evolutionary adaptation thesis is the extensive body of research literature that has accumulated over the past 30 years that demonstrates that humans are born believers. Justin Barrett (2012) has eloquently summarized this research in his groundbreaking book, *Born Believers*. During one of his many studies on the origins of parents' and their children's religious beliefs, Barrett shares an anecdote in which the mother of a 5-year-old boy was answering questions in an interview about her belief in God, responding "no" to each question. She had previously disclosed that she never spoke of religious matters with her son. During the interview, her son, who was present,

> rolled over on the floor to look his mother in the face and asked, "Mum, why are you saying 'no'? The answer should be YES!" He found his mother's obvious confusion a source of amusement throughout and kept laughing at her ridiculous answers. How could she get so wrong something that was so obvious to him?
>
> (p. 132)

Children believe in God, even when their parents do not.

One of the most convincing series of studies conducted by Barrett and his colleagues involves assessing preschool children's theory of mind. Theory of mind is the ability to determine that the beliefs in one's own mind can differ from the beliefs in another person's mind (see Baron-Cohen, 1995). Developmental psychology researchers most commonly use a false-belief task to determine whether a preschool child has theory of mind. Except in rare cases such as children diagnosed on the autism spectrum, a child demonstrates a knowledge of false beliefs at around 4 years of age. In his research studies, Barrett (2012) has sought to uncover what children seem to know about God. Do children's understanding of God's beliefs differ from their understanding of their parents' or pets' beliefs? Barrett shows the child participants ages 3–6 a cracker box with rocks inside. Closing the box, he then asks in succession what the child participant's mother, father, or pet thinks is inside the cracker box. Finally, he asks, "If God saw this closed box for the first time, what would God think was inside it?" (p. 89). By age 5, 80% of the children respond that their parents and pets would think that the cracker box contains crackers (a false belief), whereas God would think that it contains rocks (a true belief). None of these children was coached to believe that God knows everything, yet most of them knew by age 5 that God's mind belongs in a special category, distinct even from their parents' minds. In other words, these children *naturally* reason about God's mind differently than they do about their parents' minds.

Barrett (2012) summarizes many such research studies to support the conjecture that young children naturally believe in a Higher Power, and only much later do some children stop believing. In other words, believing in a Higher Power is the default position in the human mind. How then do we understand atheism? Barrett (2012) relies on the research of Baron-Cohen (2002), which suggests that individuals (both male and female) who manifest weak theory of mind abilities are what he calls "male-brained" due to higher levels of *in utero* exposure to testosterone. According to Barrett (2012):

> If theory of mind and related social cognition are so critical for theistic belief and if severe male-brained people are weak in or lack these social cognitive abilities, then we would predict that people who have always found it difficult or impossible to believe in any gods might tend to be more male-brained.
>
> (p. 205)

Thus, Barrett proposes that the default belief in God can be disrupted by abnormal levels of testosterone. Elsewhere, I have argued from an attachment perspective that early childhood relationships with rejecting caregivers might make a person prone to repress their default belief in God—in effect, rejecting God, just as they felt rejected by their caregivers (see, e.g., Goodman, 2025, Chapter 5). Regardless of the process of denial, whether *in utero* or through early interactions with caregivers, atheism and agnosticism represent aberrations from humans' default belief in religion and spirituality. Based on all the evidence, I draw the conclusion that religion and spirituality are an evolutionary adaptation that therapists need to consider when they treat *all* patients—including atheists and agnostics. If true, then therapists and pastoral care providers must formulate interventions that uniquely address not only the patient's emotional needs but also their spiritual needs. Latent spirituality can become a resource of healing not just for spiritually informed patients but also for nonspiritual patients if the psychotherapy process begins to trend in a spiritual direction.

The Role of Attachment Theory in Individualizing Spiritual Care

The range of psychiatric disorders and situational crises that therapists and pastoral care providers are confronted with is vast and complex. Can a one-size-fits-all intervention strategy effectively address this range of human suffering? For example, the pastoral care team at a church screens a 60-year-old man who is going through a divorce initiated by his spouse and wants help mourning the loss of his partner of 10 years. In fact, divorce is a bread-and-butter issue of pastoral care interventions; the issue is extensively covered in the training materials (Bretscher, 2020, pp. 609–638) of Stephen Ministry (Haugk, 2020), a popular nondenominational Christian lay ministry program. Upon intake, the team discovers that this is his fourth failed marriage, and all four spouses initiated divorce proceedings. Immediately, the team observes a pattern here. Unfortunately, in some more conservative pastoral care approaches, any exploration into the underlying pattern of failed marriages is forbidden. The pastoral care team could refer this man for psychotherapy, but how might a spiritually informed psychotherapy help him to understand this pattern and provide him with healing?

As discussed in Chapter 2, Mary Main developed an interview method for assessing attachment patterns in adolescence and adulthood (Main et al., 1985). She reasoned that infants begin to develop repositories of these expectations of caregiver behavior in their minds that she called "internal working models" (see also Bowlby, 1980) or "attachment representations." According to Main et al. (1985): "Individual differences in these internal working models will therefore be related not only to individual differences in patterns of nonverbal behavior but also to patterns of language and structures of mind" (p. 67). Main and her colleagues developed the Adult Attachment Interview (AAI; George et al., 1996) and a companion classification system (Main & Goldwyn, 1994) that yields the three traditional attachment patterns and a fourth attachment pattern associated with childhood abuse and trauma, which is the adult analogue of disorganized/disoriented attachment in infancy. Main argued that the patterns of behavior identified by Ainsworth in infancy could predict patterns of language in adulthood, which was demonstrated in a 20-year longitudinal study (Waters et al., 2000). In adulthood, behavioral assessments of attachment break down: it is doubtful that anyone reading this book right now is scanning the environment in search of their primary caregiver.

Thus, researchers use the AAI classification system to analyze how a person discusses their relationships, particularly relationships with caregivers during childhood (ages 5–12). Slade (1999) has extended this thinking about attachment patterns to what she calls a person's "primary mode of relatedness" (p. 588), in which the internal working model governs their patterns of interaction with significant others. Daniel (2015) explored these primary modes of relatedness as they relate to the four attachment patterns from the research of Main (Hesse & Main, 2000). Daniel identified nine "interpersonal markers" (p. 115) that characterize each of the four primary modes of relatedness. These markers include proximity/distance, trust/expectations of others, attitude to seeking and receiving help, expression and regulation of emotions, self-image/self-esteem, openness and self-disclosure, dependence/independence, conflict management, and empathy. Let us turn to each of the four attachment patterns and describe their corresponding prototypes based on these nine interpersonal markers.

Securely Attached Person

The securely attached person feels comfortable with proximity and physical contact with others. They find meaning in interactions with others. They generally trust others (unless given a reason not to) and hold positive expectations of others. The securely attached person is open to seeking help from others when they cannot do something by themselves. They express their emotions in a balanced manner; their self-image is generally positive, yet realistic and nuanced; and consequently, they generally have positive self-esteem. The securely attached person makes appropriate self-disclosures, neither oversharing nor being secretive about their personal self. They can depend on others for emotional support in committed relationships but can balance this tendency with self-reliance and autonomy. They can formulate creative solutions to interpersonal conflict. Relatedly, the securely attached person demonstrates empathy with and care for others as well as themselves.

Westen et al. (2006) developed the Adolescent Attachment Prototype Questionnaire (AAPQ) as an alternative method of assessing attachment patterns, creating a narrative prototype characterizing each attachment pattern. Here is their characterization of the securely attached prototype:

> Patients who match this prototype tend to expect that they can rely on the availability and sensitivity of the people they love. They are able to become emotionally close and express affection toward significant others. They tend to feel comfortable depending on others and having others depend on them, and they tend to feel calmed and comforted by contact and support they receive when distressed. They are generally sensitive to other people's "signals," tend to be empathic and emotionally "present," and are able to problem solve and think constructively when in emotionally difficult interpersonal situations. They tend to have balanced, realistic views of significant others and view themselves as lovable and worthy of care. Individuals who match this prototype are able to explore and talk openly about emotionally significant events, even when doing so is painful. They are generally able to tell coherent narratives about significant life events, answer comfortably when asked for details and examples, and reflect on their childhood and its effects on who they are today.
>
> (p. 1082)

This narrative provides some convergent validity with the narrative provided earlier based on the nine interpersonal markers of Daniel (2015) characterizing a securely attached person.

Anxious-Avoidant Person

The anxious-avoidant person feels uncomfortable with proximity and physical contact with others. They tend to dismiss or devalue interactions with others and ignore or conceal feelings of insecurity related to possible rejection or ridicule. The anxious-avoidant person prefers to work independently, even when they need help. They tend to restrict their emotional expressions, especially negative emotions, and instead present a false positivity in most interactions. The anxious-avoidant person displays an exaggerated view of themselves to compensate for low self-esteem. They seem secretive regarding personal information and value autonomy over relationship. The anxious-avoidant person tends to avoid conflict because it makes them feel uncomfortable. Their capacity for empathy is limited, expressing an interpersonal coldness.

Here is the characterization of the anxious-avoidant prototype (Westen et al., 2006):

> Patients who match this prototype tend to minimize or dismiss the importance of close relationships. They are uncomfortable with emotional intimacy, physical contact, etc. They tend to derive a sense of self-worth by being independent and self-sufficient and disparage sentimentality, tenderness, or discussion or expression of feelings. When distressed, they tend to withdraw or attempt to cope by themselves. They may overly idealize their parents or attachment figures, having trouble acknowledging their imperfections. Alternatively, they may disparage, contemptuously derogate, or belittle their parents or their role in their own development in an attempt to dismiss their importance. Patients who match this prototype have minimal access to specific memories from childhood and little interest in exploring or retrieving them. They tend to offer sparse narratives about interpersonal events and appear unwilling or unable to describe interpersonal experiences in detail or to provide specific examples. They often offer generalizations about their significant relationships that do not cohere with supporting details (e.g., they may describe their relationship with their mother as "loving" but, when pressed for specific examples, provide memories that seem distant or unpleasant). They tend to take an excessively pragmatic approach to language, having no use for "wasted words."

(pp. 1082–1083)

This narrative seems to converge with the interpersonal markers of this attachment category articulated by Daniel (2015).

Anxious-Resistant Person

The anxious-resistant person tends to dissolve interpersonal boundaries, constantly seeking proximity and physical contact but feeling dissatisfied when achieved. They feel as though they are being abandoned or losing the attention of others and expect abandonment to occur at any moment. The anxious-resistant person often feels helpless, expressing a desire for help even on tasks that they could be reasonably expected to complete themselves. They express their emotions frequently and dramatically, especially negative emotions. The anxious-resistant person experiences low self-esteem and tries to compensate by seeking interpersonal validation. They make frequent self-disclosures that seem tangential and often irrelevant to the situation and also feel dependent on others, constantly seeking out relationships. They hold resentments and often escalate conflict. The anxious-resistant person is preoccupied with others' feelings and gets entangled, often attributing their own feelings to others, which severely limits their capacity for empathy.

Here is the characterization of the anxious-resistant prototype (Westen et al., 2006):

> Individuals who match this prototype seek intense emotional intimacy with others but constantly feel ambivalent about them. They tend to experience significant others (within and without the family) as less accessible or responsive than they want them to be, leading to distress, frustration, anger, anxiety, passive helplessness, etc. They may feel smothered by significant others at the same time as never quite given enough, taken care of well enough, etc. When distressed, they turn to significant others for comfort, but they chronically feel disappointed. They may protest that they want autonomy or distance from attachment figures while behaving in ways that keep them uncomfortably involved or overinvolved. Individuals who match this prototype tend to have trouble staying on topic when discussing significant interpersonal events or relationships, often offering excessively long descriptions of events, wandering from topic to topic, crying continuously while describing past events, etc. They tend to use vague, meaningless, or empty words when describing interpersonal events (e.g., may insert nonsense words such as "dadadada" into sentences, [and] use psychobabble such as "she has a lot of material around that issue," etc.).
>
> (p. 1083)

Again, this narrative captures the same relatedness pattern articulated by the interpersonal markers of this attachment category by Daniel (2015).

Disorganized/Disoriented Person

The disorganized/disoriented person is afraid to seek proximity with others but also feels lost without that closeness. They strongly distrust others, fearing that others will violate their boundaries. Afraid to seek out help, they nevertheless feel utterly helpless. Their emotional expressions are often chaotic, without much ability to regulate them. The disorganized/disoriented person experiences low self-esteem and an incoherent self-image. They resist making self-disclosures, but involuntary idiosyncratic thoughts and feelings might break through in interpersonal exchanges. They also feel deeply conflicted between a desire for autonomy and a desire to be taken care of. The disorganized/disoriented person shows poor tolerance for inter-personal conflict, sometimes manifesting a total collapse of protective strategies and instead acting out their feelings by engaging in inappropriate behavior. Fear of interacting with others interferes with empathy with or care for others.

Here is the characterization of the disorganized/disoriented prototype (Westen et al., 2006):

> Individuals who match this prototype have had trouble getting beyond, master-ing, resolving, or making meaning of traumatic events (e.g., loss or abuse), so that they tend to respond in intimate relationships in ways that appear incon-sistent, contradictory, or dissociative. They have difficulty trusting significant others and tend to manifest contradictory responses when distressed or in need of help (e.g., pushing the other away while demanding help or responding sim-ultaneously with anger and help-seeking). They tend to be controlling in close relationships, either through hostile, critical, or punitive responses, or through overinvolved, "enmeshed," or smothering caregiving. Individuals who match this prototype experience strong emotions that often disrupt or derail their nar-rative descriptions of interpersonal events, rendering these descriptions inco-herent, difficult to follow, etc. When talking about traumatic events (e.g., loss or abuse), they tend to show signs of disorientation, disorganization, or dissoci-ation; seem to lose the capacity to keep in mind the perspective of the listener; and show signs of illogical, childish, or peculiar reasoning (e.g., indicating that a dead person is still alive in the physical sense, or appearing convinced that their thoughts or feelings killed someone in childhood). They may lapse into prolonged silences, unfinished sentences, or stilted, "eulogistic" speech when describing traumatic events or losses.

Again, the disorganized/disoriented prototype (Westen et al., 2006) aptly resem-bles the interpersonal markers of this attachment category by Daniel (2015).

What do these four attachment patterns and their interpersonal markers have to do with giving care to people who are seeking spiritual solutions to their emo-tional or spiritual problems? Patients, or anyone seeking mental health services, will respond to the therapist (Slade, 2018)—and to a Higher Power (Granqvist, 2020)—differently, depending on their attachment pattern formed during infancy and early childhood. Thus, a one-size-fits-all response such as that advocated by certain pastoral care approaches (e.g., the Stephen Ministry; Haugk, 2020) might not fit some patients. Returning to the previous illustration of the man coming to a church's pastoral care team on the eve of his fourth failed marriage, we do not know which attachment pattern he formed during childhood; we know only the outcome—that he experienced considerable upheaval in his intimate relationships. Given this tumultuous interpersonal history, we can probably rule out a secure attachment. We would not expect a securely attached person to manifest this degree of emotional upheaval. As Daniel (2015) pointed out, the securely attached person balances both positive and negative expressions of emotion and demonstrates empathy and care for others. Which of the other three attachment patterns might fit this man?

Considering the anxious-avoidant attachment pattern, we would have to inquire about this man's relationship history with his parents during the evaluation phase of the intervention, which is not part of a typical pastoral care intake interview. In addition, we would have to explore the circumstances under which these marriages failed. Did this man's partners divorce him because he was cold and aloof? Did he try to keep his emotional distance in these relationships, which frustrated his partners' need for emotional closeness? Did he avoid conflict in these relationships? Was this man stingy in the personal experiences that he shared in these relationships, causing his partners to feel shut out of his life? Were his responses to his marital partners' frustrations unempathic and insensitive? A therapist trained to pay close attention to the effects of early insecure attachment on adult interpersonal relationships would listen to these interpersonal markers and draw the tentative conclusion that this man formed an anxious-avoidant attachment pattern during childhood and was manifesting the interpersonal aspects of this attachment pattern with his marital partners.

Considering the anxious-resistant attachment pattern, we would again take a careful relationship history during the intake interview and explore the circumstances under which these marriages failed. Did this man's marital partners divorce him because he was intrusive in all aspects of their daily lives? Did he manifest strong expressions of emotion that would escalate conflict in these marriages? Did this man rely too much on his marital partners for help with things he could have done for himself? Did he often misattribute motives to his partners that reflected his own motives for behavior, thus impeding his capacity to empathize with them? Did he have trouble staying on topic when discussing significant interpersonal events or relationships with his partners, frustrating them in the process? In this scenario, the therapist would listen to these interpersonal markers and draw the tentative conclusion that this man formed an anxious-resistant attachment pattern during childhood and was manifesting the interpersonal aspects of this attachment pattern with his marital partners.

Considering the disorganized/disoriented attachment pattern, we would rely on data collected from this man's intake interview regarding his relationship history and his early relationships to his caregivers to provide clues about his current difficulties with maintaining relationships. Did this man's marital partners divorce him because he walled himself off from becoming known by them, constructing impermeable boundaries that frustrated their attempts to reach him emotionally? Did he demonstrate occasional emotional breakdowns when conflicts arose in these marriages, perhaps frightening his marital partners? Did this man demonstrate an incoherent self-image that made his marital partners wonder whether they really knew him or whether he really knew himself? Did his helplessness and simultaneous fear of receiving help hinder his empathic responses to his marital partners? In this scenario, the therapist might draw the tentative conclusion that this man formed a disorganized/disoriented attachment pattern during childhood and was displaying the interpersonal markers associated with this pattern with his marital partners.

This man's "symptom"—multiple failed marriages—might indicate that he did not develop a secure attachment in early childhood, but it does not necessarily tell us which insecure attachment he might have developed. Only targeted inquiry would give us the specific information that we would need to make an educated guess about the type of insecure attachment that might be affecting the longevity of his marriages. Could this information make a difference in how we might approach this man during the treatment phase of the intervention?

A member of a typical pastoral care team giving care to this man would have to respond using the same interventions—empathy, validation, encouragement, and spiritual tools—regardless of his insecure attachment status. A spiritually informed therapist, however, might offer a wider range of interventions that take into account the prevailing attachment pattern. Following Dozier (2003), the therapist might offer a "gentle challenge" (p. 254) to the person's primary mode of relatedness. Inevitably, this man would begin to behave toward the therapist—and perhaps has already been behaving toward his Higher Power—in the same manner that he treated his previous marital partners. If the therapist speculates that the man formed an anxious-avoidant attachment pattern during early childhood, she might anticipate that the man would eventually treat the therapist in a cold, grandiose, and dismissing manner with little empathy for the therapist. Similarly, the man probably also treats his Higher Power with disdain, holding a superficial belief that God could never reject him and concealing a deeper anxiety about the potential for divine abandonment. The therapist would need to challenge this primary mode of relatedness by surfacing the underlying fears of abandonment, rejection, resentment, and self-blame that sabotage his relationships to significant others and to his Higher Power and then working them through.

If the therapist speculates that the man formed an anxious-resistant attachment pattern during early childhood, she might anticipate that the man would eventually form a helpless, dependent relationship to the therapist, never feeling satisfied with the care he is receiving. Similarly, he would express anger toward God for constantly failing him and not following through on God's promises of security and contentment. In contrast to the previous scenario, this man's fears of abandonment are more visible, and his grievances over past slights associated with inconsistent attentiveness to his needs are more available for discussion. The therapist would need to challenge this primary mode of relatedness by maintaining strict boundaries and not surrender to the temptation to rescue him from the inevitable frustrations that will arise, for example, when he learns that the therapist will not respond to texts after the end of the workday. Gradually, the man would develop a tolerance and trust that the therapist as well as his Higher Power have his best interests in mind, even when the therapist is not available to him or when God does not answer his prayers immediately.

If the therapist speculates that the man formed a disorganized/disoriented attachment pattern during early childhood, she might anticipate that the man would eventually form a profoundly fearful, mistrusting relationship to the therapist that might require an ongoing exploration of complex trauma that encompasses multiple spheres of development (e.g., Arvidson et al., 2011). Establishing a working alliance (Horvath & Greenberg, 1989) with this man would prove especially challenging because he lacks what is known as "epistemic trust" (Fonagy & Allison, 2014)—"trust in the authenticity and personal relevance of interpersonally transmitted information" (p. 372). This man would have difficulty trusting in the goodness and genuineness of the therapist's interventions. It is also quite possible that he would be experiencing grave doubts about God's benevolence and trustworthiness, as revealed in Scripture and the teachings of clergy. The therapist must try to establish a working alliance and epistemic trust so that this man could absorb the interpretations that might be helpful to him. Cultivating a sacred space where this man could verbalize his traumatic experiences, both past and present, and re-frame his relationship to his Higher Power as a source of healing, not destruction, requires enormous and longsuffering patience. Such work is not always successful. The point is that an uncomplicated diet of empathy, validation, encouragement, and spiritual tools might not be sufficient to help such persons heal from their complex trauma.

These person-centered interventions, while well-meaning and likely helpful for most patients, might be interpreted differently by patients with different insecure attachment patterns. For example, an anxious-avoidant person might interpret validation as a pitiful expression of the therapist's weakness and desire to ingratiate themselves to this person. An anxious-resistant person might view validation as a gratification of the infantile dependent relationship that they are seeking with the therapist. A disorganized/disoriented person might perceive validation as an attempt at seducing the patient to let down their guard to gratify the therapist's needs. Without the therapist's requisite self-awareness, skill, and knowledge of the patient's attachment pattern, the person-centered interventions at the heart of a typical pastoral care program might have unintended consequences that could exacerbate the patient's problems.

The Correspondence Pathway

It is a common observation that many persons, spiritual or nonspiritual, tend to relate (or refuse to relate) to God in a manner that reflects how they relate (or refuse to relate) to significant others, especially caregivers during their childhoods. In psychoanalytic theory, we refer to this phenomenon as "transference" (Freud,

1912)—we transfer onto another person the feelings, attitudes, fantasies, wishes, and fears that we experienced with our caregivers during childhood. The correspondence pathway (Granqvist, 2020; Kirkpatrick, 2005) suggests that humans' attachment relationship to God corresponds to their attachment relationships to their caregivers during childhood. Thus, a securely attached person (see above) would likely perceive God as a safe haven and a secure base and seek God's proximity when the attachment system is activated by signals of danger, both external (e.g., an impending hurricane) and internal (e.g., an illness, exhaustion). An anxious-avoidant person (see above) would likely perceive God as rejecting and distant and therefore turn their back on God and valorize self-sufficiency, just as an anxious-avoidant infant snubs the caregiver upon reunion in the Strange Situation procedure and instead soothes themselves with toys or thumb-sucking. An anxious-resistant person (see above) would likely perceive God as inconsistent and unpredictable and thus constantly strive to earn God's approval yet doubt whether they will ever achieve it. A disorganized/disoriented person (see above) fears retribution from an ominous God and lives life in terror waiting for the existential other shoe to drop. The correspondence pathway predicts a correspondence between a person's attachment relationship formed with the caregivers during childhood and their attachment relationship to God. Later in this book, I discuss the correspondence pathway in my narrative analysis of Coretta Scott King (see Goodman, 2025, Chapter 2) and Sigmund Freud (see Goodman, 2025, Chapter 5).

In his classic text, *The Varieties of Religious Experience*, William James (1902) foreshadows the correspondence pathway, citing the description by Newman (1852) of persons on this pathway as "once-born"—meaning not having experienced a religious conversion. James suggests that these persons are "organically weighted on the side of cheer" (p. 83) and evaluates them as possessing a "healthy-mindedness to the tendency which looks on all things and sees that they are good" (p. 87). James's healthy-mindedness of the once-born seems to differ from the correspondence pathway in two critical respects. First, James describes this type of person's relationship to God as originating out of an optimistic personality trait, whereas the correspondence pathway, relying on attachment theory, understands a person's relationship to God as originating out of the critical influence of caregiving patterns of behavior during early childhood. Second, James focuses only on persons who attribute positive qualities to God, whereas the correspondence pathway predicts that a correspondence exists between a person's quality of relationship to their caregivers and the quality of relationship to God, regardless of whether these relationships have a positive or negative valence. In other words, a person who perceives their parents as punitive and vindictive would likely also regard God as punitive and vindictive, which most of us would not regard as "healthy-minded." Thus, though differing significantly from the correspondence pathway, James's views do foreshadow the correspondence pathway.

Granqvist (2020) adds a necessary complication to the correspondence pathway, which he calls "socialized correspondence" (p. 127). In addition to developing an internal working model that mirrors that of the caregivers, a child is also exposed (or not exposed) to the religiosity of the caregivers. Relying on social learning theory (Bandura &Walters, 1977), Granqvist suggests that securely attached children who are exposed to the religious practices of their parents are likely to establish a secure attachment relationship to God, while securely attached children who are not so exposed are not likely to establish an attachment relationship to God. On the other hand, parents' religious practices cannot predict insecurely attached children's relationship to God. Granqvist (2020) uses Ainsworth and her colleagues' (Ainsworth et al., 1974) understanding of socialization to explain the differences in how securely attached and insecurely attached children internalize their parents' values: "The secure child will ultimately comply ('obey' even) with the parent's behavioral norms not because of fear of punishment or to receive exogenous reward but because of mutual love and affection" (p. 130). Granqvist concludes: "Caregiver sensitivity and child security do seem to facilitate a child's behavioral adoption of parental norms" (p. 131). In other words, securely attached children, whose parents are consistently responsive in meeting their attachment needs, are more likely to adopt the religious practices of their parents than insecurely attached children, whose parents are inconsistently responsive or consistently unresponsive in meeting their attachment needs. Insecurely attached children are as likely to adopt as not to adopt the religious practices of their parents. Thus, a secure attachment provides fertile ground for learning the parents' religious practices (or lack of religious practices).

Based on this more complex understanding of the correspondence pathway, Granqvist (2020) recommends that religious educators spend as much time focusing on the quality of the parent-child relationship as they do on formal religious training; otherwise, "religious preaching and teaching may ultimately fall on deaf ears" (p. 138). Finally, the correspondence pathway is not restricted to a person's relationship to God; this pathway could also apply to other parental norms such as political, moral, and social norms.

Granqvist and his colleagues (Nkara et al., 2018) used the unpublished Religious Attachment Interview (RAI) to support the correspondence theory. Coherent descriptions of parents were correlated with coherent descriptions and the benevolence of God. In addition, Cassibba et al. (2008) reported that a highly religious group of Catholics in Italy (i.e., priests, nuns, seminary students) were coded as having more loving experiences with their mothers as well as more coherent discourse on the AAI than a group of lay Catholics. Furthermore, in both groups, securely attached participants reported having a more loving image of God than insecurely attached participants. In summary, ample evidence supports the correspondence pathway.

The Compensation Pathway

It is perhaps a less common observation that persons who have had unhappy childhoods end up experiencing the most committed relationships to a Higher Power. In other words, their relationship to God stands in sharp contrast to their relationships to their caregivers during childhood. The compensation pathway (Granqvist, 2020; Kirkpatrick, 2005) suggests that humans' attachment relationship to God compensates for their inadequate attachment relationships to their caregivers during childhood. God becomes a surrogate attachment figure Who provides a safe haven and secure base and responds to the emotional needs of these persons, whose parents were inconsistently responsive or consistently unresponsive in meeting their emotional needs during childhood. Later in this book, I discuss the compensation pathway in my narrative analysis of Anne Frank (see Goodman, 2025, Chapter 3), Bill W. (see Goodman, 2025, Chapter 4), and my patient Séamus (see Goodman, 2025, Chapter 6).

Whereas the correspondence pathway predicts a one-to-one correspondence between the attachment quality of a person's relationships to the caregivers during childhood and the attachment quality of that person's relationship to God, the compensation pathway predicts a secure attachment to God that compensates for an insecure attachment to the caregivers during childhood (either anxious-avoidant attachment, in the case of Bill W., or anxious-resistant attachment, in the case of Anne Frank). A major question that I posed in Chapter 1 is how to know which pathway will predict a person's attachment relationship to God in adulthood.

James (1902) also foreshadows the compensation pathway, citing the description by (Newman, 1852) of persons on this pathway as "twice-born"—having experienced a religious conversion. The idea of being "born again" comes from Jesus's instruction to the Pharisee Nicodemus, who came to Jesus at night (John 3:7; NIV, 1978). James suggests that twice-born persons have a sick soul in need of redemption—"not of mere reversion to natural health ... The sufferer, when saved, is saved by what seems to him a second birth, a deeper kind of conscious being than he could enjoy before" (p. 157). Unlike persons on the correspondence pathway, who seem to have an optimistic personality trait that makes them view God and the world as full of promise, persons on the compensation pathway have their "original optimism and self-satisfaction ... leveled with the dust" (p. 161). According to James (1902), "deliverance [conversion] must come in as strong a form as the complaint, if it is to take effect ... Some constitutions [personalities] need them too much" (p. 162). Elsewhere, James calls these persons "the morbid-minded" and claims that from their point of view, "healthy-mindedness pure and simple seems unspeakably blind and shallow" (p. 162). Thus, persons on the compensation pathway view God as the only solution to their "preoccupation with every unwholesome kind of misery" (p. 162).

James's morbid-mindedness of the twice-born seems to differ from the compensation pathway in one critical respect. James (1902) seems to be describing this type of person's relationship to God as originating out of a pessimistic personality trait, whereas the compensation pathway, relying on attachment theory, understands a person's relationship to God as providing a surrogate solution of attachment security to compensate for insecure attachment relationships to caregivers during childhood. Thus, relationship dynamics with caregivers during childhood determine the compensation pathway, not a personality trait. Ultimately,

James (1902) characterizes the healthy-minded from the sick soul as a contrast between "pure naturalism and pure salvationism" (p. 167). This dualistic perspective, however, has no place in the correspondence and compensation pathways because persons on the correspondence pathway (James's healthy-minded) can be securely or insecurely attached to God, depending on the quality of their attachment relationships to their caregivers during childhood. On the other hand, persons on the compensation pathway (James's morbid-minded) experience a secure attachment to God because they have substituted God as their source of attachment security for their inadequate caregivers during childhood. God as the surrogate attachment figure then gives them unconditional love and a unified self, which they never experienced in their caregiver attachment relationships during childhood.

A dramatic religious conversion is the *sine qua non* of the compensation pathway. The 12-step movement, begun in 1935 by Bill W. when he co-founded Alcoholics Anonymous with Dr. Bob, popularized the phrase "hitting rock bottom," which means that a person has reached the lowest point in their life and must either commit suicide, go insane, or surrender to a Higher Power. Bill W.'s life is an example of the person who hits rock bottom, has a conversion experience, and surrenders his life to a Higher Power, where he finds inner serenity as well as outer success (see Goodman, 2025, Chapter 4). Acute emotional turmoil and stress almost always precede the religious conversion. There is a desperate search for a way out of the agony of living. In fact, an early candidate for the official title of the Big Book of Alcoholics Anonymous (AA) was *The Way Out* (Anonymous, 2012, p. 165). Step 1 of the AA program suggests admitting to oneself the powerlessness over alcohol and the unmanageability of one's life; Step 2 suggests believing that a Higher Power can help; Step 3 suggests surrendering to the care of this Higher Power (Anonymous, 2010, p. 59). These three steps parallel the compensation pathway.

Before turning their will and their lives over to the care of God (Anonymous, 2010, p. 59), however, alcoholics have obviously surrendered to a different attachment figure—alcohol. God is only one among many surrogate attachment figures sought by persons who develop insecure attachment relationships to their caregivers during childhood. Alcohol, drugs, food, sex, gambling, and shopping can all serve as surrogate attachment figures that temporarily down-regulate stress, especially attachment-activating stress such as separation, and bring ephemeral relief. In contrast to the caregivers, these substances and behaviors are available 24 hours per day, seven days per week. The person does not need to depend on unreliable people to alter their mood. Pets, possessions, and even places can also serve as surrogate attachment figures, even though it is questionable whether some of these surrogates meet the criteria of being "stronger and wiser" (Bowlby, 1988, p. 120) and being able to protect the person from danger. In cases such as heroin, the surrogate attachment figure inevitably leads the person into grave danger, not out of it. Nevertheless, these surrogate attachment figures temporarily allay fears of rejection, betrayal, lack of control, and abandonment. Some addicts eventually recognize that their chosen surrogate attachment figure brings more trouble that it is worth and thus seek the perfect surrogate attachment figure in a Higher Power.

According to Granqvist (2020), "Regulation of severe distress is at the core of this surrogate use of God and religion" (p. 164).

Once again, Granqvist and his colleagues are at the forefront of the empirical research on the compensation pathway. Granqvist et al. (2007) established support for a link between sudden religious changes and assessments of parents' insensitivity on the AAI, with ratings of parents during childhood as less loving and less sensitive correlated with their ratings of intense increases in religiousness. In a follow-up study, Granqvist et al. (2014) observed that the intense increases in religiousness reflected "an unorthodox blend of theistic religiosity *and* New Age spirituality (Granqvist, 2020, p. 167; emphasis in original). Granqvist (2020) summarizes these research findings: "Experiences of parental insensitivity and current attachment insecurity predispose a person to 'desperate searching', in which the person grabs on to whatever religious/spiritual means are available to regulate distress" (p. 167).

If an insecurely attached person can develop either an insecure attachment relationship to God (reflecting the correspondence pathway) or a secure attachment relationship to God (reflecting the compensation pathway), then how can we make an accurate prediction regarding which pathway this person will follow? I raise this issue in Chapter 1 of Goodman (2025) in my discussion of the difficulty with this theory's falsifiability (Popper, 1959). These twin pathways of correspondence and compensation seem to be unfalsifiable: they both equivalently account for every person's insecure attachment relationships to parents and to God. Granqvist and Kirkpatrick (2018) suggest that insecurely attached persons compensate for their attachment insecurity when they "cannot bear the high levels of suffering experienced sufficiently well by employing his or her usual [insecure] strategy for managing stress" (p. 934). In bearable situations of stress, however, insecurely attached persons' relationship (or nonrelationship) to God corresponds to their insecure attachment relationships to their parents during childhood. In other words, compensation is activated *only when* insecure attachment relationships to parents during childhood *and* high levels of stress co-occur. Although not specifically addressed by Granqvist and Kirkpatrick, many factors influence pathway selection over and above the stress threshold, which includes stress intensity, frequency, and duration. Developmental phase, personality organization, defensive structure, type of insecure attachment subcategory, specific caregiver attachment relationships, nature of the relationship to the significant other with whom the stress is occurring, and genetic predisposition all contribute to pathway selection.

I want to highlight two particular factors that seem to work in tandem with unbearable stress levels to push an insecurely attached person off the correspondence pathway and onto the compensation pathway. These factors include: (1) their specific caregiver attachment relationships, and (2) their attachment subclassification. First, Daniel (2015, pp. 123–125) suggests that internal working models of attachment can be person-specific, even though the gold-standard assessment instrument of adult attachment, the AAI, yields only one attachment category. She writes that "it is not likely that adults are furnished with a single, unitary working model that is 'employed' in all relationships as a matter of course" (p. 124). In Chapter 3 of Goodman (2025), I conclude that Anne Frank developed an anxious-resistant attachment relationship to her mother and a secure attachment relationship to her father. Across all her relationships, however, Frank seems to have developed an anxious-resistant internal working model. My analysis of Frank's secure attachment relationship to God suggests that she used this relationship to compensate for the anxious-resistant attachment relationship to her mother. I could have argued that Frank's secure attachment relationship to God corresponds to her secure attachment relationship to her father. Although that interpretation is possible, the all-consuming quality of her attachment relationship to her mother, coupled with her occasional insecure attachment behavior toward her father and toward the others living in the secret annex (including Peter), suggests that her secure attachment relationship to God compensated for a more generalized anxious-resistant internal working model, or "primary mode of relatedness" to others (Slade, 1999, p. 588). The example of my own life narrative (see Goodman, 2025, Chapter 1) demonstrates how my need for an attachment relationship to God varied along with the status of my attachment relationships to my parents, to whom I developed different attachment relationships. In summary, specific caregiving relationships can determine which pathway to follow.

Second, a person's attachment subclassification might influence the selection of pathway. In Chapter 4 of Goodman (2025), I conclude that Bill W. used his secure attachment relationship to God to compensate for his anxious-avoidant attachment relationships to his parents; on the other hand, in Chapter 5 of Goodman (2025), I conclude that Sigmund Freud consciously denied the existence of God, which corresponded with his anxious-avoidant attachment relationships to his parents (his mother essentially abandoned him to a nanny and later-born children, while his father told him he would never amount to anything). How can we understand the fact that although both men developed anxious-avoidant attachment relationships to their parents, only one turned to God for help in a time of crisis? I attribute some influence to Bill W.'s raging alcoholism, which nearly killed him—an existential stressor. Something else might have been going on, however. In Chapter 4 of Goodman (2025), I argue that Bill W.'s anxious-avoidant internal working model of attachment was more brittle than Freud's and thus more vulnerable to a break-through of primary attachment need, which only God could fulfill. We do not have AAI classifications on either man; thus, I will not speculate on each man's anxious-avoidant subcategory. Is it possible, however, that certain attachment subclassifications are more brittle than others, thus leaving the person more emotionally available to having a secure attachment relationship to God? For example, the dismissing (anxious-avoidant) attachment classification has four subclassifications (Ds1, Ds2, Ds3, Ds4; Hesse, 2018, p. 565). Might one or more of these subclassifications have more brittle properties than the others?

Granqvist (2020) has proposed that stress levels of sufficiently severe intensity can disable the insecurely attached person's secondary (defensive) attachment strategy, allowing the primary attachment strategy of seeking proximity to an attachment figure to become manifest. Secondary attachment strategies come in two varieties—hyperactivating/preoccupied (i.e., overdramatizing attachment needs to maximize their fulfillment by others) and deactivating/dismissing (i.e., ignoring attachment needs to minimize rejection of their fulfillment by others). Granqvist rightly suggests that insecure attachment strategies defend against a person's awareness of primary attachment needs. Bill W. ignores his attachment needs—until the collapse of his life overthrows this strategy and exposes him to his primary needs for security and protection. Returning to my argument that the belief in and practice of spirituality are humans' default position, Bill W. rediscovered this spirituality in himself and reached out to a Higher Power to meet his primary attachment needs. His secondary (defensive) attachment strategy of anxious-avoidance was no longer working. It was too brittle to withstand the onslaught of his stressors and inevitably crumbled, triggering the dormant primary attachment strategy of seeking the proximity of a "stronger and wiser" (Bowlby, 1988, p. 120) Higher Power to be activated. In addition to confronting a different set of stressors with different levels of intensity, Freud's secondary (defensive) attachment strategy might have been less brittle and was therefore better equipped to withstand the onslaught of his stressors. The ultimate question is whether establishing (or perhaps re-establishing) a secure attachment relationship to God can adequately serve the purpose of "psychic equilibrium" (Rizzuto, 1979, p. 88). For Granqvist (2020), "Regulation of severe distress is at the core of this surrogate use of God and religion" (p. 164). In addition to the intensity of the stress level, both the quality of the attachment relationship to specific caregivers and the attachment subclassification might influence whether a person follows the correspondence pathway or experiences a spiritual conversion and puts their faith and security in a Higher Power, following the compensation pathway. Of course, following the compensation pathway might not be permanent; Granqvist (2020) suggests that placing the attachment relationship to God in the background can occur either when the person's stress level diminishes or when the person finds a new surrogate attachment figure such as a romantic partner. More research in these areas is sorely needed.

Conclusion

In this chapter, I have examined whether the capacity for religion and spirituality is an evolutionary adaptation that promotes humans' survival. I presented two lines of argument to support this position. First, I argued that religion and spirituality are universal phenomena that transcend geography, culture, and history. The religious and spiritual provision of a safe haven and secure base that reduce anxiety and enhance risk-taking, the support for a coherent set of moral norms that enhance group cohesion, and the solution to the awareness of our impending death (i.e., life after death), thus transcending the fear of death (Becker, 1973) and removing a crucial barrier to the will to survive, all point to religion and spirituality as an evolutionary adaptation and not a by-product of other, more primary adaptations. I argued that some persons from every geographical location, cultural heritage, and historical epoch do not believe or practice religion or spirituality because they are manifesting a particular attachment pattern (i.e., anxious-avoidant) toward a Higher Power that denies or is uncertain of a Higher Power's existence. Even persons who practice nontheistic religions such as Buddhism often focus their worship toward a Higher Power: "One of the most common Buddhist prayers is 'I take refuge in the Buddha'" (Granqvist, 2020, p. 67).

Second, I argued that belief in a primitive spirituality spontaneously arises in every child, regardless of geographical location, cultural heritage, and historical epoch. Barrett (2012) cites extensive research in this area (much of which he and his colleagues conducted) that supports the idea that young children are "born believers"—in other words, belief in and practice of religion and spirituality are humans' default position. Not only do children from atheistic households develop a belief in God, but they also reason about God differently than about humans, including their parents. Young children's theory of God's mind clearly differs from their theory of their parents' minds. Barrett (2012) concludes: "Children [are] born believers, with strong natural dispositions toward religious thought and practice … Though children may be born believers, whether they die believers is between them and God" (pp. 256–257).

Third, I argued that psychotherapy must consider the patient's internal working model of attachment, which helps to determine the range of interventions used by the therapist. I outlined how a person classified with each of the four attachment patterns—securely attached, anxious-avoidant, anxious-resistant, and disorganized/disoriented—might respond to psychotherapy. I argued that it is important for a therapist to tailor their interventions to accommodate the patient's "primary mode of relatedness" (Slade, 1999, p. 588) and then gradually to provide a "gentle challenge" (Dozier, 2003, p. 254) to it. The therapist's own internal working model of attachment also influences the interactions between the therapist and patient in therapy (I will discuss this issue in Chapter 6).

Fourth, I reviewed the correspondence and compensation pathways toward a belief in and practice of religion and spirituality. The therapist or pastoral counselor must not only recognize the patient's attachment pattern developed in relation to their parents during childhood but also understand how their strategy of establishing felt security with their parents has manifested in their attachment relationship (or nonrelationship) to a Higher Power. The correspondence pathway predicts that a person who is exposed to religion and spirituality and who has developed secure attachment relationships to their parents during childhood will develop a secure attachment relationship to a Higher Power (see Goodman, 2015, Chapter 2). Conversely, a person exposed to religion and spirituality and who has developed insecure attachment relationships to their parents during childhood will develop an insecure attachment relationship to a Higher Power (see Goodman, 2025, Chapter 5). The compensation pathway, however, predicts that a person who is exposed or not exposed to religion and spirituality and who has developed insecure attachment relationships to their parents during childhood will develop a secure attachment relationship to a Higher Power to compensate for the insecure attachment relationships to their parents during childhood (see Goodman, 2025, Chapters 3 and 4).

The obvious question that arose from this discussion was how to reconcile the correspondence and compensation pathways when persons developed insecure attachment relationships to their parents during childhood. The correspondence pathway predicts a transfer of this attachment insecurity to their attachment relationship to a Higher Power, while the compensation pathway predicts a compensation for this attachment insecurity to their parents during childhood with a secure attachment relationship to a Higher Power. Granqvist and Kirkpatrick (2018) and Granqvist (2020) attempt to resolve this falsifiability problem (Popper, 1959) by suggesting that life stressors that exceed a certain threshold facilitate the breakdown of the secondary (defensive) attachment strategy of insecurity, resulting in a reliance on the primary attachment strategy of proximity-seeking directed toward a Higher Power.

I introduced the consideration of the development of specific attachment relationships to parents during childhood as well as the consideration of specific attachment subclassifications as potential explanations for a person's following the correspondence or compensation pathway. A person who developed a secure attachment relationship to one parent during childhood might be able to transfer this attachment security to a Higher Power when stress levels exceed a certain threshold (see Goodman, 2025, Chapter 3), whereas a person who developed insecure attachment relationships to both parents during childhood might have a more brittle insecure internal working model of attachment and thus continue down the correspondence pathway despite intense stress levels (see Goodman, 2025, Chapter 5).

I also mentioned that attachment subclassifications might influence the eventual pathway outcome followed by the person. For example, the dismissing (anxious-avoidant) attachment classification has four subclassifications (Ds1, Ds2, Ds3, Ds4; Hesse, 2018, p. 565). I suggested that one or more of these subclassifications might have more brittle properties than the others, thus increasing the likelihood of breaking down under pressure from intense life stressors and allowing for the primary attachment strategy of proximity-seeking to be directed toward a Higher Power. Following Granqvist (2020), I also suggested that when stress levels diminish or when the person finds a new surrogate attachment figure, such as a romantic partner, persons following the compensation pathway might place their attachment relationship to a Higher Power in the background. Regardless of the person's conscious awareness of this relationship, "No child arrives at 'the house of God' without his pet God under his arm" (Rizzuto, 1979, p. 8). This pet God of early childhood exists in perpetuity. The correspondence and compensation pathways help us to understand what happens to this pet God and whether it develops into a meaningful relationship to the Divine or recedes into the background.

In Chapters 4–6, I discuss how we can use knowledge of a person's attachment pattern and the correspondence and compensation pathways to enhance our clinical work. I argue that the goal of AIP is to help the patient to achieve "earned security" (Hesse, 2018, p. 570; Main & Goldwyn, 1989) in the patient's parental attachment relationships through a process of generalizing their secure attachment relationship to a Higher Power. This process can also work in reverse: the patient can achieve earned security in their attachment relationship to a Higher Power through a process of generalizing their secure parental attachment relationships. Because of the correspondence pathway, however, the circumstances of this second process are typically associated with religious trauma (see Griffith, 2010). "Earned security" is a state of mind with respect to attachment that indicates that despite having experienced consistently unresponsive or inconsistently responsive caregiving, the person has had a "corrective emotional experience" (Alexander & French, 1946), such as a secure attachment relationship to a Higher Power, psychotherapy, a secure romantic attachment relationship, or the birth of a child that transforms the insecure internal working model of attachment into a secure one. It is "earned" because the person did something to change their insecure working model of attachment developed during childhood. Establishing a secure attachment relationship to God can transform a person's internal world. This new surrogate attachment relationship not only compensates for their insecure attachment relationships to their parents during childhood but also transforms these insecure parental attachment relationships. Thus, the person receives an "earned secure" classification of secure/autonomous on the AAI.

A person classified as earned secure from an AAI transcript speaks coherently and collaboratively about their parental attachment relationships during childhood despite having "(a) appeared to have had difficult childhood relationships with parents, and/or (b) another untoward experience such as loss or separation" (Main & Goldwyn, 1989, p. 119). There is evidence that psychotherapy can assist patients to speak coherently and collaboratively about their insecure attachment relationships to their parents during childhood. One year of twice weekly psychodynamic therapy was associated with significant increases from insecure to secure attachment classification and significant increases in mentalization compared to dialectical behavior therapy (DBT) and supportive psychotherapy (SPT) in a sample of 90 women diagnosed with borderline personality disorder (Levy et al., 2006). Research is needed to determine whether a secure surrogate attachment relationship to a Higher Power can also transform an insecure internal working model of attachment into a secure one and whether spiritually informed AIP can assist with this process. AIP is ideally suited to facilitate an exploration of a person's relationship to a Higher Power and to make connections between this relationship and relationships to significant others.

We can now apply our basic understanding of attachment patterns to parents and to God and the correspondence and compensation pathways to the therapeutic context to help spiritually curious and spiritually grounded patients to use their Higher Power as a resource for the emotional healing of their relationships to themselves and others. Other sociobiological systems might influence a person's relationships to God and to others such as the social hierarchy system (Griffith, 2010); however, this book focuses exclusively on the attachment system as being especially influential in shaping the innate spirituality common to us all. Future authors might consider the effects of these other sociobiological systems on a person's relationship to a Higher Power and to others, including the relationship to the therapist.

References

Ainsworth, M. D. S., Bell, S. M., & Stayton, D. J. (1974). Infant-mother attachment and social development: "Socialization" as a product of reciprocal responsiveness to signals. In M. P. M. Ricshards (Ed.), *The integration of a child into a social world* (pp. 99–135). Cambridge University Press.

Alexander, F., & French, T. M. (1946). *Psychoanalytic therapy: Principles and application.* Ronald Press Company.

Anonymous. (2010). *Alcoholics Anonymous* (4th ed.). Alcoholics Anonymous World Services, Inc.

Anonymous. (2012). *Alcoholics Anonymous comes of age: A brief history of A.A.* Alcoholics Anonymous World Services, Inc.

Arvidson, J., Kinniburgh, K., Howard, K., Spinazzola, J., Strothers, H., Evans, M., Andres, B., Cohen, C., & Blaustein, M. E. (2011). Treatment of complex trauma in young children: Developmental and cultural considerations in application of the ARC intervention model. *Journal of Child & Adolescent Trauma, 4,* 34–51.

Bandura, A., & Walters, R. H. (1977). *Social learning theory* (Vol. 1). Prentice-Hall.

Baron-Cohen, S. (1995). *Mindblindness: An essay on autism and theory of mind.* MIT Press/Bradford Books.

Baron-Cohen, S. (2002). The extreme male brain theory of autism. *Trends in Cognitive Sciences, 6,* 248–254.

Barrett, J. L. (2012). *Born believers: The science of children's religious belief.* Free Press.

Becker, E. (1973). *The denial of death.* Free Press.

Bellah, R. N., Madsen, R., Sullivan, W. M., Swidler, A., & Tipton, S. M. (1985). *Habits of the heart: Individualism and commitment in American life.* HarperCollins.

Bowlby, J. (1980). *Attachment and loss*: Vol. 3. *Loss, sadness and depression.* Basic Books.

Bowlby, J. (1988). *A secure base: Parent-child attachment and healthy human development.* Basic Books.

Bretscher, J. P. (Ed.). (2020). *Stephen minister training manual* (Vol. 2). Stephen Ministries.

Cassibba, R., Granqvist, P., Costantini, A., & Gatto, S. (2008). Attachment and God representations among lay Catholics, priests, and religious: A matched comparison study based on the Adult Attachment Interview. *Developmental Psychology, 44,* 1753–1763.

Daniel, S. I. F. (2015). *Adult attachment patterns in a treatment context: Relationship and narrative.* Routledge.

Dozier, M. (2003). Attachment-based treatment for vulnerable children. *Attachment and Human Development, 5,* 253–257.

Fonagy, P., & Allison, E. (2014). The role of mentalizing and epistemic trust in the therapeutic relationship. *Psychotherapy, 51,* 372–380.

Freud, S. (1912). The dynamics of transference. In J. Strachey (Ed. and Trans.), *The standard edition of the complete psychological works of Sigmund Freud* (Vol. 12, pp. 97–108). Hogarth Press.

George, C., Kaplan, N., & Main, M. (1996). *Adult Attachment Interview* (3rd ed.). Unpublished manuscript, University of California, Berkeley.

Goodman, G. (2025). *Practical applications of transforming the attachment relationship to God: Using Attachment-Informed Psychotherapy*. Routledge.

Granqvist, P. (2020). *Attachment in religion and spirituality: A wider view*. Guilford Press.

Granqvist, P., Broberg, A. G., & Hagekull, B. (2014). Attachment, religiousness, and distress among the religious and spiritual: Links between religious syncretism and compensation. *Mental Health, Religion and Culture, 17*, 726–740.

Granqvist, P., Ivarsson, T., Broberg, A. G., & Hagekull, B. (2007). Examining relations between attachment, religiosity, and New Age spirituality using the Adult Attachment Interview. *Developmental Psychology, 43*, 590–601.

Granqvist, P., & Kirkpatrick, L. A. (2018). Attachment and religious representations and behavior. In J. Cassidy & P. R. Shaver (Eds.), *Handbook of attachment: Theory, research, and clinical applications* (pp. 917–940). Guilford Press.

Griffith, J. L. (2010). *Religion that heals, religion that harms: A guide for clinical practice*. Guilford Press.

Haugk, K. C. (2020). *Christian caregiving: A way of life* (2nd ed.). Stephen Ministries.

Hesse, E. (2018). The Adult Attachment Interview: Protocol, method of analysis, and selected empirical studies: 1985–2015. In J. Cassidy & P. R. Shaver (Eds.), *Handbook of attachment: Theory, research, and clinical applications* (pp. 553–597). Guilford Press.

Hesse, E., & Main, M. (2000). Disorganized infant, child, and adult attachment: Collapse in behavioral and attentional strategies. *Journal of the American Psychoanalytic Association, 48*, 1097–1127.

Horvath, A. O., & Greenberg, L. S. (1989). Development and validation of the Working Alliance Inventory. *Journal of Counseling Psychology, 36*(2), 223–233.

Inglehart, R. (2020). Giving up on God: The global decline of religion. *Foreign Affairs, 99*, 110–118.

James, W. (1902). *The varieties of religious experience: A study in human nature*. Longmans, Green, and Co.

Jong, J., Halberstadt, J., & Bluemke, M. (2012). Foxhole atheism, revisited: The effects of mortality salience on explicit and implicit religious belief. *Journal of Experimental and Social Psychology, 48*, 983–989.

Kirkpatrick, L. A. (1998). God as a substitute AF: A longitudinal study of adult attachment style and religious change in college students. *Personality and Social Psychology Bulletin, 24*, 961–973.

Kirkpatrick, L. A. (2005). *Attachment, evolution, and the psychology of religion*. Guilford Press.

Kirkpatrick, L. A., & Shaver, P. R. (1990). Attachment theory and religion: Childhood attachments, religious beliefs, and conversion. *Journal for the Scientific Study of Religion, 29*, 315–334.

Kirkpatrick, L. A., & Shaver, P. R. (1992). An attachment-theoretical approach to romantic love and religious belief. *Personality and Social Psychology Bulletin, 18*, 266–275.

Levy, K. N., Meehan, K. B., Kelly, K. M., Reynoso, J. S., Weber, M., Clarkin, J. F., & Kernberg, O. F. (2006). Change in attachment patterns and reflective function in a randomized control trial of transference-focused psychotherapy for borderline personality disorder. *Journal of Consulting and Clinical Psychology, 74*, 1027–1040.

Lewis, C. S. (1961). *A grief observed*. Bantam Books.

Main, M., & Goldwyn, R. (1989). Adult attachment rating and classification system. Unpublished manuscript. University of California, Berkeley.

Main, M., & Goldwyn, R. (1994). Adult attachment scoring and classification systems (6th ed.). Unpublished manuscript. University College, London.

Main, M., Kaplan, N., & Cassidy, J. (1985). Security in infancy, childhood, and adulthood: A move to the level of representation. *Monographs of the Society for Research in Child Development, 50*(1–2), 66–104.

Newman, F. W. (1852). *The soul: Its sorrows and its aspirations* (3rd ed.). Chapman.

NIV (New International Version). (1978). *The holy Bible*. Zondervan.

Nkara, F., Main, M., Hesse, E., & Granqvist, P. (2018). Attachment to deities in light of attachment to parents: The religious attachment interview. Unpublished manuscript.

Popper, K. (1959). *The logic of scientific discovery*. Routledge.

Pyszczynski, T., Greenberg, J., & Solomon, S. (1999). Why do we need what we need? A terror management perspective on the roots of human social motivation. *Psychological Inquiry, 8*, 1–20.

Rizzuto, A.-M. (1979). *The birth of the living God: A psychoanalytic study*. University of Chicago Press.

Rowatt, W. C., & Kirkpatrick, L. A. (2002). Two dimensions of attachment to God and their relation to affect, religiosity, and personality constructs. *Journal for the Scientific Study of Religion, 41*, 637–651.

Slade, A. (1999). Attachment theory and research: Implications for the theory and practice of individual psychotherapy with adults. In J. Cassidy & P. R. Shaver (Eds.), *Handbook of attachment: Theory, research, and clinical applications* (pp. 575–594). Guilford Press.

Slade, A. (2018). Attachment and adult psychotherapy: Theory, research, and practice. In J. Cassidy & P. R. Shaver (Eds.), *Handbook of attachment: Theory, research, and clinical applications* (pp. 759–779). Guilford Press.

Stone, O. (Director). (1987). *Wall Street* [Film]. American Entertainment Partners; Amercent Films.

The Guardian. (2024). Taylor Swift among 141 new billionaires in "amazing year for rich people." April 2. Retrieved from www.theguardian.com/business/2024/apr/02/world-gains-141-new-billionaires-in-amazing-year-for-rich-people

Waters, E., Merrick, S., Treboux, D., Crowell, J., & Albersheim, L. (2000). Attachment security in infancy and early adulthood: A twenty-year longitudinal study. *Child Development, 71*, 684–689.

Westen, D., Nakash, O., Thomas, C., & Bradley, R. (2006). Clinical assessment of attachment patterns and personality disorder in adolescents and adults. *Journal of Consulting and Clinical Psychology, 74*, 1065–1085.

Applying Attachment-Informed Psychotherapy to Transform the Attachment Relationship to God

Chapter 4

Attachment-Informed Psychotherapy

Addressing Attachment to God Through the Therapeutic Relationship

Throughout the history of psychotherapy, clinical theoreticians have evoked various metaphors to depict the therapist-patient relationship. With the advent of attachment theory and other advances in developmental psychology in the 1950s and 1960s, a new therapeutic metaphor was born: the caregiver-infant attachment relationship. This metaphor has yielded a number of insights into the process of psychotherapy and the nature of the interactions in which the therapist and patient engage, and it is particularly relevant to a religious understanding of God. For example, God speaks to Isaiah: "As a mother comforts her child, so will I comfort you (Isaiah 66:13; NIV, 1978). In Catholicism, Jesus's mother Mary is known as the Blessed Mother or Holy Mother. In Hinduism, Parvati is the goddess of motherhood (Dabriwal, 2023). Thus, there is precedent for understanding God as the Caregiver (historically associated with mothering) and human beings as receivers of this care.

The first objective of this chapter is to illuminate both the advantages and disadvantages of using this metaphor to depict the psychology of therapeutic relationships. One distinction between this metaphor and the therapeutic relationship is the state of development of mental structures in the infant versus the patient. Whereas the caregiver is behaving in response to the infant's emotional cues not contextualized by an interactional history of expectations to guide these cues, the patient enters into a therapeutic relationship with a complex and intricate interactional history of expectations. In a relationship with God, a person usually understands that God is omniscient and thus knows a person's entire interactional history—the good and the bad—and loves all parts of the person anyway, an expression of unconditional love that many spiritually minded persons find irresistible. Many religions speak of God's unconditional love. In I John 4:16 (NIV, 1978), "and so we know and rely on the love God has for us. God is love. Whoever lives in love lives in God, and God in them." Similarly, in his autobiography, the Hindu yogi Paramahansa Yogananda writes, "God is Love; His plan for creation can be rooted only in love" (Yogananda, 1993, p. 547). Thus, in multiple religions, God provides care with a "perfect love" (e.g., I John 4:18; NIV, 1978) that takes into account the sum total of each person's interactional history. Therapists, however, can hate their patients and then use their awareness

DOI: 10.4324/9781003562924-6

of this emotional state to understand unconscious aspects of the patient's emotional state (see Winnicott, 1949). Because God is omniscient, God does not need to feel hate to read the unconscious depths of a person's mind.

The asynchrony between the caregiver-infant attachment relationship and the therapist-patient relationship requires the therapist to behave in sometimes noncomplementary ways to challenge and interpret these transferential patterns rather than simply responding to emotional cues, as a caregiver would do. These interactional expectations, typically organized around definable patterns of behavior in the therapeutic relationship, are "often neither conscious and verbalizable nor repressed in the dynamic sense" (Lyons-Ruth, 1999, p. 589), and thus pose challenges to traditional psychotherapy models that rely exclusively on symbolization to produce therapeutic change. In Judaism, God "will be like a refiner's fire or a launderer's soap" (Malachi 3:2; NIV, 1978), challenging Israel's attitudes and expectations. The psalmist writes, "For you, God, tested us; you refined us like silver" (Psalm 66:10; NIV, 1978). In Christianity, "These [trials] have come so that the proven genuineness of your faith—of greater worth than gold, which perishes even though refined by fire—may result in praise, glory and honor when Jesus Christ is revealed" (I Peter 1:7; NIV, 1978). Later in this same letter, the author writes, "Do not be surprised at the fiery ordeal that has come on you to test you" (I Peter 4:12; NIV, 1978). Thus, God perfectly loves believers while also challenging their attitudes and expectations, just as a therapist both loves and challenges their patients in psychotherapy sessions.

This understanding of therapeutic change as "gentle challenge" (Dozier, 2003, p. 254) forces therapists to focus more intensively on their own attitudes and behaviors vis-à-vis the patient as the quintessential instruments of change. Various aspects of the therapeutic relationship, in addition to verbalized interpretations of repressed conflict, have thus come under increased scrutiny. I present an attachment-informed psychotherapy model for understanding the interrelations among three relationship-based concepts used in contemporary psychotherapies: working alliance, patient attachment and therapist caregiving, and transference and countertransference. Thus, the second objective of this chapter is to sensitize therapists and psychotherapy process researchers to the structure and functioning of these interrelated concepts to increase therapeutic effectiveness.

Each of us carries with us into our therapy office a metaphor—conscious and unconscious—of our relationship to our patients. This metaphor varies both from patient to patient and within the same patient across the span of treatment. Nevertheless, the broad parameters of this metaphor probably remain constant, both within and across patients, and depend on the quality of our own attachment patterns and broader influences. Each theoretical perspective also inaugurates and sanctions its own ready-made therapeutic metaphors that we also use to help us construct our own. By examining these therapeutic metaphors, we can learn something about our representations of ourselves as therapists in relationship to our patients, and we can then evaluate whether and in what ways these metaphors serve or hinder our patients' interests.

Freud (1912b) offered the therapeutic metaphor of the surgeon-patient relationship to his disciples and fellow psychoanalysts. Freud (1915) elaborated on this metaphor in his paper on transference-love, in which he seemed to be defending against the intensity of his female patients' professions of love with a sterile, rigid set of technical guidelines. Humanistic psychologist Carl Rogers (1977) offered a radically different therapeutic metaphor of the person-person relationship, the egalitarianism of which stands in stark contrast to Freud's authoritarianism (see also Vitz, 1977). We might consider Rogers's therapeutic metaphor a reaction to the rigidity of classical psychoanalytic technique in vogue at the time. With the advent of attachment theory (e.g., Bowlby, 1973, 1980, 1982, 1988) and the psychoanalytic study of mother-infant interaction (e.g., Bowlby, 1958, 1973, 1980, 1982; Mahler et al., 1975; Stern, 1977, 1985, 1995; Winnicott, 1960, 1965), a new therapeutic metaphor was born: the caregiver-infant attachment relationship. Contemporary psychoanalysts are using this metaphor to illuminate certain aspects of the therapist-patient relationship obscured by the Freudian metaphor such as the therapeutic components of nonverbal interactions between therapist and patient, the corrective emotional experience (Alexander & French, 1946), and the noncomplementarity of the therapist-patient match (Bernier & Dozier, 2002).

Caregiver-Infant Attachment Relationship as a Metaphor for the Therapist-Patient Relationship

Bowlby (1977b, 1988) applied his own ideas about human attachment to the metaphor of the caregiver-infant relationship. He believed that the primary purpose of the therapist is to provide the patient with a secure base from which they can explore themselves and their relationships to others. In attachment theory, the secure base in the person of the caregiver serves the function of providing protection for the infant as they explore the environment. The caregiver's safe haven, a complementary concept, serves the function of comfort when internal or external threats to homeostasis cause the infant to become distressed. Concepts similar to secure base identified by other writers include conditions of safety (Weiss & Sampson, 1986), atmosphere of safety (Schafer, 1983), and background of safety (Sandler, 1960). The therapeutic relationship proceeds when the patient uses the therapist to explore themselves and their relationships to others and for comfort when confronted by distressing internal and external threats.

Attachment theory and research have spawned the application of still other facets of the caregiver-infant attachment relationship to the therapist-patient relationship (Amini et al., 1996; Diamond et al., 1999; Diamond, Clarkin, et al., 2003; Diamond, Stovall-McClough, et al., 2003; Farber et al., 1995; Holmes, 1996, 1998; Lyons & Sperling, 1996; Mackie, 1981; Mallinckrodt, 2000; Mallinckrodt et al., 1995; Mallinckrodt et al., 1998; Mallinckrodt et al., 2005; Mitchell, 1999). Parish and Eagle (2003) identified seven facets in addition to secure base and safe haven: proximity seeking, separation protest, stronger/wiser, availability, strong feelings, particularity, and mental representation.

Proximity seeking refers to the infant's need to seek proximity to the caregiver for protection when faced with an internal or external danger (Bowlby, 1982). Parish and Eagle (2003) do not define what proximity seeking looks like for the therapist-patient relationship; however, we might regard a patient's request for additional sessions after a therapist or patient vacation as an adult form of proximity seeking.

Separation protest refers to the distress experienced by the infant when separated from the caregiver and the infant's protest of it (Bowlby, 1982). In the therapist-patient relationship, the patient might protest a therapist's upcoming vacation.

One of the ingredients of an attachment relationship, according to Bowlby (1977a), is that the infant perceives the caregiver as stronger and wiser than they are. Similarly, in the therapist-patient relationship, the patient perceives the therapist as having knowledge of the patient's problems and ways to resolve them that exceed the patient's own knowledge.

Availability refers to the caregiver's emotional and physical availability to meet the infant's attachment needs (Bowlby, 1982). The therapist also meets the patient's emotional needs through attentive listening, regularly scheduled appointments, interpretations that foster a sense of being understood, and many other manifestations of therapist availability unique to each therapist-patient dyad.

An infant also expresses strong feelings toward a caregiver (Bowlby, 1982). The infant is looking for the caregiver to facilitate the regulation of these strong feelings so that he or she can begin to tolerate them. The patient also looks to the therapist for assistance with strong feelings stimulated by the therapist-patient relationship. Freud (1915) described the patient's strong feelings of romantic love for the therapist, although he did not view them as products of an attachment relationship.

Particularity refers to the child's preference for the primary caregiver over other persons, which begins practically at birth. Infants at 10 days have shown a preference to be fed by the primary caregiver rather than by a substitute (Burns et al., 1972). Patients demonstrate the same preference for their therapists. A therapist covering for a vacationing therapist meets with the vacationing therapist's patient only in an emergency. In other words, therapists are not interchangeable.

Mental representation refers to the child's reliance on an internalized image of the caregiver for comfort or guidance in the caregiver's absence (Bowlby, 1973; Mahler et al., 1975). The patient also relies on this internalized image of the therapist in certain situations outside therapy. When one of my patients diagnosed with borderline personality disorder gets an urge to drink alcohol, an image of me asking her what she is feeling at that moment comes into her mind. Mental representation resembles a safe haven as an internalized image of comfort when internal or external threats arise.

Another clinical concept from the psychoanalytic literature thought to reflect facets of an attachment relationship between the therapist and patient is the "working alliance" (e.g., Greenson, 1965; Mackie, 1981). Freud (1912a) foreshadowed the concept in his discussion of the dynamics of transference. He defined three components of transference: a negative component, a positive component, and an "unobjectionable" component (p. 105). The first two components are unconscious, and serve as resistances to the treatment, while the third component consists of friendly or affectionate feelings admissible to consciousness, which serves the treatment as its "vehicle of success" (p. 105). The unobjectionable positive transference represents "a belief in the value of treatment, based on widely held views of analysis as a discipline and of the analyst as a professional practitioner [which] facilitates the work" (Greenberg, 2001, p. 367). Greenberg (2001) has questioned whether Freud's concept has stood the test of time and has argued that the contemporary patient enters treatment seeking a relationship rather than someone who simply relieves symptoms.

Regardless of whether the patient is seeking a practitioner or a relationship, the concept seems to encompass a sense of trust in the benevolence of the therapist who "exhibits a serious interest" in and "sympathetic understanding" for the patient over time and establishes a "proper rapport" with them (Freud, 1913, pp. 139–140). Using the list of attachment concepts applicable to the therapist-patient relationship of Parish and Eagle (2003), strong feelings, stronger/wiser, secure base, and availability either are implicitly or explicitly present in Freud's original idea. Freud (1913) suggested that the patient's attachment to the therapist is a prerequisite for the emergence of the unconscious components of transference: "[The patient] will of himself form such an attachment and link the doctor up with one of the imagos of the people by whom he was accustomed to be treated with affection" (pp. 139, 140). The link between the unobjectionable positive transference and the caregiver-infant attachment relationship is implied.

The original concept of Freud (1912a) reemerged in the literature as "the therapeutic alliance" (Zetzel, 1956) and "the working alliance" (Greenson, 1965). These terms were defined as capturing elements of the real relationship to the therapist not distorted by transference. Horvath and Greenberg (1989) later sought to measure this working alliance by constructing the Working Alliance Inventory (WAI), which consists of three subscales: task, goal, and bond. "Task" refers to the level of agreement between the therapist and patient about what to do in sessions. "Goal" refers to the level of agreement about the desired outcome of treatment. "Bond" refers to the level of positive personal feelings between patient and therapist. The "bond" subscale most closely resembles the original definition by Freud (1912a) of the unobjectionable positive transference.

Research has repeatedly identified the working alliance as highly predictive of successful treatment outcome (Bordin, 1994; Horvath & Symonds, 1991; Luborsky, 1994; Martin, Garske, & Davis, 2000; Safran & Muran, 2000), and even teletherapy outcomes (although more modestly; see Aafjes-van Doorn et al., 2024). The concept of the working alliance has been associated with the concepts of secure attachment and transference because all three concepts seem to reflect similar mental representations, emotions, and strategies for emotion regulation (e.g., defensive processes and interaction structures) activated by the relationship to the therapist and its correspondence with relationships to past caregivers (Bradley et al., 2005; Westen & Gabbard, 2002). Whether these concepts overlap conceptually or operate at different levels of abstraction is a matter of debate (see below).

Limitations of the Caregiver-Infant Attachment Relationship Metaphor

Of course, every metaphor has a breaking point—a point at which the parameters no longer fit. Such is the case with the metaphor of the caregiver-infant attachment relationship. The therapist is not a caregiver per se, nor is the patient an infant. The therapist provides a service paid for by the patient, which takes place in a limited time. These treatment arrangements ironically both allow the metaphor to exist and immediately invalidate it. One of my patients diagnosed with borderline personality disorder revealed a fantasy—concretely experienced by her as an expectation—that therapists should not charge for their services. In fact, in her mind, therapists have taken a vow of poverty like Mother Teresa to conduct this work. By informing her that I would be raising my fee next year, I was invalidating this fantasy. She immediately reminded me that she had abruptly ended her previous treatment when she discovered that her previous therapist, who wanted to raise the patient's fee to $80 per session, drove a Mercedes-Benz. The fantasy of the all-nurturing, selfless caregiver conflicts with the reality of the professional aspects of the relationship. We are still working on this issue of my projected fee increase and its meanings for her.

The therapeutic relationship is unique because of financial, temporal, spatial, logistic, and ethical boundaries—boundaries that do not exist in the caregiver-infant relationship (Farber et al., 1995; Goodman, 2006). We can imagine an Orwellian world in which the mother says to the infant, "Time's up! You've had your fill of milk for the day." Or, "Stop being a baby and get off my lap!" Or, "You can't sleep in my bed; you'll get too used to that!" Anyone familiar with ferberization techniques (Ferber, 1990, 2006) will recognize the sound of these statements offered by some behaviorally oriented psychologists already applying the model of the therapeutic relationship to child-rearing practices well suited to the regimented corporate world for which these children are being trained. The establishment of boundaries such as time, money, and perhaps most important, therapist availability between sessions structures the therapeutic relationship in interesting ways. The expectations of contact-maintenance, caressing, fondling, holding, and primary caregiver preoccupation—all provided to the infant gratis—do not apply in the therapeutic context.

These arrangements—unique to the therapeutic relationship—might differentially affect patients according to their attachment quality. An anxious-resistant (preoccupied) patient (entangled in parental relationships from childhood) might respond to these boundaries with indignation and resentment and create an interaction structure in which he or she perceives the caregiver/therapist as withholding of emotional support. An anxious-avoidant (dismissing) patient (dismissing of the importance of parental relationships from childhood), on the other hand, might feel a sense of relief that strict therapeutic boundaries are in place—at least until the defensive processes against closeness to the therapist are analyzed. The therapeutic boundaries established by the therapist—fee, schedule, unavailability outside of session, lack of physical contact—are unilateral decisions that structure the responses that patients of various attachment patterns will have toward the therapy. These parameters do not exist in the caregiver-infant relationship. As therapists, we must be aware of the differential effects of these parameters on our patients, which can provide us with diagnostic and attachment-related information and strategies for intervention. The manner in which we establish and maintain these boundaries reflects our own use of secondary attachment strategies (i.e., hyperactivating/preoccupied vs. deactivating/dismissing; see Chapter 3), which interact with our patients' strategies to create unique interaction structures that can facilitate or hinder the treatment.

In addition to the parameters inherent to every therapeutic relationship, factors such as gender and race also make important contributions to the construction of the therapeutic relationship that might interact with the patient's attachment quality in interesting ways. Following the work of Jessica Benjamin (1987), the resolution of the Oedipus complex for little boys in Western society often results in a rigid identification with the father and a wholesale repudiation of the mother and, by extension, women, femininity, and dependence. Whereas the mother in infancy is typically perceived as the all-powerful primary caregiver—the secure base and safe haven—this mental representation of the mother changes as the infant enters the preschool years. Boys no longer perceive her as all-powerful and all-protecting— the hallmarks of felt security—but rather as a diminished presence in the household in comparison with the father. This transformation of the maternal representation could have an impact on the patient's perception of the female therapist. One might be less likely to feel secure in a therapeutic relationship with a woman whom society has deemed "less than." Farber and Geller (1994) have observed, "Our culture seemingly 'allows' women to serve as protectors of infants and young children but not to inhabit roles that require the provision of wisdom, strength, or protection of adults" (p. 206).

How might this clinical situation interact with the patient's attachment pattern to create a particular interaction structure? Interaction structures are patterns of reciprocal interaction between the therapist and patient that typically exist outside the awareness of this dyad (Goodman et al., 2014; Jones, 2000; see also Chapter 6). Perhaps having a female therapist would exacerbate the feelings of insecurity of the anxious-resistant patient and elicit the devaluing tendencies of the anxious-avoidant patient. Alternatively, a female therapist might provide a welcome contrast to a diminished maternal representation from childhood. These hypotheses need to be submitted to empirical testing before any definitive conclusions can be drawn regarding the interaction between the patient's attachment quality and the therapist's gender. It is instructive to consider these issues, however, as we observe our patients forming specific attachment relationships to us.

Similarly, the therapist's race also makes an important contribution to the construction of the therapeutic relationship. The imperative by Bowlby (1977a) that the infant seek an attachment figure perceived as stronger and wiser becomes complicated when applied to the therapeutic relationship because by the time the patient reaches the therapist's office, they have already had a series of social-ization experiences in the wider world that have shaped their perceptions of therapists—perceptions also situated in a particular gender, race, and class. Can an African-American therapist provide a secure base for a white patient who has been chronically exposed to the pervasive injustices visited on African Americans in this country? Certainly, African-American therapists *can* provide a secure base and safe haven for white patients, but for some white patients, their socialization process into the dominant culture—where racism is still pervasive—might present challenges to perceiving a therapist from a historically oppressed race or culture as stronger and wiser. The reaction of a white patient to a therapist of color might also depend on that patient's attachment quality. An anxious-resistant patient's inse-curity and an anxious-avoidant patient's devaluing tendencies might be elicited in this arrangement. Conversely, a patient from a historically oppressed race or cul-ture might have difficulty trusting a white therapist, who belongs to a culture his-torically identified with wielding its authority to oppress rather than to help. This dynamic can be construed in different ways, depending on the patient's attachment quality.

Financial disparities between therapists and patients also stimulate both conven-tional and idiosyncratic assumptions about social class, privilege, and access to valued commodities such as education, medical insurance coverage, and an afflu-ent living environment. These disparities can provoke feelings of admiration, com-petitiveness, envy, worthlessness, grandiosity, devaluation, anxiety, or guilt—in us as well as in our patients. McWilliams (1999) has solved this problem for herself by charging her wealthy professional patients whatever fee they charge in their own professions. Which feelings are likely to emerge in treatment because of financial disparities depends in part on the patient's preferred attachment strategy and our own. We as therapists need to pay attention to how such nonattachment dynamics interact with preexisting attachment patterns in both our patients and ourselves to produce unique interaction structures.

One of the most important differences between the therapist-patient relation-ship and the caregiver-infant attachment relationship is the difference in the mental organization of the patient versus the infant. Infant internal working models consist of expectations of caregiver responses to situations that activate the infant's attach-ment system (loss, separation, fear, stress, injury, fatigue, illness, and punishment) as well as the infant's responses to these caregiver responses (Bowlby, 1973; Main et al., 1985). Episodic memories of these caregiver responses are consolidated into semantic memory—a more generalized, abstract memory that permits expectations to form.

From these expectations, the infant can begin to predict future responses and adjust their behavior accordingly to increase the probability of terminating the attachment system when activated and eventually returning to exploration. These initial expectations, constructed through the accumulation of early experiences of caregiver-infant interaction when the attachment system is activated, form the foun-dation of the internal working model (see also Stern, 1985, pp. 97–99). Eventually, these expectations become generalized across interactions with other persons over time and become arranged into a personality organization with its own quality of mental representations of self and others, preferred defensive processes, pattern of relating to others, and emotion regulation strategy (Goodman, 2014). An infant, however, lacks this sophisticated mental organization.

When a patient enters treatment with us, we are interacting with someone who has already developed a sophisticated mental organization, which that patient wants to change. The infant, however, has no such historically structured mental organization. The expectations of caregiver responsiveness are just beginning to form through countless caregiver-infant interactions, day after day. In other words, "the infant is developing his or her past" (Tronick et al., 1998, p. 297).

This conceptual difference between the infant's and patient's mental organizations becomes problematic when the patient applies their historically developed internal working model to the therapist as caregiver. According to Dozier and Bates (2004), "Expectations of the therapist may have little to do with the therapist's actual availability, thus, the therapist must be more than sensitive to the client's needs" (p. 173). The patient signals attachment needs according to the preexisting template formed during interactions with the original caregiver, not necessarily according to the way the therapist would be naturally inclined to respond to those needs. From an attachment perspective, one of the primary tasks of psychotherapy is to change these expectations so that a patient will develop new expectations—culminating in a conscious or unconscious awareness—that their wishes and emotions will always find containment in the mind of the therapist. The therapist is not helping an infant develop expectations of containment from scratch but rather helping a patient change current expectations—already formed over years of experience with the original caregiver—to facilitate both self-containment of emotions and mutual containment of emotions through interdependence with significant others.

Consistent with this reasoning, Dozier and Tyrrell (1998) suggest:

> the mother's task is easier than the therapist's because she need not compensate for the failures of other attachment figures ... The task of therapy is often made more difficult because of the client's previous experiences with unavailable or rejecting caregivers.
>
> (p. 222)

Caregivers of infants placed in foster care most clearly illustrate this conundrum. Often abused or neglected, these infants are placed with caregivers who need to be not only sensitive to their needs but also therapeutic; in other words, "[foster] mothers need to see their infants as needy even though the behavioral evidence might suggest otherwise" (p. 244). Thus, the metaphor of the caregiver-infant attachment relationship does not precisely fit the parameters of the therapist-patient relationship because of: (1) the patient's historically determined internal working model (i.e., mental organization), and (2) the therapist's therapeutic task that transcends mere emotional sensitivity and encompasses a corrective emotional experience (Alexander & French, 1946).

Another difference between the metaphor of the caregiver-infant attachment relationship and the therapist-patient relationship is the patient's acquisition and use of language. While the infant communicates through nonverbal channels such as crying, smiling, frowning, and gesturing, the patient communicates through symbolic play or language (in most forms of psychotherapy). Indeed, Freud (1910) labeled his treatment "the talking cure" (p. 13) at the suggestion of a patient. Of course, interpretation, mediated by language, is also the vehicle he used to cure the patient. Lacan (1977) believed that the language of the father, or "the third," broke up the symbiotic relationship of mother and infant and facilitated differentiation. Symbolization creates a distance between the signifier—the word or other symbolic representation—and the signified—the thought or feeling behind the word or other symbolic representation. The communication that occurs between the caregiver and infant, however, is presymbolic. The mechanisms by which this presymbolic communication is processed in the infant's mind are not precisely known.

Members of the Process of Change Study Group in Boston have attempted to unravel this mystery. They have classified this early experience of communication as "relational procedural knowledge" and the later experience of communication as "symbolic knowledge" (e.g., Lyons-Ruth, 1999; Stern et al., 1998; Tronick et al., 1998). This group has suggested that relational procedural knowledge—the knowledge about relationships that an infant acquires in close, face-to-face interactive communication with a caregiver—develops prior to symbolic knowledge—the knowledge about relationships represented through verbal communication. Both kinds of knowledge continue to develop throughout the course of childhood. Classical psychoanalysis has targeted the domain of symbolic knowledge for therapeutic change; however, this method ignores the domain of implicit procedural knowledge formed prelinguistically.

This presymbolic form of knowledge comprises the essence of attachment patterns manifested by 12-month-old infants with expressive vocabulary words numbering in the single digits. Implicit procedural knowledge tends to reveal itself in therapist-patient interaction structures not readily available to symbolic representation—known by contemporary psychoanalysts as "enactments" (McLaughlin, 1991). According to this group, sustained therapeutic change occurs primarily within the domain of implicit relational knowledge, not verbally mediated symbolic knowledge: "Retranscription of implicit relational knowing into symbolic knowing is laborious, is not intrinsic to the affect-based relational system, is never completely accomplished, and is not how developmental change in implicit relational knowing is generally accomplished" (Lyons-Ruth, 1999, p. 579). Thus, psychotherapy, according to this point of view, needs to conform to the metaphor of the caregiver-infant attachment relationship by emphasizing change in the nonsymbolic, procedural forms of knowledge.

Working from the same assumptions, Eagle (2003) offers a pessimistic view of therapeutic change occurring within the domain of implicit procedural knowledge: "Procedural rules are especially recalcitrant ... [They] do not change that readily—even in successful treatment" (pp. 45–46). Instead, Eagle and Wolitzky (2006) suggest that therapeutic change through interpretation and acquisition of insight ("second order change," p. 14) occurs more frequently than therapeutic change through implicit procedural knowledge ("first order change," p. 14). Insight into the causal processes associated with maladaptive patterns of behavior can limit these behaviors, but the desire to engage in these behaviors usually remains because first-order change has not occurred.

While members of the Process of Change Study Group in Boston perhaps diminish the exclusive importance of "the talking cure" in favor of the contributions that therapist-patient interaction structures can make to therapeutic change, other theoreticians argue that caregiver-infant communication can serve the purposes of intrapersonal connectedness and differentiation for the infant—even before language acquisition. Benjamin (2002) describes a pattern of communication that the caregiver and infant simultaneously create and to which they surrender, which Aron (2006) has since labeled "a rhythmic third" (p. 356). This third quality of the interaction between the caregiver and infant creates a sense of connectedness between the dyadic partners.

Some Christian mystics (e.g., Edwards, 2001) emphasize the presence of the Holy Spirit as a third Person in sessions between a "spiritual director" and a "spiritual directee":

> It is a three-way relationship: among the true director who is the Holy Spirit (which in Christian tradition is the Spirit of Christ present in and among us), and the human director (who listens for the directions of the Spirit with the directee), and the directee ... The director is a companion along the pilgrim's way, wanting to be directly open along with the directee to the Spirit-undercurrents flowing through the happenings of the directee's life.
>
> (Locations 71–74)

Spiritually informed therapists could view this rhythmic sense of connectedness as the Holy Spirit working to unify the therapist and patient in their communion with the Holy Spirit. In this understanding of rhythmic third, both therapist and patient would have to share a common understanding of the connecting, unifying role of a Spiritual Being in their work together.

Benjamin (2004) also contrasts this rhythmic sense of connectedness with a sense of differentiation originating in the caregiver's marking of the infant's emotional displays. Gergely (2000; see also Fonagy et al., 2002) suggests that the sensitive caregiver mirrors the infant's negative emotional displays in such a way that the infant "knows" that the caregiver is not actually experiencing the same emotion but rather is recognizing and empathizing with the infant's emotion. He labeled this experience "marking." A caregiver's unmodulated mirroring of the infant's emotional experience (as when the caregiver expresses fright when the infant expresses a fearful response), or not mirroring the infant's emotional experience at all (as when the caregiver ignores the infant's fearful response), would equally threaten the infant's sense of security. In other words, the caregiver might exaggerate some aspect of the infant's emotional display to mark it as belonging to the infant rather than the mother, but signifying that the mother understands what the infant is experiencing. Marking is the process through which the caregiver contains and metabolizes the infant's dysregulated emotions (for an object relations perspective on the same phenomenon, see Bion, 1962, 1967). These repeated experiences of marking facilitate intrapersonal self-other differentiation and emotion regulation for the infant before the acquisition of language occurs.

In spiritual direction, this self-other differentiation is recognized as a spiritual directee's uniqueness in God's image: "[The spiritual director and spiritual directee] are pioneers together in uncharted spiritual waters, because no one has ever lived the life of this unique shaping of God's image who sits before us" (Edwards, 2001, Locations 1126–1127). The psychoanalyst Judy Kantrowitz (2001) extends this uniqueness to include the therapist-patient dyad:

> An analytic treatment is like a snowflake. Overall, it is easy to identify and distinguish. However, closer scrutiny reveals how different each one is from the others. In fact, no two are alike. Nor are any two patient-analyst pairs. In analytic treatment, the particular aspects of therapeutic action that facilitate psychological change are likely to vary from person to person.
>
> (p. 403)

Marking in a spiritually informed therapy would include upholding the patient's unique feelings without judgment because they are uniquely shaped in God's image. Honoring the innate spirituality of both therapist and patient facilitates this dual sense that there is both a primary unity with the Spirit (however conceptualized) and an essential uniqueness that characterizes each person in the dyad. Thus, for the spiritually informed therapist, the ideas of the rhythmic third and marking are an inherent part of the psychotherapy process.

After the acquisition of language, does the marking of unarticulated emotional displays have the same differentiating and emotion-regulatory properties as in infancy? Aron (2006) suggests that the therapist's verbally mediated reflections on the patient's thoughts and feelings—presented in modulated form that resembles marking—allow the patient to identify with an image of the therapist thinking about them. Fonagy et al. (2002) modifies this conceptualization by suggesting that the patient identifies instead with a more modulated image of themselves contained in the therapist's mind, which the patient then internalizes as an integrated self-representation. Both these conceptualizations apply the idea of marking, borrowed from the caregiver-infant relationship, to linguistic communication between the therapist and patient. If marking occurs during the presymbolic period of relational procedural knowing, then how can language—symbolic communication—"speak" to this layer of human experience?

Lyons-Ruth (1999) tries to answer this question with evidence from the Adult Attachment Interview (AAI; George et al., 1996), which purports to measure "enactive procedural representations" (Lyons-Ruth, 1999, p. 585). The interviewee reveals these representations in verbal dialogue on the AAI but does not necessarily represent them symbolically—"even though they may be symbolically represented by the observing researcher or psychoanalyst" (p. 585). Therapeutic change, then, would occur when the therapist uses language as a vehicle to produce the marking of dysregulated emotions to facilitate their modulation and containment. Thus, the metaphor of the caregiver-infant attachment relationship might still be relevant to the therapist-patient relationship if we view language as a conduit for communicating both connectedness and differentiation to facilitate the patient's emotion regulation and self-other differentiation.

The following clinical example illustrates this process in the therapist-patient relationship. A therapist who marks a patient's feelings of resentment toward a family member places the feelings in an intentional frame of reference without themselves becoming resentful. The modulated manner in which the therapist talks about the resentment—understanding the intentions of all parties involved—suggests to the patient that the therapist both understands the resentment (which facilitates connectedness between the patient and therapist) while not themselves reacting with resentment (which facilitates differentiation between the patient and therapist). The patient begins to identify with either an image of the therapist thinking about them (Aron, 2006) or an image of themselves contained in the therapist's mind (Fonagy et al., 2002). The patient then internalizes either image or both images to facilitate emotion regulation. The therapist's use of language to communicate with and change the implicit procedural level of knowledge requires both symbolic and nonsymbolic mental processing. Although "procedural systems influence and are influenced by symbolic systems through multiple cross-system connections" (Lyons-Ruth, 1999, p. 580), these neurocognitive and emotion-based pathways are not clearly understood by psychoanalysts or attachment researchers. Functional magnetic resonance imaging (fMRI), positron emission tomography (PET scan), and other neuroimaging techniques are beginning to reveal these interconnections using clever, sophisticated research methodologies (Schore, 2003).

Reflections on the Caregiver-Infant Attachment Relationship as a Metaphor for the God-Patient Relationship

I have discussed the limitations of the caregiver-infant attachment relationship in relation to the therapist-patient relationship. Specifically, I noted that the metaphor appears to break down when the financial, temporal, spatial, logistic, ethical, and linguistic boundaries of treatment are considered. Unlike a therapist, however, God does not charge for caring, has no temporal or spatial limitations, always interacts with humans ethically (that is God's "brand"), and, owing to God's omniscience, understands humans at both the presymbolic and symbolic levels of communication. Thus, on these dimensions, the God-patient relationship seems to conform more closely to the caregiver-infant attachment relationship than the therapist-patient relationship does.

Furthermore, the God-patient relationship transcends the metaphor of the caregiver-infant attachment relationship for one obvious reason: God's love for humans far exceeds a caregiver's love for their infant. God's love is perfectly responsive to humans' emotional needs. The psalmist writes: "How priceless is your unfailing love, O God! People take refuge in the shadow of your wings" (Psalm 36:7; NIV, 1978). Similarly, "For as high as the heavens are above the earth, so great is his love" (Psalm 103:11; NIV, 1978). From the New Testament, the author of the apostle John's first letter expresses this sentiment succinctly as "God is love" (I John 4:16; NIV, 1978). In his letter to the Romans, the apostle Paul underscores the steadfastness of God's love: "Neither death nor life, neither angels nor demons, neither the present nor the future, nor any powers, neither height nor depth, nor anything else in all creation, will be able to separate us from the love of God" (Romans 8:38–39; NIV, 1978).

The Hebrew Bible also contains many examples of God's perfect caregiving. Through the prophet Hosea, God speaks as a caregiver: "I led them with cords of human kindness, with ties of love. To them I was like one who lifts a little child to the cheek, and I bent down to feed them" (Hosea 11:4; NIV, 1978). Similarly, "As a mother comforts her child, so will I comfort you" (Isaiah 66:13; NIV, 1978). Through the prophet Isaiah, God declares that God's caregiving skills supersede those of a mother: "Can a mother forget the baby at her breast and have no compassion on the child she has borne? Though she may forget, I will not forget you" (Isaiah 49:15; NIV, 1978). Thus, according to these sacred texts, the God-patient relationship transcends the caregiver-infant attachment relationship and does not present the limitations imposed on the therapist-patient relationship. Long after the therapist-patient relationship is over, long after parents die, the God-patient relationship endures.

Thus, it would be expedient for the therapist to help the patient to connect to a Higher Power to fulfill the patient's ongoing attachment needs outside the therapy office and beyond treatment termination. As Bowlby (1977a) suggests, attachment security remains a lifelong concern "from the cradle to the grave" (p. 203). The patient's reliance on a Higher Power to meet these needs might help the patient to consolidate and sustain the psychological gains made while participating in the therapist-patient relationship. According to the psalmist, God seems to be the ultimate Container: "The Lord is compassionate and gracious, slow to anger, abounding in love … He does not treat us as our sins deserve or repay us according to our iniquities" (Psalms 103:8, 10; NIV, 1978). God is the exemplar of love, compassion, and forgiveness—emotions ideally suited to help contain a patient's emotional distress. The therapist can facilitate the transfer of this containment function from themselves to a Higher Power during the termination phase.

Are Attachment and Transference Equivalent Concepts?

The final important difference between the metaphor of the caregiver-infant attachment relationship and the therapist-patient relationship concerns the difference between the infant's feelings toward the caregiver and the patient's feelings toward the therapist. We label the infant's feelings "attachment" and the patient's feelings "transference." Are these phenomena conceptually identical, overlapping, or separate? If they are separate, do they mutually influence each other or operate as parallel systems? While a conceptual relation between the infant's attachment to the caregiver and the patient's working alliance with the therapist has received a general endorsement in the literature (see above), a conceptual relation between attachment and transference seems more equivocal.

Whether young children develop transference in psychotherapy stimulated theoretical battles between the Kleinians and the Anna Freudians in London in the middle of the last century. Melanie Klein (1927) routinely observed transference in her analysis of young children, while Anna Freud (1946) argued that transference in children does not occur because their "attachment" to their parents precludes any transfer of sexual energy onto anyone else. This dispute has been settled in favor of transference; contemporary child psychoanalysts generally recognize transference phenomena in child psychotherapy (e.g., Altman et al., 2002). If even young children can experience transference in psychotherapy, then can young children also become attached to their therapists? Or does the emergence of transference indicate that an attachment relationship has formed?

According to attachment theory (Howes, 1999), infants form attachments to one or a few persons significantly involved in their care, particularly in the attachment-activating situations mentioned above. These attachment relationships become hierarchically organized according to preference. For example, a female toddler might generally prefer sitting on her father's lap when her mother and father are present, but she might prefer the mother's lap after a bad spill or a frightening noise. The infant, however, might prefer the father to the grandmother or some other ancillary caregiver during similar attachment-activating moments. Clearly, we would include the mother and father on any short list of attachment figures, who have provided care for the infant during the organization of the attachment system, which lasts until 18 to 24 months of age (Ainsworth et al., 1974). Can subsequent attachments form? Dozier and her colleagues (Dozier et al., 2001) found that infants placed in foster care even after 18 months reorganized their attachment behavior around the emotional availability of their new caregivers. It is not known, however, whether these infants reorganize their attachment behaviors yet again when they are placed back with their biological mothers. Do remnants of these older mental organizations continue to linger and influence later behaviors?

In psychotherapy, the child patient is entering into a relationship with a potential attachment figure while maintaining an attachment to the parents. Unlike foster care, in which biological mothers perform little or no caregiving and foster mothers are solely responsible for the caregiving, the parents of the child patient continue their secure-base provision. In other words, the child establishes an attachment relationship with the therapist while maintaining an attachment relationship with the parents. Where is the child therapist in the hierarchy of attachment figures who have been present in the child's life since the moment of birth?

I am using child psychotherapy to illustrate this problem of attachment to the therapist because the child does become attached to the therapist despite primary attachments to the parents. Just this morning, the mother of a 9-year-old male patient with oppositional defiant disorder in once-weekly psychotherapy called to tell me that a car had run over his dog. The first thing he said to his mother after learning about the unfortunate news was that he wanted to speak to me. I characterize this reaction as an attachment behavior to seek vocal proximity with me. In the same manner, adult patients become attached to therapists even though they might be involved in emotionally significant relationships. If we acknowledge that attachment is a regular part of the psychotherapy relationship, then how do we understand transference and its role in psychotherapy?

A few authors have contributed to our understanding of these phenomena. One group (Henry & Strupp, 1994; Mackie, 1981; Mallinckrodt et al., 2005) argues that attachment and the working alliance are conceptually identical concepts in the sense that the spirit of "proper rapport" (Freud, 1913, p. 139) attaches the patient to the therapist and allows them to engage in a common task with a common goal (Horvath & Greenberg, 1989). In addition, some authors among this group suggest that the attachment or working alliance represents aspects of the "real," ego-based relationship with the therapist, while the transference represents aspects of the distorted, unconscious fantasies of early caregivers transferred onto the therapist. The problem with this position, as I see it, is that an insecure attachment to the therapist can include distorted, unconscious processes such as forgetting payment, coming late to session, or dismissing one's feelings toward the therapist. In addition, fantasies of crawling inside the therapist's womb or blasting off into outer space (a common fantasy of an anxious-avoidant child patient of mine) seem to contain an obvious residue of attachment and the defensive processes against it.

A second group (Eagle, 2003; Lyons-Ruth, 1999; Slade, 1999) hypothesizes a conceptual equivalence between attachment and transference because implicit procedural knowledge, the essence of internal working models, is attributed to the therapist-patient relationship and the person of the therapist. For example, Eagle (2003) regards "transference patterns ... as most representative of early procedural knowledge and rules" (p. 46), which Lyons-Ruth (1999, p. 585) characterizes as internal working models of attachment. Slade (1999) modifies the definition of transference so that it refers to the patient's "primary mode of relatedness" (p. 588) rather than the classical idea of a transfer of wishes and fears onto the therapist. The pattern of relating to an attachment figure, rather than the unacceptable aspects of the patient's own personality, is transferred onto the therapist and enacted in the therapist-patient relationship.

A third group (Bordin, 1994; Bradley et al., 2005; Diamond, Clarkin, et al., 2003; Parish & Eagle, 2003; Szajnberg & Crittenden, 1997) takes the position that attachment shares elements of both the working alliance and transference and that, indeed, these phenomena mutually influence each other. Most of these authors suggest that a positive working alliance is conceptually equivalent to a secure attachment, while a negative working alliance is conceptually equivalent to an insecure attachment. A positive transference usually occurs in the context of a secure attachment, while a negative transference usually occurs in the context of an insecure attachment. Yet a secure attachment can protect the treatment from the destructive effects of the negative transference. Diamond, Clarkin, et al. (2003) distinguish secure-base behavior in the therapist-patient relationship (the working alliance) from "recapitulated states of mind with respect to early attachment figures in the relationship with the therapist" (i.e., the transference; p. 170). Bradley and her colleagues (2005) consider all three concepts virtually interchangeable.

How Are Attachment, Working Alliance, and Transference Interrelated Concepts?

I present my own theoretical formulation of the relations among these three concepts. The working alliance includes nonattachment components, such as therapist-patient agreement on the tasks and goals of treatment, as well as a potential attachment component, the collaborative bond or rapport between the therapist and patient. This rapport, however, is not necessarily related to attachment in which the therapist is considered a secure base or safe haven. During the administration of the AAI, the interviewee's level of collaboration with the interviewer contributes to the attachment classification (Main & Goldwyn, 1994). Yet no one would suggest that the interviewee has formed an attachment to the interviewer, who is usually a stranger. The level of collaboration between the interviewee and interviewer depends on the interviewee's state of mind with respect to their attachment history with the childhood caregivers and on the interviewer's own level of collaboration, based on their attachment history.

In psychotherapy, a patient can collaborate with the therapist on their common tasks and goals without developing an attachment to them in the sense of relying on the therapist as a secure base or safe haven. It takes a history of therapist caregiving, delivered over months of exposure, to form an attachment to the therapist. In my view, treatment approaches such as cognitive-behavioral therapy (CBT) offer skills training, not caregiving per se. A working alliance is formed, yet only in rare instances would a patient treated in one of these approaches form an attachment to the therapist because these approaches do not last long enough. Thus, a working alliance is a necessary but not sufficient condition for an attachment to form—regardless of whether the attachment is secure or insecure. The quality of the working alliance depends on the patient's state of mind with respect to attachment to the caregivers during childhood and on the therapist's own state of mind with respect to their own attachment history (Tyrrell et al., 1999), not on the

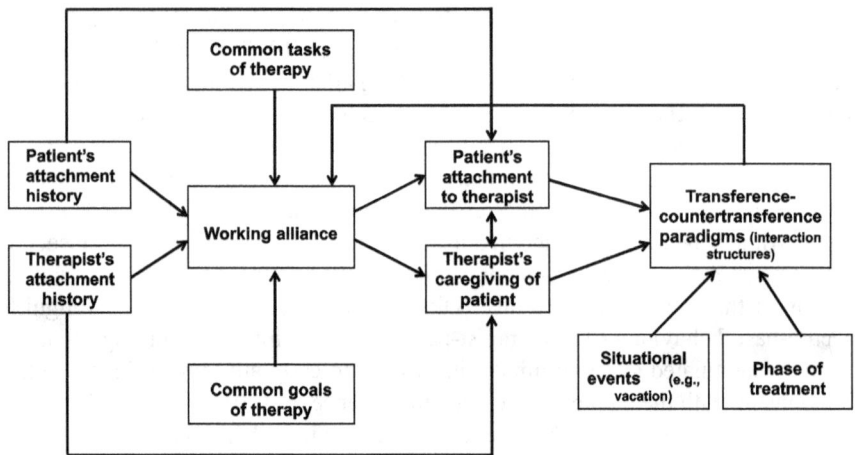

Figure 4.1 Pathways model of working alliance, patient's attachment to therapist, therapist's caregiving of patient, and transference-countertransference paradigms.

patient's state of mind with respect to attachment to the therapist (see Figure 4.1). As discussed below, noncomplementary states of mind between the therapist and patient produce a better working alliance than complementary states of mind. The reasons for this finding are not clearly understood, but one theory is that a therapist with a noncomplementary state of mind is better equipped to facilitate the patient's emotion regulation than a therapist with a complementary state of mind.

"Transference" refers to the process of transferring onto a contemporary person feelings that originally applied, and still unconsciously apply, to a person from childhood in whom the person had made an emotional investment (Freud, 1912a). The person from childhood, however, does not have to be a caregiver. Freud (1912a) stated that the "father-imago," or mental representation of a father, represents one childhood prototype on which transference is based, "but the transference is not tied to this particular prototype: it may also come about on the lines of the mother-imago or brother-imago" (p. 100). We know from attachment theory that an attachment is formed to a person who gives care in situations in which the attachment system is activated (see earlier discussion). Unless a sibling is sufficiently older to provide such care, we would not expect a sibling to use another sibling as a secure base or safe haven. Thus, siblings do not form attachments to each other in this restricted sense of the word "attachment." Consequently, the phenomenon of transference cannot be conceptually equivalent to the phenomenon of attachment.

Indeed, positive and negative transference and maternal and paternal transference (Freud, 1912a) exist and more recently, organizationally based transference: psychopathic, paranoid, and depressive transference (Kernberg, 1992) and idealizing and mirroring transference (Kohut, 1971). Furthermore, patients can exhibit different transferences at different times of the treatment or even in a single session. Kernberg and his colleagues (Clarkin et al., 2015) discuss the rapidly oscillating transferences of patients with borderline personality disorder: at one moment, the patient might be casting the therapist in the role of a persecutor, the next moment, a longed-for caregiver, and the moment after that, a defiant child. Kernberg and his colleagues articulate these oscillations using the language of projection of and identification with emotionally linked pairs of mental representations of self and others from childhood. Each role portrayed by the therapist also arouses distinct countertransference reactions because the therapist has temporarily identified with the projected mental representations of self or others. Bowlby (1980) and others (Grossmann et al., 2005; Hamilton, 2000; van IJzendoorn, 1995; Waters et al., 2000) characterize the attachment construct as generally stable over time and resistant to change. Thus, if transference can fluctuate (sometimes rapidly in a single session) and can consist of feelings originally experienced with noncaregivers, then one must conclude that transference and attachment are conceptually independent entities. Indeed, therapists' ratings of their patients' negative transference were positively correlated with the patients' ratings of their secure attachment to the therapist (Woodhouse et al., 2003).

I argue that the attachment to the therapist, developed in the context of a working alliance (see above), in turn provides a context for the entire range of transference experiences in the therapist-patient relationship (see Figure 4.1). Previously (Goodman, 2014), I argued that the preoccupied/hyperactivating (anxious-resistant) and dismissing/deactivating (anxious-avoidant) internal working models represent two distinctly different types of personality organization, both organized at a borderline level. According to Kernberg (1986a, 1986b), both borderline personality disorder and most narcissistic personality disorders (especially antisocial personality disorder) are organized at a borderline level. Borderline personality organization falls midway between the neurotic and psychotic levels of personality organization (Kernberg, 1996). What distinguishes the narcissistic personality disorders from borderline personality disorder is the presence of the pathological grandiose self. The pathological grandiose self is an admixture of idealized mental representations of others and real and idealized self-representations that compensates for a lack of integration of a normal self-concept observed in borderline personality organization, which accounts for the paradox of relatively good ego functioning and surface adaptation in the presence of primitive defensive processes, such as splitting, and contaminated, barren interpersonal relationships. I drew comparisons between borderline psychopathology and the preoccupied/hyperactivating internal working model, and between narcissistic psychopathology and the dismissing/deactivating internal working model, and provided modest empirical evidence for these assertions (Westen et al., 2006).

Briefly, borderline psychopathology shares with the preoccupied/hyperactivating internal working model the features of extreme emotion dysregulation, caregiver enmeshment, hostile dependence on significant others, and fear of abandonment. Conversely, narcissistic psychopathology shares with the dismissing/deactivating internal working model the features of emotion overregulation, dismissal or devaluation of the emotional importance of interpersonal relationships, counterdependence on others, and denial of vulnerability. These two types of personality organization lack integration and complexity at the representational level and share some of the same primitive defensive processes such as splitting (Goodman, 2014, p. 66). I also argued that mental representations of self and others are the building blocks of these personality organizations; their level of integration and complexity reflects the overall level of the personality organization.

Transference-countertransference paradigms are emotionally linked pairs of mental representations of self and others, with one of these mental representations identified with the patient and the other projected onto the therapist (Clarkin et al., 2015). These paradigms exist within a particular personality organization. For example, a psychopathic transference (Kernberg, 1992) is associated with the pathological grandiose self in a borderline personality organization. This transference consists of projecting the self-representation onto the therapist, whom the patient perceives as dishonest, exploitative, and ruthless. I am suggesting that this transference-countertransference paradigm exists within a dismissing/deactivating internal working model. Other constellations of mental representations of self and others belong to the domain of a preoccupied/hyperactivating internal working model. For example, the patient's projection onto the therapist of an infantile, dependent self-representation compels the patient to behave toward the therapist in a controlling-caregiving manner.

I am proposing that the pattern of personality organization constrains the range of representational pairs and, thus, the transference-countertransference paradigms that could emerge in a treatment. The personality organization/internal working model is therefore a necessary but not sufficient condition for a transference-countertransference paradigm to form (see Figure 4.1). In other words, the personality organization determines the level of quality, complexity, and integration of the emotionally linked pairs of mental representations of self and others manifested in the therapist-patient relationship; however, other variables such as the therapist's personality organization/internal working model, quality of caregiving (see below), phase of treatment, and situational events (e.g., the therapist's vacation) also determine which representational pairs become activated.

I want to add here that the patient's attachment system both activates and is activated by the therapist's caregiving system, reciprocal to and parallel with the attachment system. The caregiving system, according to George and Solomon (1999), is activated when the caregiver perceives "internal or external cues or stimuli ... as frightening, dangerous, or stressful for the child," associated with situations such as "separation, child endangerment, and the child's verbal and nonverbal signals of discomfort and distress" (p. 652). In the therapist-patient relationship, this caregiving takes the form of attentive listening; verbalization of emotions, needs, and the processes that inhibit the reception of caregiving; empathy; limit-setting; emotional containment; and mentalization, to name a few. These and other caregiving behaviors facilitate the patient's use of the therapist as a secure base and safe haven. George and Solomon (1999) identify four patterns of caregiving analogous to the four patterns of attachment. It is believed that caregivers' own attachment histories determine the quality of caregiving for their children. I am arguing that the therapist's caregiving of the patient mediates the influence of the therapist's own attachment history on the patient's attachment to the therapist. In addition, the patient's attachment and therapist's caregiving systems mutually influence each other (see Figure 4.1).

Thus, I am proposing a framework for understanding these relational phenomena (see Figure 4.1). The patient's and therapist's attachment relationships to caregivers during childhood, as well as their common tasks and goals, determine the quality of the working alliance, which, along with their attachment histories, determines the formation of an attachment to the therapist and caregiving of the patient. Along with other variables such as phase of treatment and situational events, this attachment formation in turn determines the range of transference-countertransference paradigms activated in the therapist-patient relationship. These transference-countertransference paradigms can in turn influence the quality of the working alliance (Bordin, 1994), which in turn influences the attachment to the therapist and caregiving of the patient. A negative transference, for example, might disrupt an already tenuous collaboration between the therapist and patient, contaminate the patient's perception of the therapist as a secure base and safe haven and the therapist's self-perception as the provider of these functions, and result in termination of the treatment. This event is most likely to occur among those patients who rely on extremely unmodulated dismissing/deactivating or preoccupied/hyperactivating attachment strategies that dramatically increase the likelihood of emotion dysregulation and resultant impulsive behavior when potentially dysregulating circumstances occur, such as a narcissistic injury or a perceived threat of abandonment.

Psychoanalysis has traditionally targeted the transference-countertransference paradigms as an intervention point of entry by translating the patient's enactments, symptoms, associations, fantasies, dreams, and other clinical material related to the therapist into symbolic knowledge through their verbal interpretation. As indicated earlier, however, some psychoanalytic and attachment theoreticians are beginning to question the exclusivity and even the primacy of symbolic knowledge as a vehicle of therapeutic change: "Representational change may be set in motion ... without necessarily assigning privileged status to a particular dimension, such as interpretation" (Lyons-Ruth, 1999, p. 601). According to Lyons-Ruth (1999), "Development does not proceed only or primarily by moving from procedural coding to symbolic coding ... Making the unconscious conscious does not adequately describe developmental or psychoanalytic change" (pp. 579, 590). Thus, we might question whether targeting transference-countertransference paradigms is the only method or even the most efficient method for producing therapeutic change. I am suggesting that implicit procedural knowledge embodied in the patient's internal working model—"often neither conscious and verbalizable nor repressed in a dynamic sense" (Lyons-Ruth, 1999, p. 589)—can also change through the therapist's reliable provision of a secure base—a nonsymbolic procedural response aimed at this level of relational knowing. Although the verbal translation of unconscious, split-off mental representations of self and others can facilitate the integration of the patient's internal working model/personality organization and restore emotion regulation, other, nonsymbolic interventions can also target the internal working model for therapeutic change.

Persons can also transfer their implicit procedural knowledge embodied in the internal working model onto God. The patient's implicit procedural knowledge can express itself in bodily sensations such as the patient in Chapter 6 of Goodman (2025), who feels kundalini energy—a divine feminine life force—gradually migrating upward in his upper chest, neck, and jaw. The internal working model of the patient's attachment relationship to God can also express itself in narrative patterns prompted by attachment-activating questions (e.g., Adult Attachment to God Interview [AAGI]; see Goodman, 2025, Chapter 6). The spiritually informed therapist who practices Attachment-Informed Psychotherapy (AIP) must consider how the patient's internal working model might influence their attachment relationship to a Higher Power.

Unless the patient believes themselves to be a conduit of God's direct communication to humanity (which could stimulate a different conversation about mental illness; see Griffith, 2010), God does not communicate verbally. At best, we experience a stirring in our souls—what the prophet Elijah experienced as "a gentle whisper" (I Kings 19:12; NIV, 1978). The classically trained psychoanalyst seldom speaks during a session for a reason: they want to act as a blank screen upon which the patient can project their own fantasies, wishes, and fears (for an explanation of therapist neutrality, see Freud, 1915). Contemporary psychoanalysis, particularly the Relational School, has come to view therapist neutrality as impossible to achieve because of the ubiquity of countertransference and, when attempted, can trigger an iatrogenic effect in the patient (e.g., fleeing treatment because of the therapist's robotic quality; for a related argument, see Kaplan, 2016).

Because God does not typically speak verbally to humans, can God's silence trigger an iatrogenic effect in humans seeking contact? If God is the Giant Rorschach Card in the Sky—the Big Blank Screen onto which we simply project our fantasies, wishes, and fears—then this nonverbal property of God might exacerbate a person's "primary mode of relatedness" (Slade, 1999, p. 588). A securely attached person might perceive God's silence as confirmation that God is pleased with them. God arranges the events in the securely attached person's life to work together for good (Romans 8:28; NIV, 1978). On the other hand, an anxious-avoidant person might use God's silence as a rejection and thus serve as a rationalization for ignoring God or establishing greater distance from God. The events of the anxious-avoidant person's life are randomly distributed like raffle tickets spun around in a raffle drum. An anxious-resistant person might interpret God's silence as the silent treatment— evidence that God is displeased with them, causing worry that they are unworthy to hear God's voice, yet always straining to listen for it. God arranges the events in the anxious-resistant person's life to signal displeasure in them. A disorganized/ disoriented person might interpret God's silence as evidence of condemnation and subsequent angry withdrawal from them. God arranges the events in the disorganized/disoriented person's life to express this condemnation, producing terror of God.

The correspondence pathway (see Chapter 3) would suggest that in people's minds, God interacts with them in ways consistent with their primary mode of relatedness. In the apostle Paul's letter to Titus, the author makes a similar observation: "To the pure, all things are pure, but to those who are corrupted and do not believe, nothing is pure. In fact, both their minds and consciences are corrupted" (Titus 1:15; NIV, 1978). There is scientific support for this observation: each attachment pattern consists of a particular psychic structure that a person coopts in their application of "confirmation bias," which can entrench the nature of their attachment relationship to God. According to the cognitive psychologist Peter Wason (1960), confirmation bias is defined as the tendency to interpret information, particularly ambiguous information, as confirming a person's pre-established beliefs and values. God's silence would fall under the category of ambiguous information. When you notice that your partner is silent, what does it mean? Does the silence indicate that your partner is contented, angry, tired, worried, sad, or perplexed? Most persons, and especially therapists, often use nonverbal cues to aid in the interpretation of silence. In the spiritual realm, these nonverbal cues might take the form of natural events in a person's life. But these events, too, have ambiguous meanings. Thus, spiritually minded persons interpret God's silence and the events that God seemingly orchestrates as confirmation of their pre-established beliefs and values founded upon their internal working model developed in relation to caregivers during childhood.

The ambiguous meaning of life events and their interpretation are addressed in a Taoist parable dating back to at least 139 BCE titled, "Sāi Wēng Lost His Horse," in *The Huainanzi* (Major et al., 2010, pp. 728–729). A poor farmer's horse runs away, and his neighbors tell him, "That's too bad." The farmer replies, "Maybe." Shortly thereafter, the horse returns, bringing another horse with it. His neighbors tell him, "Well, that's good fortune." The farmer replies, "Maybe." The following day, the farmer's son is trying to tame the new horse and falls, breaking his leg. His neighbors tell him, "Well, that's too bad." The farmer replies, "Maybe." Shortly thereafter, the emperor declares war on a neighboring nation and orders all able-bodied men to join the army. Many men die or suffer permanent injuries, but the farmer's son is unable to fight and is therefore spared because he is injured. The farmer's neighbors tell him, "Well, that's good fortune." The farmer replies, "Maybe." And so on. This securely attached—and wise—farmer understands the inherent ambiguity of the meaning of life events and knows better than to project meaning onto these events as his neighbors do. Shakespeare expresses a similar equanimity toward the meaning of life events when Hamlet tells Rosencrantz, "There is nothing either good or bad, but thinking makes it so" (Shakespeare, 1899, pp. 74–75). The internal working model often determines how a person interprets the meaning of life events as well as people's interactions and behaviors.

AIP, and psychodynamic therapy more generally, increase a patient's awareness of how and why their mind works as it does. The patient engages in and shares with the therapist ongoing interactions with significant others (including a Higher Power). The patient also engages in ongoing interactions with the therapist. The therapist might ask the patient to interpret the underlying intentions of these significant others (including a Higher Power) and of the therapist, which would enhance the patient's mentalizing capacity. Mentalization is the ability to interpret others' (and one's own) behaviors as products of others' (and one's own) mental states (i.e., wishes, desires, intentions, beliefs, fantasies; Fonagy et al., 2002). A closely related concept, theory of mind, is the ability to determine that the beliefs in one's own mind can differ from the beliefs in another person's mind (see Chapter 3; see also Baron-Cohen, 1995). A patient's belief that they can interpret the meaning of a life event as well as people's interactions and behaviors definitively might make that patient feel momentarily in control, but it diminishes the ability of a Higher Power to place that life event into a broader context that serves a greater good. In the Taoist parable, the farmer understands this truth. In his letter to the Romans, the apostle Paul also reveals his understanding of this truth: "And we know that in all things God works for the good of those who love him" (Romans 8:28; NIV, 1978), but in a different letter, he encourages the Thessalonians to "give thanks in all circumstances" (1 Thessalonians 5:18; NIV, 1978).

Working therapeutically with a patient on their understanding of God's omnibenevolence could generalize to oneself and significant others—not to trust oneself and others blindly but to learn how to give oneself and others the benefit of the doubt. Conversely, working therapeutically with a patient on their understanding of the imperfect benevolence of significant others could generalize to trusting in God's omnibenevolence. These insights might reciprocally influence each other in a bidirectional openness to new experiences unfiltered by the potential distortions directed by the patient's (and therapist's) internal working model. A goal of AIP is to develop the ability to tolerate the ambiguity of the meaning of life events as well as people's interactions and behaviors without automatically resorting to typecasting these events, interactions, and behaviors to confirm the biases pre-established by the internal working model. I explore these issues in greater depth in Chapters 5 and 6.

Limitations of this Treatment Model

I would like to make a plea for a measure of humility in the application of AIP to spiritually curious and spiritually grounded patients. This treatment model is contraindicated for patients who experience psychotic episodes (i.e., featuring poor reality testing, or the inability to distinguish fantasy from reality). Stabilizing these patients is key to their initial treatment, which might include supportive psychotherapy and an appropriate medication regimen (Griffith, 2010).

AIP is also contraindicated for patients who experience complex posttraumatic stress disorder (PTSD) or dissociative identity disorder (DID). These persons often struggle to distinguish past from present experiences, especially when they become distressed. For these persons, I would recommend a treatment model that serves to ground the person in present experience (e.g., Brand et al., 2022; Chefetz, 2015). Patients who begin to feel grounded in present experience with one of these treatment models can later benefit from AIP and the exploration of attachment relationships, including their attachment relationship to a Higher Power.

Conclusion

In summary, I argue that the metaphor of the caregiver-infant attachment relationship captures only certain features of the therapist-patient relationship—most important among them, the caregiver functions of a secure base and a safe haven. The metaphor appears to break down when the financial, temporal, spatial, logistic, and ethical boundaries of treatment are considered. I also note the vast differences between the infant's and the patient's fund of implicit procedural knowledge and linguistic knowledge. I also note that the God-patient relationship seems to conform more closely to the caregiver-infant attachment relationship than to the therapist-patient relationship does. Ultimately, the God-patient relationship transcends the metaphor of the caregiver-infant attachment relationship for one obvious reason: God's love for humans far exceeds a caregiver's love for their infant because God is the personification of love (see I John 4:16; NIV, 1978).

I also discuss the difference between the infant's attachment to the caregiver and the patient's working alliance and transference to the therapist. I propose that the working alliance and transference-countertransference paradigms are both conceptually independent of attachment phenomena embodied in internal working models but reflect the level of personality organization (psychotic, borderline, or neurotic) and the characteristic secondary attachment strategies (dismissing/deactivating or preoccupied/hyperactivating) used by the patient as an adult but originally developed out of caregiving experiences during childhood.

Finally, I discuss the varieties of emotional and interpersonal response to the reality that God does not typically speak verbally to humanity. The quality of the patient's internal working model constrains these varieties of emotional and interpersonal response by acting as a filter through which all experience is processed. Confirmation bias further solidifies these views of God such that "there is nothing either good or bad, but thinking makes it so" (Shakespeare, 1899, pp. 74–75). A spiritually informed therapist using AIP needs to: (1) recognize the influence of the internal working model on a patient's attachment relationship to God, (2) interpret the implications of their confirmation bias, which assumes that God's verbal silence can mean only one thing, and (3) provide therapeutic experiences that have the potential to override the emotional and interpersonal expectations inherent to the patient's particular internal working model. In so doing, the patient will eventually open themselves up to a multiplicity of meanings of God's verbal silence and look for God's presence in other modes of communication. Barrett (2012) instructs spiritually grounded parents to teach their children to interpret even mundane events as orchestrated by a Higher Power:

> If you believe God heals relationships and bodies, helps change people's minds, or finds you a parking space, say so in earshot of your children ... Prayer, particularly asking and thanking God for common things like family members, health, and wealth, as well as mundane events such as getting a good deal on tomatoes at the market or having a particularly enjoyable outing with friends, could help prime the one who prays to notice God's actions.
>
> (pp. 247–248)

In his first letter to the Thessalonians, the apostle Paul encouraged them to "give thanks in all circumstances" (1 Thessalonians 5:18; NIV, 1978)—not just the serendipitous ones.

I am not suggesting a teaching role for spiritually informed therapists but am instead pointing out that a Higher Power can "speak" through other modes of action. Like the Taoist farmer, whose runaway horse ultimately resulted in his son's life being spared, the spiritually informed therapist can help the patient to recognize a multiplicity of spiritual meanings of life events and tolerate the ambiguity inherent in these multiple spiritual meanings. A successful treatment will aid the patient in making this journey of spiritual meaning-making and reaching the twin goals of understanding that their Higher Power orchestrates all life events to work together for good in the long run (Romans 8:28; NIV. 1978), while simultaneously giving thanks in all circumstances (I Thessalonians 5:18; NIV, 1978). This is what a secure attachment relationship to a Higher Power would look like.

References

Aafjes-van Doorn, K., Spina, D. S., Horne, S. J., & Békés, V. (2024). The association between quality of therapeutic alliance and treatment outcomes in teletherapy: A systematic review and meta-analysis. *Clinical Psychology Review, 110*, 102430.

Ainsworth, M. D. S., Bell, S. M., & Stayton, D. J. (1974). Infant-mother attachment and social development: "Socialization" as a product of reciprocal responsiveness to signals. In M. P. M. Richards (Ed.), *The integration of a child into a social world* (pp. 99–135). Cambridge University Press.

Alexander, F., & French, T. M. (1946). *Psychoanalytic therapy: Principles and application.* Ronald.

Altman, N., Briggs, R., Frankel, J., Gensler, D., & Pantone, P. (2002). *Relational child psychotherapy.* Other Press.

Amini, F., Lewis, T., Lannon, R., Louie, A., Baumbacher, G., McGuinness, T., & Schiff, E. Z. (1996). Affect, attachment and memory: Contributions toward psychobiologic integration. *Psychiatry, 59*, 213–239.

Aron, L. (2006). Analytic impasse and the third: Clinical implications of intersubjectivity theory. *International Journal of Psycho-Analysis, 87*, 349–368.

Baron-Cohen, S. (1995). *Mindblindness: An essay on autism and theory of mind*. MIT Press/ Bradford Books.

Barrett, J. L. (2012). *Born believers: The science of children's religious belief*. Free Press.

Benjamin, J. (1987). The decline of the oedipus complex. In J. M. Broughton (Ed.), *Critical theories of psychological development* (pp. 211–244). Plenum Press.

Benjamin, J. (2002). The rhythm of recognition: Comments on the work of Louis Sander. *Psychoanalytic Dialogues, 12*, 43–53.

Benjamin, J. (2004). Beyond doer and done to: An intersubjective view of thirdness. *Psychoanalytic Quarterly, 73*, 5–46.

Bernier, A., & Dozier, M. (2002). The client-counselor match and the corrective emotional experience: Evidence from interpersonal and attachment research. *Psychotherapy: Theory/ Research/Practice/Training, 39*, 32–43.

Bion, W. R. (1962). *Learning from experience*. Heinemann.

Bion, W. R. (1967). *Second thoughts*. Heinemann.

Bordin, E. S. (1994). Theory and research on the therapeutic working alliance: New directions. In A. O. Horvath & L. S. Greenberg (Eds.), *The working alliance: Theory, research, and practice* (pp. 13–37). Wiley.

Bowlby, J. (1958). The nature of the child's tie to his mother. *International Journal of Psycho-Analysis, 39*, 350–373.

Bowlby, J. (1973). *Attachment and loss*: Vol. 2. *Separation: Anxiety and anger*. Basic Books.

Bowlby, J. (1977a). The making and breaking of affectional bonds. I. Aetiology and psychopathology in the light of attachment theory. *British Journal of Psychiatry, 130*, 201–210.

Bowlby, J. (1977b). The making and breaking of affectional bonds: II. Some principles of psychotherapy. *British Journal of Psychiatry, 130*, 421–431.

Bowlby, J. (1980). *Attachment and loss*: Vol. 3. *Loss, sadness and depression*. Basic Books.

Bowlby, J. (1982). *Attachment and loss*: Vol. 1. *Attachment* (2nd ed.). Basic Books.

Bowlby, J. (1988). *A secure base: Parent-child attachment and healthy human development*. Basic Books.

Bradley, R., Heim, A. K., & Westen, D. (2005). Transference patterns in the psychotherapy of personality disorders: Empirical investigation. *British Journal of Psychiatry, 186*, 342–349.

Brand, B. L., Schielke, H. I., Schiavone, F., & Lanius, R. A. (2022). *Finding solid ground: Overcoming obstacles in trauma treatment*. Oxford University Press.

Burns, P., Sander, L. W., Stechler, G., & Julia, H. (1972). Distress in feeding: Short-term effects of caretaker environment of the first 10 days. *Journal of the American Academy of Child Psychiatry, 11*, 427–439.

Chefetz, R. A. (2015). *Intensive psychotherapy for persistent dissociative processes: The fear of feeling real*. Norton.

Clarkin, J. F., Yeomans, F. E., & Kernberg, O. F. (2015). *Transference-focused psychotherapy for borderline personality disorder: A clinical guide*. American Psychiatric Publishing.

Dabriwal, V. (2023). *Parvati: The divine mother and universal goddess*. Amazon Books.

Diamond, D., Clarkin, J., Levine, H., Levy, K., Foelsch, P., & Yeomans, F. (1999). Borderline conditions and attachment: A preliminary report. *Psychoanalytic Inquiry, 19*, 831–884.

Diamond, D., Clarkin, J. F., Stovall-McClough, K. C., Levy, K. N., Foelsch, P. A., Levine, H., & Yeomans, F. E. (2003). Patient-therapist attachment: Impact on the therapeutic process and outcome. In M. Cortina & M. Marrone (Eds.), *Attachment theory and the psychoanalytic process*. Whurr.

Diamond, D., Stovall-McClough, C., Clarkin, J. F., & Levy, K. N. (2003). Patient-therapist attachment in the treatment of borderline personality disorder. *Bulletin of the Menninger Clinic, 67*, 227–259.

Dozier, M. (2003). Attachment-based treatment for vulnerable children. *Attachment and Human Development, 5*, 253–257.

Dozier, M., & Bates, B. C. (2004). Attachment state of mind and the treatment relationship. In L. Atkinson & S. Goldberg (Eds.), *Attachment issues in psychopathology and intervention* (pp. 167–180). Erlbaum.

Dozier, M., Stovall, K. C., Albus, K. E., & Bates, B. (2001). Attachment for infants in foster care: The role of caregiver state of mind. *Child Development, 72*, 1467–1477.

Dozier, M., & Tyrrell, C. (1998). The role of attachment in therapeutic relationships. In J. A. Simpson & W. S. Rholes (Eds.), *Attachment theory and close relationships* (pp. 221–248). Guilford Press.

Eagle, M. (2003). Clinical implications of attachment theory. *Psychoanalytic Inquiry, 23*, 27–53.

Eagle, M., & Wolitzky, D. L. (2006). The perspectives of attachment theory and psychoanalysis: Adult psychotherapy. Paper presented at conference, The perspectives of attachment theory and psychoanalysis: Adult psychotherapy. Adelphi University and the New York Attachment Consortium, Garden City, NY, November.

Edwards, T. (2001). *Spiritual director, spiritual companion: Guide to tending the soul.* Paulist Press. Kindle Edition.

Farber, B. A., & Geller, J. (1994). Gender and representation in psychotherapy. *Psychotherapy, 31*, 318–326.

Farber, B. A., Lippert, R. A., & Nevas, D. B. (1995). The therapist as attachment figure. *Psychotherapy, 32*, 204–212.

Ferber, R. (1990). Sleep schedule-dependent causes of insomnia and sleepiness in middle childhood and adolescence. *Pediatrician, 17*, 13–20.

Ferber, R. (2006). *Solve your child's sleep problems* (rev. ed.). Fireside.

Fonagy, P., Gergely, G., Jurist, E. L., & Target, M. (2002). *Affect regulation, mentalization, and the development of the self.* Other Press.

Freud, A. (1946). *The psycho-analytical treatment of children.* Imago.

Freud, S. (1910). Five lectures on psycho-analysis. In J. Strachey (Ed. and Trans.), *The standard edition of the complete psychological works of Sigmund Freud* (Vol. 11, pp. 1–56). Hogarth Press.

Freud, S. (1912a). The dynamics of transference. In J. Strachey (Ed. and Trans.), *The standard edition of the complete psychological works of Sigmund Freud* (Vol. 12, pp. 97–108). Hogarth Press.

Freud, S. (1912b). Recommendations to physicians practising psycho-analysis. In J. Strachey (Ed. and Trans.), *The standard edition of the complete psychological works of Sigmund Freud* (Vol. 12, pp. 109–120). Hogarth Press.

Freud, S. (1913). On beginning the treatment (further recommendations on the technique of psycho-analysis I). In J. Strachey (Ed. and Trans.), *The standard edition of the complete psychological works of Sigmund Freud* (Vol. 12, pp. 123–144). Hogarth Press.

Freud, S. (1915). Observations on transference-love (Further recommendations on the technique of psycho-analysis III). In J. Strachey (Ed. and Trans.), *The standard edition of the complete psychological works of Sigmund Freud* (Vol. 12, pp. 157–171). Hogarth Press.

George, C., & Solomon, J. (1999). Attachment and caregiving: The caregiving behavioral system. In J. Cassidy & P. R. Shaver (Eds.), *Handbook of attachment: Theory, research, and clinical applications* (pp. 649–670). Guilford Press.

George, C., Kaplan, N., & Main, M. (1996). Adult attachment interview (3rd ed.). Unpublished manuscript. University of California, Berkeley.

Gergely, G. (2000). Reapproaching Mahler: New perspectives on normal autism, symbiosis, splitting and libidinal object constancy from cognitive developmental theory. *Journal of the American Psychoanalytic Association, 48*, 1197–1228.

Goodman, G. (2006). Discussant [The perspectives of attachment theory and psycho-analysis: Adult psychotherapy]. Presented at conference, The perspectives of attachment theory and psychoanalysis: Adult psychotherapy. Adelphi University and the New York Attachment Consortium, Garden City, NY. November.

Goodman, G. (2014). *The internal world and attachment*. Routledge.

Goodman, G. (2025). *Practical applications of transforming the attachment relationship to God: Using attachment-informed psychotherapy*. Routledge.

Goodman, G., Edwards, K., & Chung, H. (2014). Interaction structures formed in the psychodynamic therapy of five patients with borderline personality disorder in crisis. *Psychology and Psychotherapy: Theory, Research and Practice, 87*, 15–31.

Greenberg, J. (2001). The analyst's participation: A new look. *Journal of the American Psychoanalytic Association, 49*, 359–381.

Greenson, R. R. (1965). The working alliance and the transference neurosis. *Psychoanalytic Quarterly, 34*, 155–181.

Griffith, J. L. (2010). *Religion that heals, religion that harms: A guide for clinical practice*. Guilford Press.

Grossmann, K. E., Grossmann, K., & Waters, E. (Eds.). (2005). *Attachment from infancy to adulthood: The major longitudinal studies*. Guilford Press.

Hamilton, C. E. (2000). Continuity and discontinuity of attachment from infancy through adolescence. *Child Development, 71*, 690–694.

Henry, W. P., & Strupp, H. H. (1994). The therapeutic alliance as interpersonal process. In A. O. Horvath & L. S. Greenberg (Eds.), *The working alliance: Theory, research, and practice* (pp. 51–84). Wiley.

Holmes, J. (1996). Psychotherapy and memory: An attachment perspective. *British Journal of Psychotherapy, 13*, 204–218.

Holmes, J. (1998). The changing aims of psychoanalytic psychotherapy: An integrative perspective. *International Journal of Psycho-Analysis, 79*, 227–240.

Horvath, A., & Greenberg, L. (1989). Development and validation of the working alliance inventory. *Journal of Counseling Psychology, 36*, 223–233.

Horvath, A., & Symonds, B. (1991). Relation between working alliance and outcome in psychotherapy: A meta-analysis. *Journal of Counseling Psychology, 38*, 139–149.

Howes, C. (1999). Attachment relationships in the context of multiple caregivers. In J. Cassidy & P. R. Shaver (Eds.), *Handbook of attachment: Theory, research, and clinical applications* (pp. 671–687). Guilford Press.

Jones, E. E. (2000). *Therapeutic action: A guide to psychoanalytic therapy*. Jason Aronson.

Kantrowitz, J. L. (2001). The analyst's participation: A new look [Commentary]. *Journal of the American Psychoanalytic Association, 49*, 398–406.

Kaplan, M. (2016). Clinical considerations regarding regression in psychotherapy with patients with conversion disorder. *Psychodynamic Psychiatry, 44*, 367–384.

Kernberg, O. F. (1986a). Borderline personality organization. In M. Stone (Ed.), *Essential papers on borderline disorders: One hundred years at the border* (pp. 279–319). New York University Press.

Kernberg, O. F. (1986b). Further contributions to the treatment of narcissistic personal-ities. In A. Morrison (Ed.), *Essential papers on narcissism* (pp. 245–292). New York University Press.

Kernberg, O. F. (1992). *Aggression in personality disorders and perversions.* Yale University Press.

Kernberg, O. F. (1996). A psychoanalytic theory of personality disorders. In J. F. Clarkin & M. F. Lenzenweger (Eds.), *Major theories of personality disorder* (pp. 106–140). Guilford Press.

Klein, M. (1927). Symposium on child analysis. *International Journal of Psycho-Analysis, 7*, 339–370.

Kohut, H. (1971). *The analysis of the self: A systematic approach to the psychoanalytic treatment of narcissistic personality disorders.* International Universities Press.

Lacan, J. (1977). *Écrits: A selection* (A. Sheridan, Trans.). Norton.

Luborsky, L. (1994). Therapeutic alliances as predictors of psychotherapy outcomes: Factors explaining the predictive success. In A. O. Horvath & L. S. Greenberg (Eds.), *The work-ing alliance: Theory, research, and practice* (pp. 38–50). Wiley.

Lyons, L. S., & Sperling, M. (1996). Clinical applications of attachment theory: Empirical and theoretical perspectives. In J. M. Masling & R. F. Bornstein (Eds.), *Psychoanalytic perspectives on developmental psychology* (pp. 221–256). American Psychological Association.

Lyons-Ruth, K. (1999). The two-person unconscious: Intersubjective dialogue, enactive relational representation, and the emergence of new forms of relational organization. *Psychoanalytic Inquiry, 19*, 576–617.

Mackie, A. J. (1981). Attachment theory: Its relevance to the therapeutic alliance. *British Journal of Medical Psychology, 54*, 203–212.

Mahler, M. S., Pine, F., & Bergman, A. (1975). *The psychological birth of the human infant: Symbiosis and individuation.* Basic Books.

Main, M., & Goldwyn, R. (1994). Adult attachment scoring and classification systems (6th ed.). Unpublished manuscript. University College, London.

Main, M., Kaplan, N., & Cassidy, J. (1985). Security in infancy, childhood, and adulthood: A move to the level of representation. *Monographs of the Society for Research in Child Development, 50*(1–2), 66–104..

Major, J. S., Queen, S. A., Meyer, A. S., & Roth, H. D. (2010). *The Huainanzi.* Columbia University Press.

Mallinckrodt, B. (2000). Attachment, social competencies, social support, and interpersonal process in psychotherapy. *Psychotherapy Research, 10*, 239–266.

Mallinckrodt, B., Gantt, D. L., & Coble, H. M. (1995). Attachment patterns in the psycho-therapy relationship: Development of the client attachment to therapist scale. *Journal of Counseling Psychology, 42*, 307–317.

Mallinckrodt, B., King, J. L., & Coble, H. M. (1998). Family dysfunction, alexithymia, and client attachment to therapist. *Journal of Counseling Psychology, 45*, 497–504.

Mallinckrodt, B., Porter, M. J., & Kivlighan, D. M., Jr. (2005). Client attachment to ther-apist, depth of in-session exploration, and object relations in brief psychotherapy. *Psychotherapy: Theory, Research, Practice, Training, 42*, 85–100.

Martin, D. J., Garske, J. P., & Davis, M. K. (2000). Relation of the therapeutic alliance with outcome and other variables: A meta-analytic review. *Journal of Consulting and Clinical Psychology*, *68*, 438–450.

McLaughlin, J. (1991). Clinical and theoretical aspects of enactment. *Journal of the American Psychoanalytic Association*, *39*, 595–614.

McWilliams, N. (1999). *Psychoanalytic case formulation*. Guilford Press.

Mitchell, S. (1999). Attachment theory and the psychoanalytic tradition: Reflections on human relationality. *Psychoanalytic Dialogues*, *9*, 85–107.

NIV (New International Version). (1978). *The holy Bible*. Zondervan.

Parish, M., & Eagle, M. N. (2003). Attachment to the therapist. *Psychoanalytic Psychology*, *20*, 271–286.

Rogers, C. R. (1977). *Carl Rogers on personal power*. Delacorte.

Safran, J. D., & Muran, J. C. (2000). *Negotiating the therapeutic alliance: A relational treatment guide*. Guilford Press.

Sandler, J. (1960). The background of safety. *International Journal of Psycho-Analysis*, *41*, 352–356.

Schafer, R. (1983). *The analytic attitude*. Basic Books.

Schore, A. N. (2003). *Affect regulation and the repair of the self*. Norton.

Shakespeare, W. (1899). *The tragedy of Hamlet, prince of Denmark* (E. Dowden, Ed.). Methuen and Co.

Slade, A. (1999). Attachment theory and research: Implications for the theory and practice of individual psychotherapy with adults. In J. Cassidy & P. R. Shaver (Eds.), *Handbook of attachment: Theory, research, and clinical applications* (pp. 575–594). Guilford Press.

Stern, D. N. (1977). *The first relationship: Mother and infant*. Harvard University Press.

Stern, D. N. (1985). *The interpersonal world of the infant: A view from psychoanalysis and developmental psychology*. Basic Books.

Stern, D. N. (1995). *The motherhood constellation: A unified view of parent-infant psychotherapy*. Basic Books.

Stern, D. N., Sander, L. W., Nahum, J. P., Harrison, A. M., Lyons-Ruth, K., Morgan, A. C., Bruschweiler-Stern, N., & Tronick, E. Z. (1998). Non-interpretive mechanisms in psychoanalytic therapy: The "something more" than interpretation. *International Journal of Psycho-Analysis*, *79*, 903–921.

Szajnberg, N. M., & Crittenden, P. M. (1997). The transference refracted through the lens of attachment. *Journal of the American Academy of Psychoanalysis*, *25*, 409–438.

Tronick, E. Z., Bruschweiler-Stern, N., Harrison, A. M., Lyons-Ruth, K., Morgan, A. C., Nahum, J. P., Sander, L., & Stern, D. N. (1998). Dyadically expanded states of consciousness and the process of therapeutic change. *Infant Mental Health Journal*, *19*, 290–299.

Tyrrell, C. L., Dozier, M., Teague, G. B., & Fallot, R. D. (1999). Effective treatment relationships for persons with serious psychiatric disorders: The importance of attachment states of mind. *Journal of Consulting and Clinical Psychology*, *67*, 725–733.

van IJzendoorn, M. H. (1995). Adult attachment representations, parental responsiveness, and infant attachment: A meta-analysis on the predictive validity of the Adult Attachment Interview. *Psychological Bulletin*, *117*, 387–403.

Vitz, P. C. (1977). *Psychology as religion: The cult of self-worship*. William B. Eerdmans.

Wason, P. C. (1960). On the failure to eliminate hypotheses in a conceptual task. *Quarterly Journal of Experimental Psychology*, *12*, 129–140.

Waters, E., Merrick, S., Treboux, D., Crowell, J., & Albersheim, L. (2000). Attachment security in infancy and early adulthood: A twenty-year longitudinal study. *Child Development, 71*, 684–689.

Weiss, J., & Sampson, H. (1986). *The psychoanalytic process: Theory, clinical observation, and empirical research*. Guilford Press.

Westen, D., & Gabbard, G. O. (2002). Developments in cognitive neuroscience: II. Implications for theories of transference. *Journal of the American Psychoanalytic Association, 50*, 99–134.

Westen, D., Nakash, O., Thomas, C., & Bradley, R. (2006). Clinical assessment of attachment patterns and personality disorder in adolescents and adults. *Journal of Consulting and Clinical Psychology, 74*, 1065–1085.

Winnicott, D. W. (1949). Hate in the counter-transference. *International Journal of Psycho-Analysis, 30*, 69–74.

Winnicott, D. W. (1960). The theory of the parent-infant relationship. *International Journal of Psycho-Analysis, 41*, 585–595.

Winnicott, D. W. (1965). *The maturational processes and the facilitating environment: Studies in the theory of emotional development*. International Universities Press.

Woodhouse, S. S., Schlosser, L. Z., Crook, R. E., Ligiero, D. P., & Gelso, C. J. (2003). Client attachment to therapist: Relations to transference and client recollections of parental caregiving. *Journal of Counseling Psychology, 50*, 395–408.

Yogananda, P. (1993). *Autobiography of a yogi* (12th ed.). Self-Realisation Fellowship.

Zetzel, E. R. (1956). Current concepts of transference. *International Journal of Psycho-Analysis, 37*, 369–375.

Chapter 5

The Therapist's Secure Base Provision and the Patient's Underlying Attachment Needs

In Chapter 4, I suggested (with others like Bowlby, 1988; Parish & Eagle, 2003) that one of the therapist's most important functions in producing therapeutic change is to provide a secure base for the patient. Providing a secure base, however, is not identical to emotional sensitivity and responsiveness. In examining the mediating role of caregiver sensitivity in the well-established relation between the caregiver's attachment organization and the infant's attachment organization, de Wolff and van IJzendoorn (1997) conducted a meta-analytic study in which they concluded, "[Caregiver] sensitivity has lost its privileged position as the only important causal factor" (p. 583) in determining attachment security in infancy. Referred to as a "transmission gap," the other causal factors besides parenting behavior that account for the quality of infant attachment have puzzled attachment researchers because classical attachment theory has always asserted that caregiver sensitivity to the infant's emotional needs helps the infant develop expectations of caregiver reliability and security, which in turn coalesces into a secure attachment by 12 months.

One solution to this transmission gap is to consider only caregiving behavior in attachment-activating situations as influencing the quality of infant attachment (Cassidy et al., 2005). For example, an otherwise insensitive caregiver mobilizes their latent emotional responsiveness and understanding when the infant falls off the bed and hurts their knee, offering comfort, consolation, and holding contact. It is secure base provision—the extent to which the caregiver provides a secure base in moments of fear, injury, or loss—that determines the quality of infant attachment, not emotional sensitivity and responsiveness when the attachment system is not activated (e.g., when the infant is eating with the family).

In the same manner, the therapist's provision of a secure base must meet the specific needs of the patient in moments of crisis. The therapist must discern these specific needs even though the patient might miscue the therapist and obscure these needs (Cooper et al., 2005; Eagle, 2006; Hoffman et al., 2006). A therapist could respond to a patient in line with that patient's expectations developed from childhood experiences when the attachment system was activated, or respond in defiance of these expectations. The quality of the secure base, which the therapist

DOI: 10.4324/9781003562924-7

provides, is likely to determine whether a sufficient context for therapeutic change is established.

The therapist's ability to discern a patient's attachment needs gently whispering beneath the din of defensive processes clamoring to distract from hearing them depends on various factors, some of which have nothing to do with the patient, others of which interact with the patient's characteristics to produce interaction structures (Jones, 2000) unique to the therapeutic dyad. These interaction structures (patterns of reciprocal interaction; see Chapter 4) can facilitate or disrupt the therapist's secure base provision. Sometimes a therapist's own personality organization can interact with their theoretical orientation to limit the treatment's effectiveness (Crastnopol, 2001; Kantrowitz, 1995). For example, a therapist alienated from their feelings practices cognitive behavioral therapy (CBT), a treatment model that de-emphasizes the processing of feelings. Whether the therapist and patient's characteristics are complementary or noncomplementary, and how this matching influences treatment process and outcome, have recently garnered considerable attention in the psychotherapy research literature. Freud's one-size-fits-all technical recommendations failed to account for therapist-patient matching that undoubtedly affects treatment outcomes.

Since Luborsky et al. (1975) first claimed that all psychotherapy models produce generally equivalent outcomes (see also Rosenzweig, 1936), psychotherapy researchers have attempted to identify therapist and patient characteristics that might improve treatment effectiveness. Out of over 200 therapist and patient characteristics studied, therapist-patient matching accounts for a higher proportion of variance in treatment outcomes than any therapist or patient characteristic (Beutler, 1991). Matching on demographic variables such as gender, ethnicity, and first language is associated with successful treatment outcomes (Berzins, 1977; Beutler et al., 1991; Flaskerud, 1990; Nelson & Neufeldt, 1996). Similarly, matching on personal values, beliefs, attitudes, coping styles, expectations, and self-concept is also associated with successful treatment outcomes (Beutler et al., 1986; Nelson & Neufeldt, 1996; Reis & Brown, 1999; Talley et al., 1990).

On interpersonal variables, however, it is therapist-patient *mismatching* that produces successful treatment outcomes (Arizmendi et al., 1985; Beutler et al., 1991; Charone, 1981). For example, dissimilarity on values related to interpersonal security and sexual relationships produces successful treatment outcomes (Beutler et al., 1978). Similarly, treatments are more effective when therapists who value autonomy are matched with dependent patients, or when therapists who value connection are matched with patients who value autonomy, than when both parties have similar interpersonal traits (Berzins, 1977). Evidently, these contrasting interpersonal traits between the therapist and patient provide the patient with the corrective emotional experience (Alexander & French, 1946) required for a successful treatment outcome (Bernier & Dozier, 2002).

The therapeutic principle of noncomplementarity has also emerged in the attachment literature (Bernier & Dozier, 2002; Bernier et al., 2005; Dozier, 2003; Dozier & Bates, 2004; Dozier et al., 1994; Dozier & Tyrrell, 1998; Tyrrell et al.,

1999). Dozier and her colleagues have demonstrated that noncomplementary secondary (defensive) attachment strategies (see Chapter 3) between case managers and patients produced more successful treatment outcomes than complementary secondary attachment strategies. In their first study, Dozier et al. (1994) administered the AAI to 27 patients diagnosed with thought or mood disorders and 18 case managers of these patients to determine their attachment patterns using the Attachment Q-Set (AQS; Kobak et al., 1993). The AQS codes AAI narratives on two orthogonal dimensions: security-insecurity (primary attachment strategy) and deactivating-hyperactivating (secondary attachment strategy). Dozier et al. (1994) interviewed the case managers regarding their most recent interventions with their patients. These interviews were coded for depth of intervention and attention to dependency needs.

The results indicated that case managers rated as insecurely attached intervened in greater depth with the hyperactivating (anxious-resistant) patients than case managers rated as securely attached, who tended to intervene in less depth with this same type of patient. Similarly, case managers rated as insecurely attached attended more to the greater dependency needs of their hyperactivating (anxious-resistant) patients than case managers rated as securely attached, who attended to fewer dependency needs in this same type of patient. In their discussion, the authors concluded that securely attached case managers "seem able to attend and respond to clients' underlying needs, whereas case managers who are more insecure respond to the most obvious presentation of needs" (Dozier et al., 1994, p. 798). These insecurely attached case managers have difficulty resisting "the strong pull from the client to respond in ways that confirm existing [internal working] models" (p. 793). In other words, offering a noncomplementary relational experience to the patient is more likely to occur with a securely attached therapist because of "their willingness to intervene in ways that may be uncomfortable for themselves" (p. 798). The authors also pointed out that securely attached case managers responded more to the dependency needs of deactivating (anxious-avoidant) patients than those of hyperactivating (anxious-resistant) patients.

This idea is consistent with the work of Diamond et al. (2003), who, in their work with patients with borderline personality disorder, "remain attuned to the often fleeting emergence of ... secure states [of mind] that may emerge" (p. 167). Like a "gentle whisper" (I Kings 19:12; NIV, 1978), the need to rely on the therapist or a Higher Power as a secure base is often hard to hear above the din of noise—the denials of dependency—that distracts the therapist from making a noncomplementary intervention. One of my analytic patients, diagnosed with borderline personality disorder, denied that she missed me after vacations (for a full discussion of this case, see Goodman, 2010, Chapter 3). According to her, she enjoyed sleeping in and not having to analyze everything. Despite this patient's dismissing attitude, she came four times per week, seldom missed a session, and was seldom late. She called me once to tell me that she was feeling ill and was canceling the following day's session. At our next session, she chastised me for not calling her back to check on her. It took several days for us to work through what she perceived as my unavailability to her. It is not my practice to call patients back under such circumstances, but in retrospect, I agree that I should have called back this patient because, unbeknownst to me, she was using me as a safe haven during her illness. In subsequent sessions, she ignored such interpretations and focused instead on my "obligation" to patients to return their telephone calls. All therapists have had similar experiences in their practices. The question is whether therapists can allow themselves to respond differentially to patients based on their patients' secondary attachment strategies—to nurture the gentle whisper of secure attachment behavior and its associated state of mind rather than silence it.

The therapeutic principle of noncomplementarity makes intuitive clinical sense. The therapist responds to the patient's underlying needs, not to his or her miscues (Cooper et al., 2005; Eagle, 2006; Hoffman et al., 2006) governed by defensive processes. Securely attached therapists are more likely to tolerate discomfort in the interaction and challenge the patient's characteristic mode of relatedness to others than insecurely attached therapists. Do we know, however, whether noncomplementary interventions actually produce more successful treatment outcomes than complementary interventions?

In their second study, Tyrrell et al. (1999) administered the AAI to 54 patients diagnosed with thought or mood disorders and 21 case managers of these patients to determine their attachment patterns with the AQS (Kobak et al., 1993). The study design differed from the first study, however, because the case managers assessed treatment outcomes, defined as the quality of working alliance, global life satisfaction, and global assessment of functioning (GAF). Deactivating (anxious-avoidant) case managers and their hyperactivating (anxious-resistant) patients tended to have a higher quality of working alliance than deactivating (anxious-avoidant) case managers and their deactivating (anxious-avoidant) patients. Conversely, hyperactivating (anxious-resistant) case managers and their deactivating (anxious-avoidant) patients tended to have a higher quality of working alliance than hyperactivating (anxious-resistant) case managers and their hyperactivating (anxious-resistant) patients. Patients who belonged to noncomplementary dyads also experienced greater global life satisfaction and higher GAF than patients who belonged to complementary dyads. The authors (Tyrrell et al., 1999) argue that this study provides empirical evidence for the therapeutic goal of Bowlby (1988) to disconfirm the patient's usual interpersonal and emotional strategies and expectations. In noncomplementary dyads, this goal is accomplished because case managers "have different ways of approaching relationships and regulating emotions than their clients ... The development of these more effective strategies can then lead to enhanced quality of life and better psychological, social, and occupational functioning for clients" (Tyrrell et al., 1999, pp. 731–732).

One of the fascinating facets of this study is that therapist-patient correspondence on attachment patterns predicted treatment outcomes without any knowledge of the nature of the interventions made by the therapists. The authors (Tyrrell et al., 1999) conclude, "The therapeutic process that mediates the relationship between client-case manager attachment dissimilarity and positive treatment outcomes needs to be investigated more thoroughly" (p. 732). I suspect that emotion regulation, produced by a noncomplementary correspondence on attachment patterns, occurs through behavioral as well as verbal channels of communication. A therapist's facial expressions, body language, tone of voice, and the office's seating arrangement all communicate a level of tolerance or intolerance of a patient's pattern of emotion regulation. The timing of the therapist's verbal interventions also communicates this tolerance or intolerance, irrespective of verbal content. The findings of this study suggest that a corrective emotional experience (Alexander & French, 1946), mediated by a noncomplementary correspondence of attachment patterns, produces enhanced treatment outcomes. In other words, new implicit procedural knowledge (see Chapter 4), acquired by the patient through the nonverbal emotion-regulatory interactions with the therapist, can produce therapeutic change independent of the acquisition of new symbolic (verbal) knowledge that can increase insight.

These important studies conducted by Dozier and her colleagues need to be replicated with skilled therapists in traditional psychotherapy settings with less disturbed patients to improve the generalizability of the results (Diamond et al., 2003; Dozier et al., 1994). Toward this end, Bernier et al. (2005) conducted a similar study with 90 first-year college students and 10 professors who volunteered as academic counselors. The counselor-professors worked together with the students in regularly scheduled one-to-one sessions throughout the fall semester to provide mentoring and to discuss social and emotional adjustment problems. Students were administered the AAI, while counselor-professors completed a self-report attachment questionnaire. The authors assessed outcomes as students' adaptive behaviors and perceptions in mentoring and grade-point average at the end of the semester.

The results paralleled those of the previous studies: hyperactivating (anxious-resistant) students paired with deactivating (anxious-avoidant) counselor-professors tended to have more adaptive behaviors and perceptions in mentoring and higher grades than deactivating (anxious-avoidant) students paired with deactivating (anxious-avoidant) counselor-professors. Conversely, deactivating (anxious-avoidant) students paired with hyperactivating (anxious-resistant) counselor-professors tended to have more adaptive behaviors and perceptions in mentoring and higher grades than hyperactivating (anxious-resistant) students paired with hyperactivating (anxious-resistant) counselor-professors. Thus, Bernier and her colleagues (2005) essentially replicated the findings of Dozier and her colleagues (Dozier et al., 1994; Tyrrell et al., 1999) with a sample of college students receiving academic mentoring. Unfortunately, a self-report attachment questionnaire was administered to the counselor-professors, which renders the study's findings suspect because of the low correlation ($r = .09$) between the AAI and self-report measures of attachment (Roisman et al., 2007).

These empirical findings suggest that the therapist must respond differently to patients, depending on their mode of emotion regulation. Because a therapist typically uses only one secondary (defensive) attachment strategy (hyperactivating or deactivating), while his or her patients use either strategy, both complementary and noncomplementary dyadic therapy relationships will be established in any given patient caseload. With noncomplementary patients, therefore, a therapist "must have the ego strength and flexibility necessary to respond to the client ... even if it is uncomfortable for the clinician at the time" (Dozier & Tyrrell, 1998, p. 240). If we acknowledge that "the clinician's state of mind ... affects the client's expectation of availability" (Dozier & Bates, 2004, p. 173), then therapists need to have their own personal psychotherapy experience and self-analysis to acquaint themselves with their preferred attachment strategies and modes of emotion regulation—something that psychoanalytic institutes have incorporated into their training programs for almost 100 years (Freud, 1912; Szajnberg & Crittenden, 1997).

Applying these insights to Attachment-Informed Psychotherapy (AIP) for spiritually curious or spiritually grounded patients, the therapist must assess not only the patient's and their own secondary (defensive) attachment strategies used in their attachment relationships to the caregivers during childhood but also the patient's and their own secondary (defensive) attachment strategies used in their attachment relationship to God. As the reader already knows from Chapter 4, the attachment relationship to God can correspond with or compensate for the attachment relationships to the caregivers during childhood. The therapist's awareness of the quality of their own attachment relationship to a Higher Power can aid in the selection of appropriate interventions that can provide a "gentle challenge" (Dozier & Bates, 2004, p. 174; see also Dozier, 2003, p. 254) to the patient's secondary attachment strategy in their attachment relationship to God.

Let me provide a brief illustration. A therapist (perhaps belonging to a church that emphasizes doctrinal purity or ritual) is aware of having developed an anxiousavoidant (dismissing) attachment relationship to God, while the patient (perhaps belonging to a church that emphasizes cathartic emotional expression) has developed an anxious-resistant (preoccupied) attachment relationship to God. The therapist must assemble an array of intervention strategies consistent with their anxious-avoidant (dismissing) mode of relatedness that might help the patient to shift into a more reflective mode of mental functioning and ultimately, a more secure attachment relationship to God. Because the compensation pathway predicts that the quality of a person's attachment relationships to their caregivers during childhood might differ qualitatively from the quality of the person's attachment relationship to God, the therapist must select intervention strategies that gently challenge the insecure attachment relationship under discussion—either to the caregivers during childhood or to a Higher Power.

In the illustration above, the therapist must rely on their awareness of their preferred secondary (defensive) attachment strategy of anxious-avoidance to select intervention strategies that will aid in transforming the patient's anxious-resistant internal working models of both their attachment relationships to their caregivers during childhood and their attachment relationship to God to secure internal working models. If the patient's attachment relationships to the caregivers during childhood are insecure, while the attachment relationship to God is secure, then the therapist would be using intervention strategies to gently challenge the insecure attachment relationships to the caregivers during childhood as well as using the secure attachment relationships to both God and the therapist to generalize to these insecure caregiver attachment relationships so that the patient's internal working models are consistently secure. The added layer of complexity comes with the therapist's awareness of the quality of their own attachment relationship to God and their use of this awareness to formulate intervention strategies that gently challenge the patient's insecure (anxious-avoidant or anxious-resistant) attachment relationship to God. The goal is to create a noncomplementary therapeutic experience that produces a transformation in all internal working models from insecure to secure (for a full discussion, see Chapter 6).

Treatment Modality, Secondary Attachment Strategies, and Treatment Outcome

I propose that we classify not only therapists but also treatment modalities as hyperactivating or deactivating in their technical approach. In Chapter 5 of Goodman (2025), I argue that Freud's technical recommendations tended toward the deactivating end of the continuum. I would also classify cognitive therapy (Beck, 1976) and behaviorism (Skinner, 1974) as treatment modalities on the extreme deactivating end of the continuum. On the other hand, primal therapy (Janov, 1970) and accelerated experiential-dynamic psychotherapy (Fosha, 2000) fall on the extreme hyperactivating end of the continuum. Object relations and relational therapies would fall somewhere in the middle, balancing emotional containment with emotional expression. Further exploration would probably reveal that therapists self-select the treatment modality they practice based partly on the fit between their secondary attachment strategy and the treatment modalities that share their own patterns of emotion regulation. Deactivating (anxious-avoidant) therapists would be naturally attracted to treatment modalities that emphasize rationality, cognition, and distance, while hyperactivating (anxious-resistant) therapists would be naturally attracted to treatment modalities that emphasize irrationality, emotional discharge, and mutual closeness.

The therapeutic success of treatment of patients with severe personality disorders by both Kernberg (1975) and Kohut (1971), despite the apparently irreconcilable differences in theory and clinical technique between the two modalities, spawned controversy in the 1970s and 1980s (Glassman, 1988; Munich, 1993). Perhaps one secret to the success of both modalities in spite of their theoretical and technical differences is the patient population that each one treated and the fit that resulted between the treatment modality and the internal working model of the targeted population. It is already recognized that patients with different diagnostic features of borderline personality disorder require different treatment approaches (Munich, 1993). Kernberg, who developed his treatment modality to target patients with borderline personality disorder, used confrontation of hostile mental representations of self and others (Clarkin et al., 2015) and an inflexible treatment frame (Yeomans et al., 1992) to achieve therapeutic results. Kohut, who developed his treatment modality to target patients with narcissistic personality disorder, used empathy (Kohut, 1984) and a flexible treatment frame (Kohut, 1981) to achieve therapeutic results.

If we assume that patients with borderline personality disorder generally rely on hyperactivating strategies of emotion regulation and that patients with narcissistic personality disorder generally rely on deactivating strategies of emotion regulation (Goodman, 2014), then perhaps Kernberg's confrontational stance provides a noncomplementary therapeutic experience for patients with borderline personality disorder, and Kohut's empathic stance a noncomplementary therapeutic experience for patients with narcissistic personality disorder. In other words, these two treatment modalities succeed perhaps because each one corrects for the specific deficit in pattern of emotion regulation presented by the population that each treatment modality was designed to target: emotional containment for the patients with borderline personality disorder and emotional expression for the patients with narcissistic personality disorder.

Despite the compelling evidence in support of the therapeutic benefit of noncomplementary therapist-patient matching on attachment pattern, the therapist needs to engage in complementary interpersonal interactions with the patient in the early phase of treatment (Tracey, 1987; Tracey & Ray, 1984). Kohut (1984) intuitively sensed that a shift must take place from a complementary position vis-à-vis the patient to a noncomplementary position and divided these positions into two phases of treatment—the understanding phase (dominated by empathic understanding) and the explanatory phase (dominated by explanation through interpretation). A noncomplementary stance, therefore, would be therapeutic only after a working alliance and an attachment to the therapist have been firmly established (see Chapter 4). Under those conditions, the therapist's secure base function would permit the patient to explore with the therapist alternative models of intrapersonal and interpersonal interaction and alternative modes of emotion regulation. A noncomplementary stance prior to the establishment of a working alliance and attachment to the therapist, however, could cause the patient's false compliance or premature termination of treatment.

Although a "gentle challenge" to the patient's preferred pattern of emotion regulation is associated with positive therapeutic change (Dozier, 2003, p. 254), especially in long-term intensive psychotherapy, where internal working models can be worked through in depth (Dozier & Tyrrell, 1998), other research groups (e.g., McBride et al., 2006) have concluded that a *complementary* pairing of treatment modality with the patient's attachment pattern yields the most successful treatment outcome for patients with depression—regardless of the treatment phase. This research group randomly assigned 56 patients with major depressive disorder to one of three treatment conditions—CBT, interpersonal psychotherapy (IPT), or medication. Patients were informed that they would be receiving 16–20 sessions of treatment in the CBT or IPT condition, and "if a patient had not achieved treatment response by 20 weeks, treatment was terminated" (p. 1044). Patients completed a self-report measure of attachment at intake and two self-report measures of depression at intake and within one week of termination. Avoidant (dismissing) attachment moderated the relation between treatment condition and depression. Specifically, avoidantly attached patients paired with CBT experienced a greater reduction in depressive symptoms than avoidantly attached patients paired with IPT. McBride et al. (2006) interpreted their results: CBT "may appeal to avoidantly attached individuals who may emphasize narrowly the importance of cognition as a way to remove themselves from interpersonal concerns" (p. 1051), whereas IPT "might ... prove too threatening for individuals who regulate [emotion] by deactivating relationship issues" (p. 1050).

This finding appears to support my hypothesis, stated earlier, that treatment modalities can function to deactivate or hyperactivate a patient's attachment system and thus underregulate or overregulate emotion. Contrary to the therapeutic principle of noncomplementarity, however, CBT—a deactivating treatment modality—matched with deactivating (avoidantly attached) patients, produced a reduction in depressive symptoms. This finding is not surprising, however, when we consider the treatment length (16–20 sessions) and the fact that patients were informed that the treatment would not continue beyond that range. Who among us would want to form an attachment to someone we would never see again after five months? I am suggesting that 16–20 sessions coincides with an early, complementary treatment phase. A working alliance has been established, but an attachment is just beginning to form. The later, noncomplementary treatment phase begins after the attachment to the therapist has formed. During this second treatment phase, the therapist can challenge the patient's implicit procedural knowledge through both verbal and nonverbal interactions with the patient (see Chapter 4). These noncomplementary interactions have therapeutic value precisely because the therapist is an attachment figure who observes deficits in the patient's emotion regulation and uses the secure base function to modulate the intense emotions that inevitably emerge in attachment relationships.

During the early, complementary treatment phase, before an attachment to the therapist has formed, the sheer presence of a working alliance can serve to strengthen the patient's defensive processes, which in turn can reduce symptoms. Commenting on the study by McBride et al. (2006), Eagle (2006) observed, "CBT was more effective for the avoidant patients because it helped to prop up and strengthen defenses that had been failing. Or, at least, it did not threaten these defenses" (p. 1092). In the absence of an attachment to the therapist, perhaps this is all that time-limited psychotherapies can offer—support for the defensive structure through a complementary working alliance and temporary relief from symptomatology. A follow-up assessment at one year would have told us whether the patients had maintained their symptom reduction. A study of long-term psychotherapy in which patients form an attachment to the therapist would also have told us whether a noncomplementary match between the treatment modality and the patient's attachment pattern would have outperformed a complementary match of these conditions—an outcome that I would predict based on our theoretical and empirical knowledge about noncomplementary matching.

The question whether to provide the patient with a noncomplementary match or a complementary match—in both treatment modality and therapist attachment pattern—is related to an earlier question I raised: to what extent should the therapist allow the patient to experience them as a caregiver from childhood? And to what extent should the therapist allow the patient to experience them as a new, unfamiliar caregiver—a secure base and safe haven? A complementary pairing of treatment modality, therapist, and patient would allow the patient to experience the therapist as an old, familiar caregiver. For example, a deactivating (anxious-avoidant) therapist who refuses to explore the patient's underlying feelings related to the therapist's upcoming vacation perfectly complements a deactivating (anxious-avoidant) patient who responds to the news of the vacation by announcing that they will now be able to sleep in during session times. The therapist's behavior thus repeats the caregiver's behavior from childhood when the caregiver demonstrated no concern about the possible effects of a weeks-long separation from the child. On the other hand, the patient needs to experience the therapist as a caregiver from childhood first so that the therapist can then respond differently and thereby disconfirm these ancient caregiver expectations. This idea resembles primary task of the therapist, according to Winnicott (1971): to survive the attacks of the patient without withdrawal, collapse, or retaliation, which the caregivers had done.

A noncomplementary pairing of treatment modality, therapist, and patient would allow the patient to experience the therapist as a new, unfamiliar caregiver who could disconfirm ancient caregiver expectations. For example, a hyperactivating (anxious-resistant) therapist who explores the patient's underlying feelings related to the therapist's vacation defies the expectations of a deactivating (anxious-avoidant) patient who responds by devaluing the therapist, calling him "a man with a vagina" (true story, see Goodman, 2010, Chapter 3). As Dozier and Tyrrell (1998) pointed out, it is the therapist's responsibility to respond to the patient in a noncomplementary manner, "even if it is uncomfortable for the clinician at the time" (p. 240). On the other hand, the therapist who never allows the patient to experience him or her as a caregiver from childhood never has the opportunity to defy the patient's ancient childhood expectations, and therapeutic change never occurs.

Greenberg (1986) argues for a balance between danger and safety in the therapeutic situation. Translated into attachment language, this phrase means that the therapist must allow the patient to experience themselves as an *insecure* base from which transference-countertransference paradigms characterized by patient splitting (i.e., all-good/all-bad thinking) and projection (i.e., it's not me, it's you) predominate. As an insecure base in the patient's eyes, how will the therapist respond? Will the therapist confirm this status with complementary behavior, or disconfirm it with noncomplementary behavior? In the previous example, I decided to explore the feelings about my vacation even though I knew that my patient was going to devalue me. I needed to be an insecure base and temporarily abandon her by taking a vacation before I could disconfirm the anxious-avoidant internal working model of her attachment relationship to me by showing concern about her feelings about it. Consciously, she needed to protect herself from my move toward connectedness (asking her about her feelings) by creating distance from me (devaluation). Unconsciously, however, she wanted me to show concern for her feelings—something she had never experienced from her childhood caregivers. Her hostile defense against closeness belies the intensity of her wish to be cared for.

Earlier, I alluded to the idea that religious institutions, like treatment modalities, also fall on this deactivating-hyperactivating continuum of emotion regulation. Using Christianity as an example, churches that emphasize doctrinal purity and ritual (privileging "correct" theology, religious dogma, or tightly scripted liturgy) would fall on the deactivating end of this continuum, while churches that empha- size a cathartic emotional expression (privileging glossolalia, ecstatic prophecy, or "falling out") would fall on the hyperactivating end of the spectrum. Occasionally, churches can vacillate between the deactivating and hyperactivating ends of the spectrum.

Although I am unaware of any research studies exploring the connection between the quality of internal working models of attachment relationships and church denomination, I would hypothesize that if someone were to conduct such a study, church membership would correspond to the person's secondary attach- ment strategy of anxious-avoidance or anxious-resistance. It is for two reasons that I mention this possible correspondence between the mode of relatedness espoused by the religious institution and the congregant's mode of relatedness as captured by the continuum of emotion regulation: (1) church membership might provide clues regarding the quality of the person's attachment relationship to God; and (2) if asked by the patient, the therapist can recommend a church or church denomination that would gently challenge the patient's prevailing attachment relationship to God. Thus, a person who developed an anxious-avoidant attachment relationship to God might benefit from attending a more emotionally expressive church, while a person who developed an anxious-resistant attachment relationship to God might benefit from attending a more doctrinaire church. A flexible, balanced ability to regulate emotions expressed toward God would reflect a secure attachment relationship to God. Just like the selection of treatment modality, the selection of worship venue might aid in the person's reliance on the more secure, primary attachment strat- egies, such as proximity-seeking and open communication and using God as a safe haven and secure base.

Pouring New Wine into Old Wineskins or New Wineskins?

Psychodynamic theoreticians have made us aware of the simultaneous tasks of the therapist: (1) to permit the emergence of the transference (i.e., to permit oneself to be used as an old, familiar caregiver), and (2) to respond differently to the patient than the old, familiar caregivers did (i.e., behaving as a new, unfamiliar caregiver). How does the therapist determine when to behave like an old, familiar caregiver and when to behave like a new, unfamiliar one? In other words, when does the ther- apist behave in a complementary manner, and when does the therapist behave in a noncomplementary manner? First, the therapist must clinically assess the patient's attachment pattern—whether he or she tends to use deactivating (anxious-avoidant) or hyperactivating (anxious-resistant) strategies to interact with significant others, including the therapist. Slade (1999) has presented a superb description of these strategies as they appear in the therapist-patient relationship—what she calls a patient's "primary mode of relatedness" (p. 588). The therapist needs to know about these secondary attachment strategies because they help define what would be considered complementary or noncomplementary behavior. The therapist who calls a patient who missed a session without calling to cancel would be demonstrating complementary behavior with a hyperactivating (anxious-resistant) patient and noncomplementary behavior with a deactivating (anxious-avoidant) patient.

Second, the therapist must know about their own secondary attachment strategy because it also helps define what would be considered complementary or noncomplementary behavior. If the deactivating (anxious-avoidant) therapist's natural tendency is to withdraw emotionally and become uncharacteristically quiet after the patient devalues him or her, then the therapist needs to "be aware of and monitor one's fundamental strategies and reactions for the patient's sake" (Szajnberg & Crittenden, 1997, p. 435). Clinical training is a necessary but not a sufficient condition to facilitate noncomplementary behavior among therapists. Experienced therapists responded to patients in a complementary manner even though they had been trained to understand and resist the patient's maladaptive relational patterns (Henry et al., 1993). For over 100 years, psychoanalytic training programs have required candidates to "have undergone a psycho-analytic purification and have become aware of those complexes of his own which would be apt to interfere with his grasp of what the patient tells him" (Freud, 1912, p. 116). Perhaps other treatment modalities should consider adopting a personal therapy requirement so that the therapist is in a more enlightened position to determine whether they are engaging in complementary or noncomplementary behavior vis-à-vis the patient's verbal and nonverbal behavior.

Third, the therapist needs to consider the treatment phase because the therapist's response to the nature of the relationship with the patient varies with the treatment phase. As I mentioned earlier, a treatment could be divided into complementary and noncomplementary phases. The complementary phase constitutes the early treatment phase, when the working alliance is established and an attachment to the therapist is beginning to form. The patient needs to begin to experience the therapist as a childhood caregiver: an attachment figure. After the attachment to the therapist has formed, the therapist can then move into the noncomplementary phase, when they begin to challenge the patient's secondary attachment strategy by facilitating either the expression of unacceptable attachment needs (for a deactivating/anxious-avoidant patient) or their containment (for a hyperactivating/anxious-resistant patient). In the language of Alexander and French (1946), the therapist is providing a "corrective emotional experience" (p. 294).

Fourth, the therapist needs to consider the treatment goals because the patient might not be seeking personality change at the level of implicit procedural knowledge. Instead, the patient might simply want immediate relief from their symptoms. The treatment goal might dictate that a complementary treatment phase comprise the entire course of treatment. I argued earlier that the positive outcome from a complementary interaction between CBT and deactivating (anxious-avoidant) patients with depression (McBride et al., 2006) represented the strengthening of the patient's defensive processes and subsequent symptom reduction. For patients who seek a lasting, generalized personality change, however, "long-term intensive therapy may be required" (Dozier & Tyrrell, 1998, p. 224). This intensive psychotherapy requires the therapist to adopt a noncomplementary stance vis-à-vis the patient to achieve the patient's goal of enduring personality change.

Fifth, the therapist needs to consider the treatment length because insurance companies often do not reimburse the therapist beyond a certain number of sessions—too few for an attachment to the therapist to form. Under these conditions, the therapist can commence only a complementary treatment phase. The insurance companies fail to understand that a corrective emotional experience can never take place because the patient is not in treatment long enough to form an attachment to the therapist. Consequently, the patient experiences only temporary relief, and when their benefits renew on the policy renewal date, they will be seeking another round of short-term treatment from the insurance company. Insurance companies could avoid funding a revolving door if they realized that it is more cost-effective to reimburse for one long-term intensive treatment that provides a corrective emotional experience than it is to reimburse for multiple short-term superficial treatments over the course of the policyholder's lifetime (for a patient horror story manufactured by an insurance company, see Clark et al., 2018).

Sixth, the therapist needs to consider the patient's potential to comply with the therapist's noncomplementary stance rather than respond authentically. The patient who feels that the therapist's secure base function could fail might conform to the therapist's noncomplementary intervention just to preserve the attachment. Eagle (2003) has suggested that the patient wants not only to please the therapist but also to create a feeling of being understood and accepted. It is critical that the therapist recognize the profound power that they wield as a secure base and safe haven for their patients.

For example, a patient fearful of abandonment might agree to pay the therapist a fee increase that the patient is unable to afford to prevent the therapist from carrying out what the patient perceives to be an imminent abandonment if they resist. The therapist's intervention is noncomplementary because it communicates to the hyperactivating (anxious-resistant) patient that the therapist is a separate person, has financial needs, and is temporarily relinquishing the caregiver role to assert that the patient meet these needs. The patient could comply to avoid a feared abandonment rather than authentically recognize that the therapist is indeed a separate person with a separate set of needs that exist independently of the patient's attachment to the therapist. The treatment frame (Langs, 1976; Langs & Stone, 1980) needs to be a focal point of discussion whenever the therapist or patient suggests changes to it so that the therapist can identify patient compliance and help the patient to understand it in the context of the power dynamic intrinsic to any attachment relationship.

Finally, the therapist needs to remember this paradox: to be both an old, familiar and a new, unfamiliar caregiver, to behave in both a complementary and a noncomplementary manner, to accept the patient's projections and to interpret them. The effective therapist first allows the patient to transform them into the "ghosts in the nursery" (Fraiberg et al., 1975)—the imperfect attachment figures from the past—and then mentally contains the image of the patient in relation to these attachment figures by reflecting on the experience rather than reacting reflexively (Bion, 1962, 1967; Dozier et al., 1994). This mental containment detoxifies the old, familiar childhood experiences of an insecure base and unsafe haven and repairs them so that the patient can begin to use the relationship to the therapist and other meaningful relationships as a secure base and a safe haven during moments of distress. The patient thus discovers what it means to depend on a separate person for comfort and safety. The capacity to depend on others as separate persons is considered a hallmark of integrated object relations (Kernberg, 1986).

Perhaps Casement (2001) expresses the same ideas more eloquently:

An analytic "good object" ... is that which can tolerate being used to represent the worst in a patient's experience ... [and] can bear to feel that despair, along with them, and yet find the courage to go on with the analysis.

(pp. 384, 385)

Too often, the therapist rushes in to rescue the patient from the old, familiar caregivers, thereby avoiding the punishing or despondent transferences (and withdrawing, collapsing, or retaliatory countertransferences) and depriving the patient of an opportunity to face their ghosts. It is in the bearing of the patient's despair and "nameless dread" (Bion, 1967, p. 116)—rather than fulfilling the patient's expectation of withdrawing, collapsing, or retaliating—that the therapist becomes a new, unfamiliar caregiver by adopting a noncomplementary stance vis-à-vis the patient.

God can also serve as an old, familiar caregiver or a new, unfamiliar caregiver for patients (as well as therapists). Patients sometimes associate God with a wounded childhood, where they felt judged or not accepted. I can clearly remember as a high school student growing a long beard and hearing a church member tell me to shave it off after a church service. At the time, I was thinking, "If Jesus is depicted in every painting as having a beard, why is this guy so bothered by my beard?" I can imagine the response I would have received in this conservative Baptist church if I had come out as gay, lesbian, or, God forbid, trans. This is the experience of many youth in today's conservative churches. These youth are associating God with intolerance, judgment, and even hatred, despite Jesus's command to "love one another. As I have loved you, so you must love one another" (John 13:34; NIV, 1978). The old, familiar God for these persons might be a judgmental, vengeful, or rejecting God. Helping these persons to experience God as a new, unfamiliar caregiver—accepting, forgiving, compassionate, loving—requires unraveling the childhood experiences that prompted their initial perception and then using non-complementary therapeutic strategies to help these persons to view God as a new, unfamiliar caregiver. Disentangling the views of other religious persons ("get a haircut!") from the views of God ("I love you regardless of your facial hair") can be a long, arduous process that requires patience and persistence.

Paradoxically, the precursors of a noncomplementary therapeutic stance originate in the caregiver-infant attachment relationship. Dozier and her colleagues (Bernier & Dozier, 2002; Bernier et al., 2005; Dozier, 2003; Dozier & Bates, 2004; Dozier et al., 1994; Dozier & Tyrrell, 1998; Tyrrell et al., 1999) argue that therapeutic change occurs when the therapist gently challenges the patient's expectations of how others respond to them in relationships. These expectations form in the crucible of the caregiver-infant attachment relationship over the course of many experiences of care in times of distress and discomfort. If the caregiver refuses to pick up the infant when they are distressed, then the infant will grow up to expect no such care from anyone else. If the caregiver picks up the infant inconsistently when they are distressed, then the infant will grow up to expect care only when he or she dramatizes the distress. A noncomplementary stance, therefore, would be giving care when care is needed but not expected or titrating care to correspond to the actual need. Caregivers who function as a secure base and safe haven, however, also provide noncomplementary care to their infants.

In Chapter 4, I discussed the concept of "marking"—the caregiver's attempt to empathize with the infant's pain and simultaneously to convey to the infant a dissimilarity in the caregiver's own emotional state (Fonagy et al., 2002; Gergely, 2000). This subtle differentiation between the disorganized feelings of the infant and the organized yet empathic feelings of the caregiver produces the emotional containment and regulation sought by the infant. How does this process relate to the therapist's noncomplementary stance? The caregiver is not withdrawing, collapsing, or retaliating against the infant's primitive emotional displays but rather is responding creatively by incorporating the infant's feelings (helplessness, fear, anger) and their own feelings (concern, calmness) into a unique emotional display that neither disregards the infant's feelings nor reflects them back. The caregiver marks the infant's feelings as known to them but different from their own.

The therapist also conveys an empathic understanding of the patient's emotional displays but also challenges their gravity just by tolerating them—something that the caregivers during childhood were unable or unwilling to do. The patient who reminded me that she had abruptly ended her previous treatment after a fee increase was struggling with the fact that her mother was asking her for money to support a lavish lifestyle (see Goodman, 2010, Chapter 3). My patient resented her mother's requests for financial support, not only because the mother did not need it, but also because she unconsciously resented her mother for physically abusing and ignoring her as a child. Because the mother never met my patient's emotional needs, my patient felt that her mother should not have been asking my patient to meet *her* needs. Resenting my projected fee increase the following year, the patient cast me in the role of the old, familiar caregiver—her greedy, depriving mother—and herself in the role of the deprived, neglected child.

Because of the exploitative and neglectful manner in which my patient's mother treated her as a child (and continued to treat her as an adult), my patient felt entitled to compensation from caregivers, including me. In the past, she emphatically stated that mental healthcare providers, like Mother Teresa, should take a vow of poverty and offer their services free of charge. My projected fee increase contradicted one fantasy of me—and all caregivers—as a breast with an infinite supply of milk, and refuted her expectation that she was entitled to special dispensation from her therapist-caregiver. Of course, the expectation of perfect care disguised the unbearably painful underlying expectation of no care at all. I could have confirmed her expectation of entitlement and dropped the projected fee increase, but that would not have promoted any therapeutic change. Proceeding with the fee increase introduced the painful awareness of reality—that I am a separate person with limitations and needs.

Using the concept of "marking," how should I have proceeded with my patient? I needed to use my skill and creativity to show my patient that I understood and empathized with her childhood resentment, its influences on her fantasies of entitlement to omnipotent caregiving, and her painful awareness that I am separate and not omnipotent. At the same time, I needed to show my patient that my understanding of these issues comes out of a position of difference—that I neither shared her wish for omnipotent caregiving nor expected myself to be able to fulfill it. In other words, I was tolerating the expression of her wish without actually fulfilling it. Later in the treatment, this same patient requested to move up our Thursday appointment time from 7:15 a.m. to 7 a.m. because it would facilitate her work schedule (yet note that one of her reasons for wanting to end the analysis was to get more sleep). I agreed to the time change. At the end of the session, she asked me to remind her of the Thursday time change in Wednesday morning's session. I reflected back that it was her suggestion to change the time. She responded that she would write down the time change. I could have agreed to remind her, but then I would have been assuming the role of the omnipotent caregiver, and she the role of the perfectly cared-for child. I chose instead to invalidate her expectation, which I believed, in this patient with borderline personality disorder, would promote therapeutic growth over time. A patient with narcissistic or paranoid personality disorder might require a different therapeutic approach based on a different set of wishes and expectations.

I have been arguing that this sense of emotional containment (Bion, 1962, 1967) comes about through the moment-by-moment process of "empathic emotion-reflective interactions" (Gergely, 2000, p. 1208) that consist of marking the infant's/patient's emotions as understood and tolerated by the caregiver/therapist but belonging to the infant/patient. According to Bion (1962, 1967), the "K link" represents the process by which the infant engages in emotional communication through projective identification (see also Ogden, 1979), activating the caregiver's capacity to receive and modify the communication through metabolization (i.e., digestion of raw sensory impressions). In projective identi-fication, the infant projects hostile, persecutory "beta elements" (i.e., raw sensory impressions that have no meaning) into the caregiver to regain a feeling of control. The emotionally responsive caregiver, interpreting the projective iden-tification as a message of distress (e.g., hunger, discomfort, the need for protec-tion), acts as a container of these raw sensory impressions and transforms them through the "alpha function" (i.e., meaning-making through self-reflection) into modulated, coherent emotions. The infant then introjects these metabolized emo-tions, thus accumulating experiences that ultimately form a mental representa-tion "capable of self-knowledge and communication between different aspects of themselves" (Britton, 1998, p. 23).

Thus, the K link serves the purpose of transforming raw sensory impressions of extremely negative emotional valence into integrated, modulated mental repre-sentations of self and others through integration with raw sensory impressions of extremely positive emotional valence. This transformation of beta elements through the alpha function takes place through the moment-by-moment marking described by Gergely and his colleagues (Gergely, 2000; see also Fonagy et al., 2002).

If, as I am arguing, this process of marking is as vitally important to the psy-chotherapy process as it is to the caregiving process, then how does the therapist go about marking the patient's emotions? Recalling my earlier discussion about implicit procedural knowledge and symbolic knowledge (see Chapter 4), therapists need to target both areas to facilitate therapeutic change (Lyons-Ruth, 1999). In the symbolic realm (i.e., narrative exchange), the therapist uses clarification, con-frontation, and interpretation (Clarkin et al., 2015) to communicate to the patient their empathic understanding of the patient's distress as well as the differentiation between the therapist's feelings and the patient's feelings. In the clinical vignette with my patient, I was communicating to her both my empathic understanding and my separateness by announcing a fee increase and discussing it with her using the symbolic medium of words.

This increase in symbolic knowledge—what Eagle and Wolitzky (2006) refer to as "second order change" (p. 14)—facilitates emotional containment and regu-lation by attaching meaning to emotional experiences, which binds and therefore modulates the unsymbolized emotions. I expect my clarifications, confronta-tions, and interpretations to modulate my patient's resentment over the projected fee increase by providing a symbolic network of verbally mediated explanations for her reaction. This symbolic network of explanations should include all of the following: (1) her attachment to me; (2) her expectation that attachment figures should offer their services free of charge; (3) her rage, disappointment, and resent-ment toward her mother for returning her love with physical abuse and neglect; (4) her transfer of these feelings toward her mother onto me when I announced the fee increase; (5) her need to preserve a sense of symbiotic unity between us; (6) her sense of envy and guilt over the fact that I have helped her in my separateness; and (7) her need to avoid mourning my loss as a breast with an infinite supply of milk. Successfully working through the patient's resentment toward me could take the form of all these explanations and many others that I have not listed and have not thought of.

A secure attachment relationship to God might have accelerated this patient's restoration to wholeness if she believed in God's forgiveness. Therapists can forgive a patient only imperfectly (despite working through this issue with her, I nevertheless experienced lingering feelings of resentment toward her), but God forgives perfectly. The psalmist writes, "As far as the east is from the west, so far has [God] removed our transgressions from us" (Psalm 103:12; NIV, 1978). This verse from the Hebrew Bible is the most poetic, and poignant, description of God's perfect forgiveness that I have ever read. Providing a noncomplementary therapeutic stance is critical to rehabilitating a patient's old, familiar attachment relationship to God (see earlier discussion).

I am making connections among all these various meanings to help build a symbolic network that my patient can then use to modulate her distressing emotions and respond more reflectively to significant others who assert their separateness. Simultaneously, my patient is internalizing a therapist-patient relationship that she can retrieve during emotionally charged moments to help her to regulate distressing emotions.

How does this process of marking take place in the implicit procedural realm? We recall that changes in implicit procedural knowledge—what Eagle and Wolitzky (2006) referred to as "first order change" (p. 14)—facilitate emotional containment and regulation by modifying the rules by which the patient organizes relational understanding—"how to do things with others" (Lyons-Ruth, 1999, p. 585). This change comes about through creating "increasingly collaborative forms of dialogue" (p. 610). Taking this perspective, enactments (McLaughlin, 1991; see also Chapter 4) would constitute one form of uncollaborative dialogue.

Here is an example of an attempted enactment from my private practice (see Goodman, 2010, Chapter 2): a narcissistic patient with borderline features in four times per week psychoanalysis announced that she was giving me a $5 per week fee increase (as a psychoanalytic candidate, I had been charging her $135 per week). I felt simultaneously gratified and devalued by the paltry increase. When I asked her about it, she replied only that she felt grateful for the progress she was making and that I deserved it. One week later, she asked whether we could begin meeting again in my former office in midtown Manhattan. I informed her that the former office was no longer available, and I wondered why she wanted to move. She responded that she was planning to move to Staten Island, and seeing me in midtown Manhattan would be more convenient for her than seeing me on the Upper East Side of Manhattan.

I quickly formed a hypothesis about this request and asked her whether her raising my fee had anything to do with it. With some interpretive assistance, she acknowledged that she had raised my fee to manipulate me into doing her bidding—moving my office to midtown Manhattan to treat her. This interaction is what I would call a failed enactment. What was probably therapeutic, however, was not my catching her in her attempted manipulation but rather my identifying my countertransference feelings of devaluation, realizing that she was casting me in the role of the humiliated child, and her in the role of the manipulative mother. I responded to her role as the manipulative mother without adopting a masochistic position as the patient had done in relation to her mother throughout her child-hood. I refrained from capitulating and moving mountains to see her in midtown Manhattan.

Nor did I adopt a sadistic position by assuming the role of her mother and casting her in the role of the child—meaning that I did not threaten to end the treatment but responded to her request instead with curiosity—a desire to understand what she was communicating to me. The mother had forced the patient's submission as a child by often threatening to leave home, suitcase packed and coat on. Through the clinical work, the patient could begin to see how she was treating me and relate it to her childhood relationship to her mother.

From an attachment perspective, I could interpret this enactment on an uncon-scious level as meaning that the patient was seeking reassurance that I cared enough about her to move my office, which would have increased my physical proximity to her. The patient, who was anxious-avoidant and therefore tended to dismiss her attachment needs, was unable to ask for reassurance directly and instead attempted to enact an answer from me. Gratifying her surface needs—moving my office—would have shown her that I was in fact not a secure base who wants to understand her but an insecure base who wants to please her. Retaliating against her surface needs also would have shown her that I was an insecure base who wants to pun-ish her.

Through a collaborative dialogue (Lyons-Ruth, 1999), I empathized with her need to feel closer to me as well as my need for us to continue working in my cur-rent office. One question that I posed to my patient ("How does it feel to you that I will be staying in this office?") suggests a concern for her feelings, even though I decided not to fulfill her request. I am saying, "I feel your feelings, but I also feel something different from you." The dialogue between my patient and me infiltrates the implicit procedural realm not through the narrative content but through the intersubjective rhythm created between my patient and me (Aron, 2006).

Transforming the Dark Matter

In addition to enactments, what are some other ways that therapists can reach the implicit procedural realm and transform it? Implicit procedural knowledge is like dark matter in the universe—invisible yet comprising the vast majority of mass in the knowable universe. The term serves as an expression of science's ignor-ance: no one can see dark matter, so no one can describe it. We know it exists only because science can infer it from measuring the rotations and velocities of galaxies (Anonymous, 2007). Because implicit procedural knowledge is unsymbolized and not conscious (Lyons-Ruth, 1999; Stern et al., 1998), therapists cannot "see" implicit procedural knowledge either. Therapists instead feel it in their conscious and unconscious countertransference reactions, in the process of the interactions with their patients rather than in their narrative content. I will attempt to outline below what the dark matter of implicit procedural knowledge is for me and how therapists work with it to produce therapeutic change.

The process by which the caregiver repairs ruptures in their interactions with their infant contributes to the pattern that the infant's internal working model ultimately forms (Solomon & George, 1999; Stern et al., 1998). Applied to the therapist-patient relationship, the process by which the therapist repairs ruptures in their interactions with their patient can contribute to changes in implicit procedural expectations of how others respond when a rupture in a meaningful relationship takes place. When I announced to my patient that I would be raising my fee, a rupture in the working alliance took place. How I respond to this rupture, day by day, determines whether my patient's implicit relational knowing can shift from a general expectation of physical abuse or neglect to a less draconian one.

The therapist's reliability—their consistent presence—is unconsciously registered in the patient's implicit relational knowing. Aspects of the treatment frame (Langs, 1976; Langs & Stone, 1980)—punctuality, an unchanging office space, a consistent session length, day, and time, a routine billing procedure—are all background (Stern et al., 1998) events that infiltrate the patient's implicit procedural knowledge and either confirm or disconfirm the expectations contained therein. These events are not conscious—not in the sense that they are dynamically repressed (Stern et al., 1998)—but not usually noticed. The patient does not notice that the therapist starts every session on time until that one time when the therapist is late. The patient must have been registering the session starts, however, because the late session start stands out in their mind.

How the therapist announces and discusses vacations with the patient is also registered in the patient's implicit procedural unconscious mind. Preparing the patient for a separation can facilitate the preservation of the therapist's secure base function for the patient and repair the expectations of rejection, emotional inconsistency, abandonment, or unavailability that emerge in the context of the therapist's (or patient's) leaving or absence. The therapist needs to remember that the patient's needs for trustworthiness, reliability, stability, and emotional availability coincide with these expectations of insecurity. The patient needs to experience their therapist as considering their attachment needs, not confirming their expectations.

The therapist's availability during emergencies also communicates security in the implicit procedural realm. Some therapists suggest minimal contact with patients with borderline personality disorder outside of sessions, and indeed, under certain circumstances, inform the patient in advance that the therapist will be terminating the treatment if the patient contacts the therapist in a life-threatening emergency (Clarkin et al., 2015). Other therapists place no such restrictions on outside contact with these patients (Linehan, 1993). Regardless of the procedures followed for availability during emergencies, the therapist needs to consider the impact of their response to emergencies when the attachment system is activated and the patient is seeking proximity for the sake of protection—even from themselves. The therapist's response or lack of response is bound to affect the patient's implicit procedural knowledge in profound ways. When the emergency is self-destructive behavior, the therapist needs to consider whether a response to the patient's dramatically presented attachment need would represent a repetition of the childhood caregiver's pattern to respond to the patient only in dramatic situations. Under these circumstances, the patient is forcing the therapist to behave in a complementary manner. On the other hand, if the patient knows that the therapist's policy is to respond whenever a life-threatening emergency arises, the patient might feel less of a need to make the therapist prove himself or herself as a safe haven.

Other behaviors that register in the patient's implicit procedural realm include vocal tone and prosody, body posture and gestures, muscle tone, and facial expressions. The patient might not consciously notice these emotional indicators, but they still communicate whether the therapist is functioning as a secure base and safe haven. A patient of mine became surly toward me in the middle of a session. Later in the session, I asked her whether she had noticed that her attitude toward me had shifted. She too had noticed it but could not figure out why. Together, we traced the shift back to a comment I had made that she reasoned she must have heard as sarcastic. My patient was not aware that she had heard my comment as sarcastic, nor was she repressing the sarcastic tone she had heard. Nevertheless, it influenced her attitude toward me.

In this situation, we were able to convert the implicit procedural knowledge into symbolic, verbally mediated knowledge through an analysis of our interactions earlier in the session. Lyons-Ruth (1999) points out, however, that "retranscription of implicit relational knowing into symbolic knowing is ... not how developmental change in implicit relational knowing is generally accomplished" (p. 579). Making this conversion to symbolic knowing made it possible for my patient and me to discuss the role I was playing for her at that moment, which increased her understanding. Our collaboration on figuring out together when and how her attitude shifted, however, communicated my secure base function to her in the implicit procedural realm. Words were a necessary substrate on which the collaboration developed, but not sufficient to register in my patient's implicit procedural realm. "Something more" (Stern et al., 1998) than the words of interpretation was needed to communicate to my patient on this "dark matter" level of knowledge.

Of course, the therapist and patient can also interpret this dark matter as the movement of the Spirit in the therapeutic process. I would define the Spirit as the manifestation of God in all persons as beings created in God's image (Genesis 1:27; NIV, 1978). In Chapter 3, I argued in favor of an innate spirituality present in all human beings—a bona fide evolutionary adaptation, not just a curiously quirky evolutionary by-product. According to contemplative writer Beverly Lanzetta (2019), " 'The spirit' is intrinsic to all people and all human endeavors ... Creation is not alone, separate from its source, but deeply and mysteriously imbued with spirit in every aspect of mind, soul, and matter" (pp. 2, 7).

If this argument is valid, then this Spirit is always flowing through both the therapist and the patient, regardless of any religious or spiritual beliefs or nonbelief consciously held by either one. The best therapists can harness this spiritual energy through a heightened self and other-awareness and love that transcend words, venturing into the realm of intuition and spirituality. The best therapists are like jazz musicians, improvising their solos to express their moment-to-moment feelings in the context of the other band members. The best jazz musicians go wherever the Spirit leads them. In a recent interview, jazz singer Dianne Reeves explained:

> Jazz, specifically for me, is a very spiritual music because it's beyond the page. It's this intimate exchange of ideas that is a language without words, that you can feel, that you can speak through an instrument, that you can share. And it becomes a spirit-to-spirit, soul-to-soul experience with your audience. It's because of these things that I know there's something greater than I am.
>
> (quoted in Thomas, 2024)

The best therapists channel this spiritual energy into plumbing the depths of the patient's—and their own—soul to discover modes of relatedness unknown to both participants. This is what it means to be an effective therapist.

Perhaps the most valuable way that a therapist can communicate to the patient in the implicit procedural realm is to bear the negative transference and not withdraw from it, be crushed by it, or be moved to retaliate against it (see Casement, 2001; Winnicott, 1971). The therapist's secure base function amid the patient's rage "speaks" to the implicit procedural realm like no verbally mediated intervention. The use of words can facilitate this secure base function, but the therapist's unwavering presence speaks even louder than words. With patients who have historically experienced words as attacks, lies, and manipulation, perhaps only the nonsymbolic channels of communication can convince these patients of the therapist's trustworthiness, reliability, and good will. The therapist's constant benevolent presence with the patient, whatever the emotional circumstances, might be the only mode of therapeutic change available.

Conclusion: The Clinical Illustration of Devon

Devon (a pseudonym), a 5-year-old boy in foster care because of parental neglect and exposure to domestic violence, was seeing me in once-weekly psychotherapy (for a full discussion of this case, see Goodman, 2014). In one session, Devon was portraying his older brother as aggressive, hostile, and provocative—in much the same way that he had portrayed his father in previous sessions. When I interpreted that he must hate his brother for acting this way toward him, Devon looked worried and apologized. The interpretation had obviously aroused feelings of guilt. He ended our role-play and precariously perched himself on top of a chair, looking to see if I would intervene with a prohibition. When none was immediately forthcoming, Devon asked whether I was going to stop him. I interpreted that Devon was concerned about whether I was concerned enough about him to protect him from danger. Devon then got off the chair and went to the telephone. He asked if he could call 911. I interpreted that Devon was feeling as though he needed me to rescue him. Could he trust me to help him with his feelings, especially his angry feelings? Devon asked if he could press numbers other than 911. He pretended to talk to me over the telephone.

Devon wanted to know whether I would still be a secure base and safe haven for him, even though he was expressing anger, which I told him that I recognized. I suspect that Devon expected that any expression of his anger would result in the emotional or physical withdrawal of the attachment figure—probably a historical fact in his short but eventful life. Was I going to withdraw from him like his parents, or panic like his foster mother, or pass this test (Weiss & Sampson, 1986) by demonstrating that I could be a secure base without withdrawing or panicking? I believe that I passed this particular test. Perhaps I failed other tests. Our words and behaviors as therapists need to work in synchrony to mark the patient's emotions as understood by us but not exactly shared by us. I communicated simultaneously (1) my concern about Devon's worry about whether I was going to rescue him and (2) my sense that he was not in imminent danger. I believe that this interaction and many others like it produced lasting, first-order therapeutic change in Devon's implicit procedural knowledge. Perhaps he could begin to listen for the Spirit stirring within him and follow along.

References

Alexander, F., & French, T. M. (1946). *Psychoanalytic therapy: Principles and application.* Ronald.

Anonymous. (2007). Dark matter. Retrieved July 21, 2007, from http://en.wikipedia.org/wiki/Dark_matter

Arizmendi, T., Beutler, L., Shanfield, S., Crago, M., & Hagaman, R. (1985). Client-therapist value similarity and psychotherapy outcome: A microscopic analysis. *Psychotherapy, 22,* 16–21.

Aron, L. (2006). Analytic impasse and the third: Clinical implications of intersubjectivity theory. *International Journal of Psycho-Analysis, 87,* 349–368.

Beck, A. T. (1976). *Cognitive therapy and the emotional disorders.* International Universities Press.

Bernier, A., & Dozier, M. (2002). The client-counselor match and the corrective emotional experience: Evidence from interpersonal and attachment research. *Psychotherapy: Theory/Research/Practice/Training, 39,* 32–43.

Bernier, A., Larose, S., & Soucy, N. (2005). Academic mentoring in college: The interactive role of student's and mentor's interpersonal dispositions. *Research in Higher Education, 46,* 29–51.

Berzins, J. I. (1977). Therapist-patient matching. In A. S. Gurman & A. M. Razin (Eds.), *Effective psychotherapy: A handbook of research* (pp. 222–251). Pergamon.

Beutler, L. E. (1991). Have all won and must all have prizes? Revisiting Luborsky et al.'s verdict. *Journal of Consulting and Clinical Psychology, 59,* 226–232.

Beutler, L. E., Clarkin, J. F., Crago, M., & Bergan, J. (1991). Client-therapist matching. In C. R. Snyder & D. R. Forsyth (Eds.), *Handbook of social and clinical psychology: The health perspective* (pp. 699–716). Pergamon.

Beutler, L. E., Crago, M., & Arizmendi, T. G. (1986). Therapist variables in psychotherapy process and outcome. In S. L. Garfield & A. E. Bergin (Eds.), *Handbook of psychotherapy and behavior change* (3rd ed., pp. 257–310). Wiley.

Beutler, L. E., Pollack, S., & Jobe, A. M. (1978). "Acceptance," values, and therapeutic change. *Journal of Consulting and Clinical Psychology, 46*, 198–199.

Bion, W. R. (1962). *Learning from experience.* Heinemann.

Bion, W. R. (1967). *Second thoughts.* Heinemann.

Bowlby, J. (1988). *A secure base: Parent-child attachment and healthy human development.* Basic Books.

Britton, R. (1998). *Belief and imagination: Exploration in psychoanalysis.* Tavistock/ Routledge.

Casement, P. J. (2001). The analyst's participation: A new look [Commentary]. *Journal of the American Psychoanalytic Association, 49*, 381–386.

Cassidy, J., Woodhouse, S. S., Cooper, G., Hoffman, K., Powell, B., & Rodenberg, M. (2005). Examination of the precursors of infant attachment security: Implications for early intervention and intervention research. In L. J. Berlin, Y. Ziv, L. Amaya-Jackson, & M. T. Greenberg (Eds.), *Enhancing early attachments: Theory, research, intervention, and policy* (pp. 34–60). Guilford Press.

Charone, J. K. (1981). Patient and therapist treatment goals related to psychotherapy outcome (Doctoral dissertation, Yeshiva University). *Dissertation Abstracts International, 42*(1-B), 365.

Clark, A., Goodman, G., & Petitti, C. (2018). The persistent case of major depression: An argument for long-term treatment. *Journal of Contemporary Psychotherapy, 48*, 33–40.

Clarkin, J. F., Yeomans, F. E., & Kernberg, O. F. (2015). *Transference-focused psychotherapy for borderline personality disorder: A clinical guide.* American Psychiatric Publishing.

Cooper, G., Hoffman, K., Powell, B., & Marvin, R. (2005). The Circle of Security Intervention: Differential diagnosis and differential treatment. In L. J. Berlin, Y. Ziv, L. Amaya-Jackson, & M. T. Greenberg (Eds.), *Enhancing early attachments: Theory, research, intervention, and policy* (pp. 127–151). Guilford Press.

Crastnopol, M. (2001). The analyst's participation: A new look [Commentary]. *Journal of the American Psychoanalytic Association, 49*, 386–398.

de Wolff, M., & van IJzendoorn, M. H. (1997). Sensitivity and attachment: A meta-analysis on parental antecedents of infant attachment. *Child Development, 68*, 571–591.

Diamond, D., Clarkin, J. F., Stovall-McClough, K. C., Levy, K. N., Foelsch, P. A., Levine, H., & Yeomans, F. E. (2003). Patient-therapist attachment: Impact on the therapeutic process and outcome. In M. Cortina & M. Marrone (Eds.), *Attachment theory and the psychoanalytic process.* Whurr.

Dozier, M. (2003). Attachment-based treatment for vulnerable children. *Attachment and Human Development, 5*, 253–257.

Dozier, M., & Bates, B. C. (2004). Attachment state of mind and the treatment relationship. In L. Atkinson & S. Goldberg (Eds.), *Attachment issues in psychopathology and intervention* (pp. 167–180). Erlbaum.

Dozier, M., & Tyrrell, C. (1998). The role of attachment in therapeutic relationships. In J. A. Simpson & W. S. Rholes (Eds.), *Attachment theory and close relationships* (pp. 221–248). Guilford Press.

Dozier, M., Cue, K. L., & Barnett, L. (1994). Clinicians as caregivers: Role of attachment organization in treatment. *Journal of Consulting and Clinical Psychology, 62*, 793–800.

Eagle, M. (2003). Clinical implications of attachment theory. *Psychoanalytic Inquiry*, *23*, 27–53.

Eagle, M. (2006). Attachment, psychotherapy, and assessment: A commentary. *Journal of Consulting and Clinical Psychology*, *74*, 1086–1097.

Eagle, M., & Wolitzky, D. L. (2006). The perspectives of attachment theory and psycho-analysis: Adult psychotherapy. Paper presented at conference, The perspectives of attachment theory and psychoanalysis: Adult psychotherapy. Adelphi University and the New York Attachment Consortium, Garden City, NY. November.

Flaskerud, J. H. (1990). Matching client and therapist ethnicity, language, and gender: A review of research. *Issues in Mental Health Nursing*, *11*, 321–336.

Fonagy, P., Gergely, G., Jurist, E. L., & Target, M. (2002). *Affect regulation, mentalization, and the development of the self*. Other Press.

Fosha, D. (2000). *The transforming power of affect: A model for accelerated change*. Basic Books.

Fraiberg, S., Adelson, E., & Shapiro, V. (1975). Ghosts in the nursery: A psychoanalytic approach to impaired infant-mother relationships. *Journal of the American Academy of Child Psychiatry*, *14*, 1387–1422.

Freud, S. (1912). Recommendations to physicians practising psycho-analysis. In J. Strachey (Ed. and Trans.), *The standard edition of the complete psychological works of Sigmund Freud* (Vol. 12, pp. 109–120). Hogarth Press.

Gergely, G. (2000). Reapproaching Mahler: New perspectives on normal autism, symbiosis, splitting and libidinal object constancy from cognitive developmental theory. *Journal of the American Psychoanalytic Association*, *48*, 1197–1228.

Glassman, M. (1988). Kernberg and Kohut: A test of competing psychoanalytic models of narcissism. *Journal of the American Psychoanalytic Association*, *36*, 597–625.

Goodman, G. (2010). *Transforming the internal world and attachment: Clinical applications* (Vol. 2). Jason Aronson.

Goodman, G. (2014). *The internal world and attachment*. Routledge.

Goodman, G. (2025). *Practical applications of transforming the attachment relationship to God: Using Attachment-Informed Psychotherapy*. Routledge.

Greenberg, J. R. (1986). Theoretical models and the analyst's neutrality. *Contemporary Psychoanalysis*, *22*, 89–106.

Henry, W. P., Strupp, H. H., Butler, S. F., Schacht, T. E., & Binder, J. L. (1993). Effects of training in time-limited dynamic psychotherapy: Changes in therapist behavior. *Journal of Consulting and Clinical Psychology*, *61*, 434–440.

Hoffman, K. T., Marvin, R. S., Cooper, G., & Powell, B. (2006). Changing toddlers' and preschoolers' attachment classifications: The Circle of Security intervention. *Journal of Consulting and Clinical Psychology*, *74*, 1017–1026.

Janov, A. (1970). *The primal scream; primal therapy: The cure for neurosis*. Putnam.

Jones, E. E. (2000). *Therapeutic action: A guide to psychoanalytic therapy*. Jason Aronson.

Kantrowitz, J. (1995). The beneficial aspects of the patient-analyst match. *International Journal of Psycho-Analysis*, *76*, 299–313.

Kernberg, O. F. (1975). *Borderline conditions and pathological narcissism*. Jason Aronson.

Kernberg, O. F. (1986). Further contributions to the treatment of narcissistic personalities. In A. Morrison (Ed.), *Essential papers on narcissism* (pp. 245–292). New York University Press.

Kobak, R. R., Cole, H. E., Ferenz-Gillies, R., Fleming, W. S., & Gamble, W. (1993). Attachment and emotion regulation during mother-teen problem solving: A control theory analysis. *Child Development, 64,* 231–245.

Kohut, H. (1971). *The analysis of the self: A systematic approach to the psychoanalytic treatment of narcissistic personality disorders.* International Universities Press.

Kohut, H. (1981). Remarks on empathy. Paper presented at the Conference on Self Psychology, Berkeley, CA. October 4.

Kohut, H. (1984). *How does analysis cure?* University of Chicago Press.

Langs, R. (1976). *The bipersonal field.* Jason Aronson.

Langs, R., & Stone, L. (1980). *The therapeutic experience and its setting: A clinical dialogue.* Jason Aronson.

Lanzetta, B. (2019). *Foundations in spiritual direction: Sharing the sacred across traditions.* Blue Sapphire Books.

Linehan, M. M. (1993). *Cognitive-behavioral treatment of borderline personality disorder.* Guilford Press.

Luborsky, L., Singer, B., & Luborsky, L. (1975). Comparative studies of psychotherapies: Is it true that "everyone has won and all must have prizes"? *Archives of General Psychiatry, 32,* 995–1008.

Lyons-Ruth, K. (1999). The two-person unconscious: Intersubjective dialogue, enactive relational representation, and the emergence of new forms of relational organization. *Psychoanalytic Inquiry, 19,* 576–617.

McBride, C., Atkinson, L., Quilty, L. C., & Bagby, R. M. (2006). Attachment as moderator of treatment outcome in major depression: A randomized control trial of interpersonal psychotherapy versus cognitive behavior therapy. *Journal of Consulting and Clinical Psychology, 74,* 1041–1054.

McLaughlin, J. (1991). Clinical and theoretical aspects of enactment. *Journal of the American Psychoanalytic Association, 39,* 595–614.

Munich, R. L. (1993). Conceptual issues in the psychoanalytic psychotherapy of patients with borderline personality disorder. In W. H. Sledge & A. Tasman (Eds.), *Clinical challenges in psychiatry* (pp. 61–87). American Psychiatric Press.

Nelson, M. L., & Neufeldt, S. A. (1996). Building on an empirical foundation: Strategies to enhance good practice. *Journal of Counseling and Development, 74,* 609–615.

NIV (New International Version). (1978). *The holy Bible.* Zondervan.

Ogden, T. H. (1979). On projective identification. *International Journal of Psycho-Analysis, 60,* 357–373.

Parish, M., & Eagle, M. N. (2003). Attachment to the therapist. *Psychoanalytic Psychology, 20,* 271–286.

Reis, B. F., & Brown, L. G. (1999). Reducing psychotherapy dropouts: Maximizing perspective convergence in the psychotherapy dyad. *Psychotherapy, 36,* 123–136.

Roisman, G. I., Holland, A., Fortuna, K., Fraley, R. C., Clausell, E., & Clarke, A. (2007). The Adult Attachment Interview and self-reports of attachment style: An empirical rapprochement. *Journal of Personality and Social Psychology, 92,* 678–697.

Rosenzweig, S. (1936). Some implicit common factors in diverse methods of psychotherapy. *American Journal of Orthopsychiatry, 6,* 412–415.

Skinner, B. F. (1974). *About behaviorism.* Vintage Books.

Slade, A. (1999). Attachment theory and research: Implications for the theory and practice of individual psychotherapy with adults. In J. Cassidy & P. R. Shaver (Eds.), *Handbook of attachment: Theory, research, and clinical applications* (pp. 575–594). Guilford Press.

Solomon, J., & George, C. (1999). The place of disorganization in attachment theory: Linking classic observations with contemporary findings. In J. Solomon & C. George (Eds.), *Attachment disorganization* (pp. 3–32). Guilford Press.

Stern, D. N., Sander, L. W., Nahum, J. P., Harrison, A. M., Lyons-Ruth, K., Morgan, A. C., Bruschweiler-Stern, N., & Tronick, E. Z. (1998). Non-interpretive mechanisms in psychoanalytic therapy: The "something more" than interpretation. *International Journal of Psycho-Analysis, 79*, 903–921.

Szajnberg, N. M., & Crittenden, P. M. (1997). The transference refracted through the lens of attachment. *Journal of the American Academy of Psychoanalysis, 25*, 409–438.

Talley, P. F., Strupp, H. H., & Morey, L. C. (1990). Match-making in psychotherapy: Patient-therapist dimensions and their impact on outcome. *Journal of Consulting and Clinical Psychology, 58*, 182–188.

Thomas, M. (2024, April 29). Dianne Reeves lauds the spiritual power of jazz that goes "beyond the page." Chicago Symphony Orchestra Experience webpage. Retrieved May 17, 2024, from https://cso.org/experience/article/9432/dianne-reeves-lauds-the-spiritual-power-of-ja

Tracey, T. J. (1987). Stage differences in the dependencies of topic initiation and topic following behavior. *Journal of Counseling Psychology, 34*, 123–131.

Tracey, T. J., & Ray, P. B. (1984). Stages of successful time-limited counseling: An interactional examination. *Journal of Counseling Psychology, 31*, 13–27.

Tyrrell, C. L., Dozier, M., Teague, G. B., & Fallot, R. D. (1999). Effective treatment relationships for persons with serious psychiatric disorders: The importance of attachment states of mind. *Journal of Consulting and Clinical Psychology, 67*, 725–733.

Weiss, J., & Sampson, H. (1986). *The psychoanalytic process: Theory, clinical observation, and empirical research*. Guilford Press.

Winnicott, D. W. (1971). *Playing and reality*. Basic Books.

Yeomans, F. E., Selzer, M. A., & Clarkin, J. F. (1992). *Treating the borderline patient: A contract-based approach*. Basic Books.

Chapter 6

Interaction Structures Formed by Therapist and Patient Secondary Attachment Strategies

While Freud focused on the therapist's technical behaviors in characterizing the nature of clinical practice, the (albeit sparse) literature on the role of attachment relationships in therapist-patient relationships suggests that the attachment histories of both the therapist and the patient influence not only the process but also the outcome of treatment (Bernier & Dozier, 2002; Bernier et al., 2005; Dozier, 2003; Dozier & Bates, 2004; Dozier et al., 1994; Dozier & Tyrrell, 1998; Tyrrell et al., 1999). Dozier and her colleagues articulate the principle of noncomplementarity to characterize the optimal therapist-patient match vis-à-vis internal working models of attachment relationships (see Chapter 4). Their research suggests that therapists are optimally effective with patients whose secondary (defensive) attachment strategy differs from their own. Conversely, therapists are less effective with patients whose secondary attachment strategy resembles their own. These secondary attachment strategies are patterns of emotion regulation and modes of relatedness to others, based on attachment-activating experiences with the caregivers during childhood.

In those situations in which the caregiver does not provide a secure base or safe haven, the child goes to "Plan B"—an alternative to the straightforward proximity-seeking and contact-maintaining behaviors that represent the hallmarks of secure attachment relationships. Plan B comes in two varieties: deactivating and hyperactivating (Kobak et al., 1993). When proximity-seeking and contact-maintaining behaviors fail to deactivate the attachment system, the child can deactivate the attachment system by dismissing their attachment needs and avoiding the caregiver. Adults who routinely use this secondary attachment strategy minimize, devalue, or dismiss the emotional importance of attachment relationships (Main & Goldwyn, 1994). The child can also hyperactivate the attachment system by exaggerating their attachment needs and expressing anger toward the caregiver. Adults who routinely use this secondary attachment strategy are angrily preoccupied with attachment relationships (Main & Goldwyn, 1994).

Although we would expect most therapists to have secure states of mind with respect to attachment (Diamond et al., 2003; Tyrrell et al., 1999), either by virtue of having had emotionally responsive caregivers during childhood or a long-term, intensive psychotherapy where a corrective emotional experience could occur,

DOI: 10.4324/9781003562924-8

most therapists also sometimes use a secondary attachment strategy. For secure adults, these secondary attachment strategies are partially captured in the Adult Attachment Interview (AAI) secure subclassifications (Main & Goldwyn, 1994), which range from F1 (somewhat restricting or setting aside of attachment) to F5 (somewhat resentful or preoccupied with attachment). Wherever therapists lie on this deactivating-hyperactivating continuum partially determines how they regulate their emotional lives and relate to others (Kobak et al., 1993; Slade, 1999). Patients also use these secondary attachment strategies. Anxious-avoidant (dismissing) patients use the deactivating strategy, while anxious-resistant (preoccupied) patients use the hyperactivating strategy.

The essence of Attachment-Informed Psychotherapy (AIP) is the therapist's awareness of these interaction structures and the application of this awareness in formulating therapeutic interventions. I am proposing a 2 x 2 typology of interaction structures formed by these therapist and patient secondary attachment strategies (see Table 6.1). Four possible cells exist: deactivating therapists paired with deactivating patients (cell 1), hyperactivating therapists paired with deactivating patients (cell 2), deactivating therapists paired with hyperactivating patients (cell 3), and hyperactivating therapists paired with hyperactivating patients (cell 4). Psychoanalysts from the relational school (e.g., Greenberg, 2001; Hoffman, 1994; Kantrowitz, 2001) argue in favor of the uniqueness of the therapist-patient relationship, which has been compared to "a snowflake" in which "no two are alike" (Kantrowitz, 2001, p. 403). If the therapist-patient relationship is unique, then it follows that the processes that facilitate therapeutic change would also vary from

Table 6.1 Typology presenting four interaction structures based on the secondary attachment strategies of therapist and patient

	Therapist	
Patient	*Deactivating Dismissing (Ds)*	*Hyperactivating Preoccupied (E)*
Deactivating Dismissing (Ds)	(1) Sterile (complementary): low depth, high smoothness, low arousal, rigid boundaries, overdifferentiation, overregulated emotion	(2) Expressive (noncomplementary): high depth, high smoothness, moderate arousal, flexible boundaries, optimal differentiation, expressed affect
Hyperactivating Preoccupied (E)	(3) Containing (noncomplementary): high depth, high smoothness, moderate arousal, firm boundaries, optimal differentiation, contained emotion	(4) Chaotic (complementary): high depth, low smoothness, high arousal, loose boundaries, undifferentiation, underregulated affect

relationship to relationship. Nevertheless, just as every snowflake has six sides, so too does every therapist-patient relationship have a particular shape.

In fact, I am proposing that every therapist-patient relationship can have four possible shapes. Specifying a range of shapes can also help to specify a range of clinical interventions that accompany each of these shapes. I have not conceptualized these four broadly defined shapes to minimize the uniqueness of the therapist-patient relationship but rather to delineate patterns within the uniqueness that could facilitate the development of broadly defined technical principles that therapists could use beyond a single case.

Of course, this 2 x 2 typology of interaction structures also applies to the therapist's and patient's attachment relationships to a Higher Power. In most cases, the quality of attachment relationships to the caregivers during childhood and to a Higher Power correspond to each other; thus, the four possible cells created by this typology also apply to the therapist's and patient's secondary attachment strategies used to regulate emotions in their attachment relationship to God (for discussion about the correspondence pathway, see Chapter 3). In some cases, however, the quality of attachment relationship to a Higher Power compensates for the quality of attachment relationships to the caregivers during childhood; thus, the four possible cells created by this typology might not apply to the therapist's and patient's secondary attachment strategies used to regulate emotions in their attachment relationship to God (for discussion about the compensation pathway, see Chapter 3). When the compensation pathway accounts for the therapist's or patient's attachment relationship to God, the quality of attachment relationship to God is typically secure, while the quality of attachment relationships to the caregivers during childhood is typically insecure (i.e., anxious-avoidant, anxious-resistant, or disorganized/disoriented).

Conversely, secure attachment relationships to the caregivers during childhood and an insecure attachment relationship to a Higher Power (typically anxious-avoidant) would occur only when the caregivers are not religious or spiritual (see the socialized correspondence theory of Granqvist [2020] discussed in Chapter 3). Only when suffering from an adjustment disorder (caused by overwhelming psychosocial stressors that produce psychiatric symptoms) would a securely attached patient seek psychotherapy because most securely attached patients, having experienced emotionally responsive caregiving, do not experience a pattern of emotional dysregulation implicated in most psychiatric illnesses. Thus, when a patient's attachment relationship to a Higher Power is insecure, it is likely that this person's attachment relationship to the caregivers during childhood is also insecure (unless the caregivers during childhood were not religious or spiritual). This 2 x 2 typology would therefore also apply to the therapist's and patient's attachment relationship to a Higher Power.

I have divided the four cells into two groups: complementary interaction structures and noncomplementary interaction structures (interaction structures are patterns of reciprocal interaction; see Chapter 4). Complementary interaction structures are patterns of reciprocal therapist-patient interaction in which the therapist and patient match on their secondary attachment strategy (cells 1 and 4; see Table 6.1). Conversely, noncomplementary interaction structures are patterns of reciprocal therapist-patient interaction in which the therapist and patient do not match on their secondary attachment strategy (cells 2 and 3; see Table 6.1). Dozier and her colleagues (Bernier & Dozier, 2002; Bernier et al., 2005; Dozier, 2003; Dozier & Bates, 2004; Dozier et al., 1994; Dozier & Tyrrell, 1998; Tyrrell et al., 1999) suggest that noncomplementary matches are more therapeutically effective than complementary matches.

I incorporate this idea into my typology of therapist-patient interaction structures. My descriptions of these four interaction structures are necessarily caricatured to increase their heuristic value; however, from my experience as a therapist, clinical supervisor, and psychotherapy process researcher, therapist-patient relationships that broadly resemble the ones depicted here actually do exist. Identifying these interaction structures in the early treatment phase can aid therapists in selecting the most effective intervention strategies for transforming a patient's attachment relationships both to the caregivers during childhood and to a Higher Power from insecure to secure.

Sterile Interaction Structure (Cell 1): Deactivating Therapist and Deactivating Patient

This complementary interaction structure, formed by a therapist and a patient who both tend to use a deactivating attachment strategy in their emotion regulation and mode of relatedness, is characterized by a sterile, lifeless treatment in which both partners avoid intense emotions and deeply conflictual issues. The low arousal level (see Allen, 2003) observed in these sessions reflects a low level of depth coupled with a high level of smoothness—what Mallinckrodt and his colleagues (Mallinckrodt et al., 2005) might call "coasting" (p. 87). The consequence is a superficial therapy experience with little mobilization of anxiety and minimal personality change.

McBride and her colleagues (McBride et al., 2006) found that deactivating patients paired with cognitive-behavioral therapy (CBT) for depression (a treatment that deemphasizes interpersonal connections) experienced greater symptom relief than deactivating patients paired with interpersonal psychotherapy (IPT) treatment for depression (a treatment that emphasizes interpersonal connections). Previously, I argued that the matching of deactivating patients with CBT is a complementary correspondence because this treatment model does not challenge the patient's deactivating strategy. Symptom relief occurred because this treatment merely strengthened failing defenses rather than producing lasting personality change (Eagle, 2006). Similarly, a sterile interaction structure strengthens the patient's defensive processes and never challenges the denial of attachment needs and vulnerability consistent with a false self (Winnicott, 1960).

Another feature of a sterile interaction structure is an air of formality in which the therapist maintains rigid boundaries and permits long silences. The therapist does not perceive themselves as a caregiver per se but rather perhaps as a surgeon excising a tumor (see Freud, 1912; see also Goodman, 2025, Chapter 5). There is a palpable lack of warmth or affection between the two partners, who seem invested in maintaining the status quo. The therapist or patient might be late to sessions without exploration of its potential meanings. The therapist or patient might also cancel sessions at the last minute and generally behave in a rejecting manner toward each other because each partner deactivates the other's emotional needs. The patient denies their attachment needs and ignores any anxiety associated with vacations and other separations from the therapist; the therapist denies their caregiving needs and ignores any subtle patient cues that might suggest vulnerability associated with attachment to the therapist.

For example, the patient arrives 15 minutes late to a session immediately following a week-long therapist vacation. The therapist ignores the patient's lateness as a cue that the separation had been unconsciously upsetting to the patient. By not exploring the patient's feelings, the therapist confirms the patient's expectations that others are rejecting of their attachment needs and that interdependent relationships are unimportant, overvalued, or nonexistent. Thus, the patient defensively excludes these needs, just as they did during childhood. I suspect that this interaction structure produces a high dropout rate.

From a spiritually informed point of view, these treatments are most likely devoid of any discussion of the patient's spirituality or religious affiliation. "See no spirit, hear no spirit" seems to be the motto of this therapeutic dyad. The attachment relationship to a Higher Power is not important to either the therapist or the patient. Both of them appear to be spiritually impoverished—alienated from the Divine within themselves. In this context, the patient's anxious-avoidant (dismissing) attachment relationship to a Higher Power is unlikely to change, which is also probably true for the therapist.

Chaotic Interaction Structure (Cell 4): Hyperactivating Therapist and Hyperactivating Patient

This complementary interaction structure, formed by a therapist and a patient who both tend to use a hyperactivating attachment strategy in their emotion regulation and mode of relatedness, is characterized by a chaotic, entangled treatment in which both partners rely on each other for support in an intensely emotional climate. The high arousal level (see Allen, 2003) observed in these sessions reflects a high level of depth coupled with a low level of smoothness—what Mallinckrodt and his colleagues (Mallinckrodt et al., 2005) might call "heavy going" (p. 87). The consequence is an intense, overstimulating, enmeshed therapy experience with high mobilization of anxiety and minimal personality change. The therapist and patient engage in mutual caregiving, thus reducing the role distinctions between the two partners.

Another feature of a chaotic interaction structure is an air of informality in which the therapist maintains loose boundaries, makes frequent self-disclosures, and talks incessantly. The therapist perceives themselves alternately as a caregiver and as a child, who feels overwhelmed by the patient's material and sometimes looks to the patient for comfort. The sessions contain high emotional content that might include physical affection as well as arguments and occasional cold silences between the two partners. The therapist reacts reflexively to the patient's material rather than reflecting on it. Mirroring of the patient's needs lacks differentiation and marking (Fonagy et al., 2002; Gergely, 2000).

For example, the patient discloses that her physician has scheduled her for a breast biopsy, which makes her feel terrified. The patient wants the therapist to sit closer to her in session and wants to talk to the therapist later that evening if the panicky feelings persist. The therapist gives her his home telephone number, sits next to her, and discloses that he too feels terrified about it. The therapist fails to contain the patient's anxiety and provide an experience of marking in which the patient senses that the therapist understands her terrified feelings but also feels something else (e.g., reassured that a biopsy is not the equivalent of having cancer). By feeling overwhelmed by the patient's feelings, the therapist confirms the patient's expectations that others are too fragile and undependable to contain attachment anxiety; therefore, the patient continues to feel fragmented. I suspect that this interaction structure might persist because the patient feels too vulnerable to leave treatment.

From a spiritually informed point of view, these treatments are more likely to include explicit references to spirituality. Rather than helping the patient to regulate their anxiety related to God as a perfectionist who punishes those who do not live up to certain unattainable standards, the therapist might also experience these same anxieties and therefore simply reflect back this same anxiety unmodulated by any awareness that God is compassionate and forgiving of those persons who fail to meet certain moral standards. In this context, the patient might find themselves comforting the therapist almost as often as the therapist comforts the patient. Like the previous example, the patient's anxious-resistant (preoccupied) attachment relationship to a Higher Power is unlikely to change, which is also probably true for the therapist.

Expressive Interaction Structure (Cell 2): Hyperactivating Therapist and Deactivating Patient

This noncomplementary interaction structure, formed by a therapist who tends to use a hyperactivating attachment strategy and a patient who tends to use a deactivating attachment strategy in their emotion regulation and mode of relatedness, is characterized by an expressive treatment in which the therapist helps the patient to express their emotional needs, particularly attachment needs and feelings of vulnerability. The moderate arousal level (see Allen, 2003) observed in these sessions reflects a high level of depth coupled with a high level of smoothness—what Mallinckrodt and his colleagues (Mallinckrodt et al., 2005) might call "smooth sailing" (p. 87). The consequence is a gentle exploration of vulnerability with optimal mobilization of anxiety and the potential for personality change. This interaction structure gently challenges the patient's defensive processes (Dozier, 2003, p. 254), especially the denial of attachment needs and vulnerability consistent with a false self (Winnicott, 1960).

Another feature of an expressive interaction structure is the establishment of flexible boundaries that challenge the patient's rigid invulnerability. The therapist balances silences with emotion-focused conversation that increases the patient's awareness of the therapist's recognition of attachment needs as a legitimate and valuable part of relating to others. The therapist perceives themselves as a responsive caregiver trying to connect emotionally with a young child who miscues (see Cooper et al., 2005, p. 136) independence and self-sufficiency but whose underlying attachment needs signal desire for security and closeness. Marking consists of acknowledging the patient's perception of a lack of attachment needs but also expressing the absent feelings on behalf of the patient. This marking creates a differentiated third point between therapist and patient that facilitates mentalization and emotion regulation (Aron, 2006).

For example, the therapist inquires about the patient's lateness or missed appointments and explores feelings related to vacations and other separations, even though the patient might dismiss their feelings about these events or devalue the therapist's exploration of this material. The therapist also demonstrates an openness, warmth, and affection for the patient even though the patient ignores or avoids these experiences. As often as possible, the therapist needs to disconfirm the patient's expectations that others are rejecting of attachment needs and that interdependent relationships are unimportant, overvalued, or nonexistent.

I am treating a 17-year-old boy diagnosed with Level 1 (high-functioning) autism spectrum disorder in once-weekly psychotherapy, whose parents forced him to enter therapy because he had become belligerent with his mother. As we might expect, I found it extraordinarily difficult to establish a rapport with him, not only because of his illness but also because his parents forced him into therapy. I felt chronically rejected by him in sessions. He often stated, "I don't want to be here; this is a waste of time." Long silences sometimes filled the space between us. When I asked him what he would normally be doing at 12:45 p.m. on a Saturday afternoon, he replied, "Sleeping." Gradually, I was able to develop enough of a working alliance to get him to tell me what was going on between his mother and him. I learned that his mother is a chronic alcoholic who behaves erratically around him and denigrates him when she is intoxicated. I wondered whether she might have untreated bipolar disorder. I fought through my negative countertransference reactions and kept reaching out to him, even though he kept rejecting me. Eventually, he began to open up to me about his long-term goals, which include college and living on his own. When I did not see him for two weeks, I always inquired about how he felt about the missed session even though I knew the answer would always be, "I got to sleep in last weekend." I suspect that this expressive interaction structure kept him in therapy because I encouraged him—and permitted him—to express feelings of vulnerability, which he began to value.

From a spiritually informed point of view, these treatments initially lack a focus on spiritual issues. The therapist must create a space for the patient to feel comfortable discussing their spirituality. For example, I am treating a 30-year-old nurse who has never discussed her spirituality with me. In our most recent session, she started by stating that she had nothing to talk about. I proceeded to ask her what she believes her life purpose is. She replied, "I don't know." After an unusually long pause, she acknowledged, "I don't like thinking about it because it makes me feel anxious." Now, spirituality is implicitly part of the conversation. I can mobilize this patient's anxiety to break down her secondary (defensive) attachment strategy of deactivating her attachment needs and instead activate her primary attachment strategy of proximity-seeking, perhaps later directed toward a Higher Power (see Chapter 3). With my question, I activated the patient's attachment system by increasing the patient's arousal level that challenged her rigid invulnerability to the uncertainty inherent in implicit spiritual matters. In an expressive interaction structure, therapeutic change is possible because the therapist is gently challenging the patient's deactivating secondary attachment strategy.

Containing Interaction Structure (Cell 3): Deactivating Therapist and Hyperactivating Patient

This noncomplementary interaction structure, formed by a therapist who tends to use a deactivating attachment strategy and a patient who tends to use a hyperactivating attachment strategy in their emotion regulation and mode of relatedness, is characterized by a containing (Bion, 1962, p. 102) treatment in which the therapist helps the patient to contain his or her emotions and thus facilitates their regulation. Like the expressive interaction structure, the moderate arousal level (see Allen, 2003) observed in these sessions reflects a high level of depth coupled with a high level of smoothness—"smooth sailing" (Mallinckrodt et al., 2005, p. 87). The consequence is a gentle, reflective, nonreactive exploration with optimal mobilization of anxiety and the potential for personality change. This interaction structure gently challenges the patient's emotion dysregulation by facilitating mutual dyadic regulation.

Another feature of a containing interaction structure is the establishment of firm boundaries that challenge the patient's desire for an undifferentiated experience with the therapist. The therapist balances silences with clarifications, confrontations, and interpretations in the context of the patient's emotion dysregulation, especially within the therapist-patient relationship. The therapist labels mental representations of self and others and the emotions linking them to provide an integrative experience and thereby facilitate emotion regulation. This process will help the patient to build internal structures and diminish their experiences of fragmentation. The therapist perceives themselves as a responsive caregiver trying to contain the distress of a young child who "miscues" (see Cooper et al., 2005, p. 136) dependence and clinging but whose underlying needs signal the child's desire for exploration and differentiation. Marking consists of acknowledging the patient's perception of distress but also communicating through a calm demeanor that the patient, like the child, "is not dying and will get over it" (Aron, 2006, p. 358). This marking creates a differentiated third point between therapist and patient that facilitates mentalization and emotion regulation (Aron, 2006). The therapist listens to and absorbs the patient's anger related to vacations and other separations and responds with an emotional reserve that communicates to the patient that the intensity of distress is disproportionate to the event. As often as possible, the therapist needs to disconfirm the patient's expectations that others are too fragile and undependable to contain attachment anxiety.

I treated a psychiatrically hospitalized woman diagnosed with borderline personality disorder who yelled at me for almost an entire 45-minute session after I had returned from a one-week vacation. I bided my time, listening and waiting for the storm to pass. In the next session, we were able to process her reaction to my absence without the emotion dysregulation that accompanied the session that had immediately followed my return. I could identify with her feelings of longing and frustration, but my calm demeanor suggested that my emotional response was differentiated from hers. My initial countertransference reaction was to defend myself, and I fantasized saying something like "Don't I have a right to get away from you every once in a while?" I fought through my countertransference reaction and stayed calm long enough to allow myself to be a container for her rage. Over time, these accumulated experiences of containment helped her to realize that her rage was not toxic, as she had thought. I disappointed her at times, but my emotional availability was "good enough" (Winnicott, 1965, p. 57) to allow her to modulate her own emotional reactions to ungratified attachment needs and to increase her awareness of simultaneous needs for differentiation and autonomy. I suspect that this containing interaction structure kept my patient from leaving the hospital against medical advice (which she had considered) because she experienced relief that I had survived the negative transference without collapsing, withdrawing, or retaliating (Casement, 2001). She found that she could become a separate person without either one of us dying.

From a spiritually informed point of view, these treatments often focus on intense spiritual experiences that produce acute anxiety. The therapist must contain this anxiety and allow the patient to discover for themselves a compassionate, loving Higher Power Who has their best interests in mind. For example, I am treating a 41-year-old finance executive (see Goodman, 2025, Chapter 6), whose chief complaint is explicitly spiritual: he identified an energy located in his pelvis that shouts, "I'm gay!" A part-time yoga instructor who has studied yogic philosophy, he refers to this energy as kundalini energy—a feminine energy in Hinduism—that is being blocked from "bursting forth" by anger and sadness. According to him, release of this energy would restore his connection to God. Administration of the AAI revealed that this man had developed anxious-resistant (preoccupied) attachment relationships to his caregivers during childhood; thus, he demonstrates a hyperactivating secondary attachment strategy, which is also evident in some aspects of his attachment relationship to a Higher Power. He describes feeling tortured by this energy, which, during the treatment course, has migrated upward from his groin to his upper chest, neck, and jaw, keeping him awake for hours at night. I have sought to contain the anxiety associated with this symptom and make connections between the symptom's features and certain memories related to his relationship to his father. I am down-regulating his attachment system so that he has mental space to reflect on a Higher Power that provides protection and concern rather than torture and self-doubt about his sexual orientation. In a containing interaction structure, therapeutic change is possible because the therapist is gently challenging the patient's hyperactivating secondary attachment strategy.

Conclusion

The four interaction structures I have outlined—sterile, chaotic, expressive, and containing—are, of course, caricatures of therapy sessions conducted by fictitious therapists and patients, each of whom falls on one of two ends of a continuum of secondary attachment strategies that range from deactivating to hyperactivating (Kobak et al., 1993, p. 235). Ideally, a therapist is sufficiently secure and flexible in their attachment pattern that they can challenge whatever strategy a patient presents by adopting a noncomplementary strategy to provide a corrective emotional experience for the patient (Alexander & French, 1946). A therapist who tends to use a hyperactivating attachment strategy must behave in a slightly deactivating manner with a hyperactivating patient to produce effective personality change, not only in declarative symbolic knowledge but also in implicit procedural knowledge.

Conversely, a therapist who tends to use a deactivating attachment strategy must behave in a slightly hyperactivating manner with a deactivating patient to produce effective personality change. Researchers could assign therapists and patients randomly to these four cells to verify the principle of noncomplementarity (Bernier & Dozier, 2002; Bernier et al., 2005; Dozier, 2003; Dozier & Bates, 2004; Dozier et al., 1994; Dozier & Tyrrell, 1998; Tyrrell et al., 1999). Clinical training programs could assess the attachment pattern of trainees (and their supervisors) and patients and use this information to help trainees learn how to provide noncomplementary psychotherapy experiences for their patients. However instructive these four broadly outlined interaction structures might be for the conduct of and training in psychotherapy, they can never substitute for the unique shape of each individual therapist-patient attachment relationship.

As I have illustrated, the spiritually informed therapist can also use this typology in planning intervention strategies for working with patients who have insecure attachment relationships to their Higher Power. Secondary attachment strategies (i.e., deactivating and hyperactivating) can gently challenge the patient's noncomplementary secondary attachment strategies to assist the patient in relying on the primary attachment strategy of proximity-seeking and finding protection and comfort in their attachment relationship to their Higher Power. The therapist uses these same strategies that they use when the patient is discussing their attachment relationships to the caregivers during childhood. I have found that these noncomplementary intervention strategies can produce effective change in the patient's attachment relationship to their Higher Power, not only in declarative symbolic knowledge but also in implicit procedural knowledge of this Higher Power.

Despite my promotion of one particular treatment model—AIP—I want to make a plea for a measure of flexibility in the treatment of patients. Freud (1913) was right that psychotherapy is like a game of chess in which there are an "infinite variety of moves" (p. 123) that can lead to therapeutic success. Despite diagnostic similarities, patients' needs and responses to therapeutic interventions vary widely, regardless of whether the patient is working on their relationships to significant others, the therapist (often a symbolic representative of caregivers during childhood), or a Higher Power. To meet these diverse needs, therapists need to implement intervention strategies tailored to the unique characteristics of each patient rather than boilerplate strategies designed for every patient. Therapeutically effective therapists adjust their technical approaches "on the fly" when they feel that their patients can benefit from a change in their intervention strategies. These technical modifications do not come from a treatment manual but from clinical intuition—the reflection on one's own countertransference reactions, or possibly a more broadly conceptualized empathic connection with the patient.

The contemplative Christian tradition has produced a model of spiritual intervention called "spiritual direction" that relies on waiting on the Holy Spirit to provide spiritual awareness and direction to the directee (Edwards, 2001; see Chapter 4). In a spiritual direction session, the spiritual director and directee together wait for the Holy Spirit to manifest the divine Presence by "listen[ing] for the movements of the Holy Spirit in all areas of [the directee's] life" (Location 70). This intuition-based spiritual process relies on the two participants being open to the movements of "Spirit-undercurrents flowing through the happenings of the directee's life" (Location 74). The spiritually informed therapist could benefit from harnessing this spirit-led intuition in psychotherapy sessions. As I mentioned in Chapter 5, intuitive therapists are like jazz musicians, improvising their solos to express their moment-to-moment feelings in the context of the other band members. Just as the best jazz musicians go wherever the Spirit leads them, so too do the best spiritually informed therapists rely on their spiritual intuition to intervene based on the moment-to-moment feelings experienced by the patient. Setting a session agenda and rigidly following it without any input from this spiritual Presence restrict the possibility of therapeutic or spiritual change taking place. The spiritually informed therapist must simultaneously account for many variables that affect the treatment, but ultimately, they must know how to act (or not act) in every moment of a session. To do this, they must be in tune with the spiritual forces operating both within themselves and within their patients.

Specifically, treatments of patients with various levels of disturbance or different constellations of symptoms, treatments in various settings (e.g., inpatient, day treatment, outpatient), and treatments that systematically take advantage of pairings of therapist and patient attachment relationships (reflecting patterns of emotion regulation) are beginning to yield findings in which adherence to particular treatment modalities varies according to "conditions on the ground" (i.e., movements of "Spirit-undercurrents"). Slavish adherence to a boilerplate training manual can spell disaster, as Castonguay and his colleagues (Castonguay et al., 1996) learned. While taking this inexorable journey, we have discovered an important clinical reality: treatment purity (whether psychoanalysis or CBT) might not be most effective for certain types of patients. Trainees need to be empathically and spiritually attuned to their patients' unique emotional and spiritual needs so that they can become aware when their treatment approach becomes counterproductive. Training in global clinical skills such as empathy, countertransference awareness (including spiritual countertransference awareness; see also Goodman, 2025, Chapter 6), and awareness of potential interaction structures (i.e., enactments) would more suitably position trainees to become effective therapists than training them how to apply a treatment manual. Instead of training trainees to be slaves to a treatment manual, clinical supervisors need to be training them to be its master. The field needs fewer technicians and more artists.

Finally, teaching therapist adherence to two or three broad treatment approaches (e.g., psychodynamic therapy and CBT) should become a vital aspect of clinical training; however, teaching therapist adherence to narrowly focused treatment models such as bedtime noncompliance (Ferber, 2006) ensnares the field in the "narcissism of minor differences" (Freud, 1918, p. 199) and immerses trainees in memorizing procedures rather than experiencing relationships and paying attention to the movements of "Spirit-undercurrents." The endless proliferation of manualized psychotherapies that emphasize their uniqueness obscures the broadly conceptualized therapeutic processes common to all effective psychotherapies. Psychotherapy process researchers need to focus on the common therapeutic ingredients of all effective psychotherapies and organize under a unified banner rather than splinter the field by promoting one's own treatment approach. Examining therapeutic processes that actually work moves the field "beyond brand names" and inevitable sectarian strife and instead unites the field in a common objective—to help relieve patients of their suffering, both emotional and spiritual.

Attachment-Informed Psychotherapy (AIP)—the treatment model I espouse in this book—is sufficiently broad to leverage global clinical skills such as empathy, countertransference awareness, and awareness of potential interaction structures to facilitate the emotional and spiritual journey of healing in patients. Perhaps most important, AIP easily accommodates the therapist's awareness of their own and their patients' attachment relationships to a Higher Power in promoting the spiritual journey of healing that can activate the healing of the whole person—body, mind, and soul. Healing of the attachment relationships to the caregivers during childhood and healing of the attachment relationship to a Higher Power synergize each other in spiritually grounded and spiritually curious patients. Why would we even consider working with only one type of attachment relationship at the expense of the other?

References

Alexander, F., & French, T. M. (1946). *Psychoanalytic therapy: Principles and application.* Ronald.

Allen, J. G. (2003). Mentalizing. *Bulletin of the Menninger Clinic, 67,* 91–112.

Aron, L. (2006). Analytic impasse and the third: Clinical implications of intersubjectivity theory. *International Journal of Psycho-Analysis, 87,* 349–368.

Bernier, A., & Dozier, M. (2002). The client-counselor match and the corrective emotional experience: Evidence from interpersonal and attachment research. *Psychotherapy: Theory/Research/Practice/Training, 39,* 32–43.

Bernier, A., Larose, S., & Soucy, N. (2005). Academic mentoring in college: The interactive role of student's and mentor's interpersonal dispositions. *Research in Higher Education, 46,* 29–51.

Bion, W. R. (1962). *Learning from experience.* Heinemann.

Casement, P. J. (2001). The analyst's participation: A new look [Commentary]. *Journal of the American Psychoanalytic Association, 49,* 381–386.

Castonguay, L. G., Goldfried, M. R., Wiser, S., Raue, P. J., & Hayes, A. M. (1996). Predicting the effect of cognitive therapy for depression: A study of unique and common factors. *Journal of Consulting and Clinical Psychology, 64,* 497–504.

Cooper, G., Hoffman, K., Powell, B., & Marvin, R. (2005). The Circle of Security Intervention: Differential diagnosis and differential treatment. In L. J. Berlin, Y. Ziv, L. Amaya-Jackson, & M. T. Greenberg (Eds.), *Enhancing early attachments: Theory, research, intervention, and policy* (pp. 127–151). Guilford Press.

Diamond, D., Stovall-McClough, C., Clarkin, J. F., & Levy, K. N. (2003). Patient-therapist attachment in the treatment of borderline personality disorder. *Bulletin of the Menninger Clinic, 67,* 227–259.

Dozier, M. (2003). Attachment-based treatment for vulnerable children. *Attachment and Human Development, 5,* 253–257.

Dozier, M., & Bates, B. C. (2004). Attachment state of mind and the treatment relationship. In L. Atkinson & S. Goldberg (Eds.), *Attachment issues in psychopathology and intervention* (pp. 167–180). Erlbaum.

Dozier, M., Cue, K. L., & Barnett, L. (1994). Clinicians as caregivers: Role of attachment organization in treatment. *Journal of Consulting and Clinical Psychology, 62,* 793–800.

Dozier, M., & Tyrrell, C. (1998). The role of attachment in therapeutic relationships. In J. A. Simpson & W. S. Rholes (Eds.), *Attachment theory and close relationships* (pp. 221–248). Guilford Press.

Eagle, M. N. (2006). Attachment, psychotherapy, and assessment: A commentary. *Journal of Consulting and Clinical Psychology, 74,* 1086–1097.

Edwards, T. (2001). *Spiritual director, spiritual companion: Guide to tending the soul.* Paulist Press. Kindle Edition.

Ferber, R. (2006). *Solve your child's sleep problems* (2nd ed.). Fireside.

Fonagy, P., Gergely, G., Jurist, E. L., & Target, M. (2002). *Affect regulation, mentalization, and the development of the self.* Other Press.

Freud, S. (1912). Recommendations to physicians practising psycho-analysis. In J. Strachey (Ed. and Trans.), *The standard edition of the complete psychological works of Sigmund Freud* (Vol. 12, pp. 109–120). Hogarth Press.

Freud, S. (1913). On beginning the treatment (Further recommendations on the technique of psycho-analysis I). In J. Strachey (Ed. and Trans.), *The standard edition of the complete psychological works of Sigmund Freud* (Vol. 12, pp. 123–144). Hogarth Press.

Freud, S. (1918). The taboo of virginity (Contributions to the psychology of love III). In J. Strachey (Ed. and Trans.), *The standard edition of the complete psychological works of Sigmund Freud* (Vol. 11, pp. 191–208). Hogarth Press.

Gergely, G. (2000). Reapproaching Mahler: New perspectives on normal autism, symbiosis, splitting and libidinal object constancy from cognitive developmental theory. *Journal of the American Psychoanalytic Association, 48*, 1197–1228.

Goodman, G. (2025). *Practical applications of transforming the attachment relationship to God: Using Attachment-Informed Psychotherapy*. Routledge.

Granqvist, P. (2020). *Attachment in religion and spirituality: A wider view*. Guilford Press.

Greenberg, J. (2001). The analyst's participation: A new look. *Journal of the American Psychoanalytic Association, 49*, 359–381.

Hoffman, I. Z. (1994). Dialectical thinking and therapeutic action in the psychoanalytic process. *Psychoanalytic Quarterly, 63*, 187–218.

Kantrowitz, J. L. (2001). The analyst's participation: A new look [Commentary]. *Journal of the American Psychoanalytic Association, 49*, 398–406.

Kobak, R. R., Cole, H. E., Ferenz-Gillies, R., Fleming, W. S., & Gamble, W. (1993). Attachment and emotion regulation during mother-teen problem solving: A control theory analysis. *Child Development, 64*, 231–245.

Main, M., & Goldwyn, R. (1994). Adult attachment scoring and classification systems (6th ed.). Unpublished manuscript. University College, London.

Mallinckrodt, B., Porter, M. J., & Kivlighan, D. M., Jr. (2005). Client attachment to therapist, depth of in-session exploration, and object relations in brief psychotherapy. *Psychotherapy: Theory, Research, Practice, Training, 42*, 85–100.

McBride, C., Atkinson, L., Quilty, L. C., & Bagby, R. M. (2006). Attachment as moderator of treatment outcome in major depression: A randomized control trial of interpersonal psychotherapy versus cognitive behavior therapy. *Journal of Consulting and Clinical Psychology, 74*, 1041–1054.

Slade, A. (1999). Attachment theory and research: Implications for the theory and practice of individual psychotherapy with adults. In J. Cassidy & P. R. Shaver (Eds.), *Handbook of attachment: Theory, research, and clinical applications* (pp. 575–594). Guilford Press.

Tyrrell, C. L., Dozier, M., Teague, G. B., & Fallot, R. D. (1999). Effective treatment relationships for persons with serious psychiatric disorders: The importance of attachment states of mind. *Journal of Consulting and Clinical Psychology, 67*, 725–733.

Winnicott, D. W. (1960). The theory of the parent-infant relationship. *International Journal of Psycho-Analysis, 41*, 585–595.

Winnicott, D. W. (1965). *The maturational processes and the facilitating environment: Studies in the theory of emotional development*. International Universities Press.

Chapter 7

Final Thoughts on Transforming Attachment Relationships to God

In the Beginning Was Attachment Theory

As the foregoing heading so beautifully conveys, attachment to a Higher Power is the cornerstone of religious and spiritual experience. The aim of this book has been to apply attachment theory to the experience of being in a relationship to God and for the reader to become aware that, typically, the quality of this relationship is closely related to the quality of a person's relationships to their caregivers during childhood. In psychotherapy, we can harness the power of this relationship to improve the quality of both relationships. In other words, working on understanding our relationships to our caregivers during childhood can improve our understanding of our relationship to a Higher Power, and working on understanding our relationship to a Higher Power can improve our understanding of our relationships to our caregivers during childhood. The reason for this inevitable association is that infants and young children gradually develop expectations of their caregivers' emotional responsiveness (or nonresponsiveness), which become organized into an internal working model of these early caregiver relationships (see Chapter 2). The purpose of this internal working model is to generalize the rules of these relationships to persons outside the parental relationships. For example, a child as young as 12 months old might learn experientially that when feeling scared by separation from the caregiver, they must turn away from the caregiver to avoid outright rejection. This rule, adopted by anxious-avoidant infants, is then applied to interactions with others, including romantic relationships in later life and, inevitably to a person's relationship to a Higher Power. These are the foundational concepts presented in this book.

Because attachment theory is so vital to understanding the nature of human beings' relationship to a Higher Power, let us review the basics of attachment theory here in this final chapter. We started with evolutionary theory and the generally accepted view that human beings are genetically programmed to survive in the environments in which they evolved. Survival includes protection from predators that could end a person's life long before they ever got the opportunity to reproduce their genes in adulthood. The hallmarks of the attachment system—proximity-seeking and contact maintenance—are infant and child

DOI: 10.4324/9781003562924-9

behaviors genetically designed to capitalize on the caregivers' superior strength and wisdom to protect them from predators and other external threats to off-spring safety (e.g., separation, unfamiliarity, injury) when the attachment system is activated. Of course, caregivers are also genetically designed to provide this protection when their caregiving system is activated under these same conditions of external threat. Specifically, the caregiving system activates altruistic behavior directed toward the helpless offspring, who otherwise would not survive to pass on the caregivers' genetic material in adulthood.

Caregivers provide both a safe haven for the infant and young child ("Shelter from the Storm," Dylan, 1975) and a secure base from which the infant and young child can explore the environment when their exploratory system is activated and when external threats are absent. When the exploratory system is activated, the infant and young child can interact with caregiver-sanctioned others and learn about the world outside the caregivers' warm embrace.

The attachment system becomes operational by 12 months of age and is con-spicuous for its distinctive behaviors (proximity-seeking and contact mainten-ance in the context of external threats). Bowlby (1980), the founder of attachment theory, observed that the infant forms attachments to caregivers hierarchically. For example, in a patriarchal society, where a gender-specific division of labor exists, the mother is typically the primary caregiver and the person whom the infant pre-fers when the attachment system is activated. Secondary and tertiary caregivers such as fathers and grandparents can also fill the role of attachment figure when the mother is physically unavailable. Bowlby believed that the number of attach-ment figures who provide care and protection for the infant is quite small. Virtually every child also develops an idiosyncratic relationship to a Higher Power (Rizzuto, 1979). Preschool-age children believe that God is stronger and wiser than even their parents (Barrett, 2012); thus, from an early age, God can serve as a surrogate attachment figure.

Attachment relationships do not all look the same. Researchers (Ainsworth et al., 1978; Main & Solomon, 1990) have identified four different types of attachment patterns observed in the Strange Situation procedure, where the infant's attachment system is experimentally activated, and these relationship patterns with the care-giver are forced to express themselves. These four relationship patterns are known as secure, anxious-resistant, anxious-avoidant, and disorganized/disoriented.

The hallmarks of a *secure attachment relationship* include a feeling of confi-dence that the other person (including God): (1) will be emotionally available and responsive when the person feels a threat to their physical, emotional, or interper-sonal well-being, and (2) will be able to help the person to restore their emotional equilibrium to a feeling of security. In therapy (and life), regulated emotions and coherence characterize such a person's interpersonal interactions and narrative of their attachment relationships (see also Goodman, 2025, Chapter 2). Caregivers during childhood were emotionally responsive, especially during attachment-activating situations.

The hallmarks of an *anxious-resistant attachment relationship* include a feeling of ambivalence and uncertainty about whether the other person (including God): (1) will be emotionally available and responsive, and (2) will be able to help the person to restore their emotional equilibrium. In therapy (and life), dysregulated emotions and meandering and resentful reminiscences of negative interactions characterize such a person's interpersonal interactions and narrative of their attachment relationships. Interactions, even though they took place years ago, seem entangled with the present (see also Goodman, 2025, Chapters 3 and 6). Caregivers during childhood were inconsistently emotionally responsive, especially during attachment-activating situations.

The hallmarks of an *anxious-avoidant attachment relationship* include a feeling of dismissal of the emotional significance of the relationship because the other person (including God): (1) will be emotionally unavailable and unresponsive, and (2) will be unable to help the person restore their emotional equilibrium—which they must therefore accomplish by themselves. In therapy (and life), constricted emotional expression and short, schematic descriptions of the relationship devoid of emotional meaning and vulnerability characterize such a person's interpersonal interactions and narrative of their attachment relationships. Interactions seem not to matter (see also Goodman, 2025, Chapters 4 and 5). Caregivers during childhood were consistently emotionally unresponsive, especially during attachment-activating situations.

Finally, the hallmarks of a *disorganized/disoriented attachment relationship* include a feeling of contradictory impulses both to seek and reject emotionally significant relationships because the other person (including God): (1) is perceived as simultaneously the source of comfort and the source of alarm, and (2) will cause a temporary collapse of strategies for coping with attachment-related stressors. In therapy (and life), the person typically discusses attachment relationships, particularly losses and trauma, with noticeable lapses in their ability to monitor their own reasoning and discourse. Emotions are overregulated through "freezing," because interactions are fraught with fear. Caregivers during childhood engaged in frightening or frightened behaviors, especially during attachment-activating situations.

A survey of human history and culture strongly suggests that the concept of a Higher Power has been a constant fixture of human civilization, probably even preceding civilization. In every historical epoch, in every cultural milieu, God has been there. The psalmist writes, "Where can I go from your Spirit? Where can I flee from your presence?" (Psalm 139:7; NIV, 1978). Every society contains atheists—persons who do not believe in a Higher Power—but their presence is the exception that proves the rule. As I have shown (see Chapter 3), relationship to a Higher Power is a universal phenomenon. Even persons who practice so-called "atheistic religions" such as Buddhism say the common prayer, "'I take refuge in the Buddha'" (Granqvist, 2020, p. 67). Due to their insecure (most likely anxious-avoidant) attachment relationships to their caregivers during childhood, atheists disavow their earlier understanding of a Higher Power formed during early childhood.

Attachment to a Higher Power is not an evolutionary by-product but rather a bona fide evolutionary adaptation, a phenomenon that enhances human survival and reproductive fitness. Attachment to a Higher Power promotes safe haven and secure base behaviors that permit human beings to take risks in the service of their own survival and reproduction. Even beyond that, though, attachment to a Higher Power provides human beings with a coherent set of moral norms supporting a cooperative attitude that promotes survival. Finally, as far as we know, human beings are the only members of the animal kingdom who attain an awareness of their own mortality. Attachment to a Higher Power mitigates the anxiety associated with this awareness, thus making it tolerable. Less anxiety means more concentration on survival and reproduction.

From these key points, I concluded that all human beings (and perhaps other intelligent mammalian species such as elephants, who incidentally have their own burial rituals; see Kaswan & Roy, 2024) have an innate predisposition to spirituality that has evolved over thousands of years. This innate predisposition manifests in the formation of an attachment to a Higher Power. According to contemporary Christian mystic Rohr (2016), "We're all united to God, but only some of us know it. Most of us deny it and doubt it" (p. 109).

I concluded that from an early age (Barrett, 2012; Rizzuto, 1979), children develop an attachment relationship to a Higher Power that resembles their attachment relationships to their parents in important respects. Later, through a conversion process, the attachment relationship to a Higher Power might transform from insecure to secure to compensate for the insecure attachment relationships to their parents.

The Two Pathways Toward Relationship (or Nonrelationship) to a Higher Power

The research literature (e.g., Granqvist, 2020; Granqvist & Kirkpatrick, 2018; Kirkpatrick, 2005) suggests two pathways characterizing the relationship between the quality of attachment relationships to the caregivers during childhood and the quality of attachment relationship to a Higher Power. The great German philosopher Ludwig Feuerbach (1841) argued that God is an expression of human emotion, desire, and fear. In his famous monograph, *Totem and Taboo*, Freud (1913) first analyzed this resemblance between the image of the father and the image of God:

> The psycho-analysis of individual human beings, however, teaches us with quite special insistence that the god of each of them is formed in the likeness of his father, that his personal relation to God depends on his relation to his father in the flesh and oscillates and changes along with that relation, and that at bottom God is nothing other than an exalted father.
>
> (p. 147)

Sixty-six years later, Rizzuto (1979) conducted a careful ethnographic study of four psychiatric inpatients' images of God, their parents, and themselves. She found that these patients constructed their God images out of experiences and fantasies generated in their relationship to the parents and the self. She concluded that these patients' official God image, introduced by the church, synagogue, mosque, or temple during religious education, is superimposed on this earlier God image constructed out of a composite of the parental and self-images. Unlike Freud, however, Rizzuto was careful not to conclude that belief in the God image is false; after all, as the apostle Paul writes, "We see only a reflection [of God] as in a mirror; then we shall see face to face" (I Corinthians 13:12; NIV, 1978).

Correspondence Pathway

As I carefully documented in Chapter 3, Kirkpatrick and Shaver (1990) were the first researchers to apply the Bowlby/Ainsworth/Main attachment paradigm to human beings' relationship to God. That key insight produced the idea of the correspondence and compensation pathways (Kirkpatrick, 1998), foreshadowed by the typology of "once-born" and "twice-born" characters of William James (1902, p. 80). The correspondence pathway represents the transfer of the quality of attachment relationships to the caregivers during childhood onto the attachment relationship to a Higher Power (see Chapter 3). Thus, secure attachment breeds secure attachment, anxious-resistant attachment breeds anxious-resistant attachment, and so on (see also Goodman, 2025, Chapters 2 and 5). Both Kirkpatrick (2005) and Granqvist (2020) cite plenty of evidence to support the validity of this pathway.

Granqvist (2020) adds the caveat that the correspondence pathway also depends on "socialized correspondence" (p. 127; see Chapter 3). In addition to developing an internal working model of attachment that reflects that of the caregivers (i.e., intergenerational transmission of attachment quality), a child is exposed (or not exposed) to the religiosity of the caregivers. The socialization into or not into a religion also influences the vicissitudes of the correspondence pathway. For example, the child who develops secure attachment relationships to both parents but has no opportunity to develop any such attachment relationship to a Higher Power will have what might appear to be an anxious-avoidant attachment relationship to a Higher Power—distant, remote, unmeaningful.

According to Kirkpatrick (2005) and Granqvist (2020), the correspondence pathway holds when the child experiences relatively minor stressful events over the course of their lives. For example, a child who has developed anxious-avoidant attachment relationships to their parents and who has experienced few negative major life events is more likely to be attracted to atheism or agnosticism, in which God is distant, remote, and unmeaningful. In this scenario, the person would find using their innate spiritual resources challenging and perhaps even repulsive. A child who has experienced many serious major life events, however, is more likely to be attracted to spirituality as embodied in a Higher Power to compensate for the breakdown of the secondary (defensive) attachment strategy of deactivating their attachment needs by activating their primary attachment strategy of proximity-seeking directed toward this Higher Power. When the negative major life events become overwhelming, the insecurely attached person is more likely to seek out a secure attachment relationship to a Higher Power.

Compensation Pathway

The second pathway that spans the distance between the attachment relationships to the caregivers during childhood and the attachment relationship to a Higher Power reflects how an insecurely attached person can use this latter attachment relationship to compensate for the earlier attachment insecurity (see Chapter 3). God becomes a surrogate attachment figure to Whom the person can direct their dormant primary attachment strategy of proximity-seeking and finding protection and comfort in their attachment relationship to a Higher Power (see also Goodman, 2025, Chapters 1, 3, 4, and 6). There are two conditions under which this conversion process takes place. First, as described in the previous paragraph, negative major life events can overwhelm the person's secondary (defensive) attachment strategy of anxious-avoidance or anxious-resistance and force a reliance on the primary attachment strategy of proximity-seeking. Second, a brittle attachment subclassification (e.g., Ds1, Ds2, Ds3, or Ds4) might make a person more prone to using God as a surrogate attachment figure to compensate for the secondary (defensive) attachment strategy that succeeded in protecting the child from an inconsistently responsive or consistently unresponsive caregiver during childhood. Both overwhelmingly negative major life events and a brittle attachment subclassification (see Chapter 3) can contribute to the breakdown of the secondary attachment strategy and the subsequent search for a surrogate attachment figure such as God. When a person's mortality is threatened, there really are no atheists in the foxhole.

Finally, it is also important to recognize that the quality of attachment relationships are caregiver-specific in infancy. Although attachment researchers such as Slade (1999, p. 588) argue that these caregiver-specific attachment relationships typically develop into a "primary mode of relatedness" and generalized emotion regulation strategy, Daniel (2015, pp. 123–125) points out that even into adulthood, a person can use multiple internal working models of attachment relationships based on different qualities of attachment relationships to the caregivers during childhood. These multiple internal working models of attachment relationships can complicate a person's use of the compensation pathway (see also Goodman, 2025, Chapters 1, 3, and 6). Turning to God as a surrogate attachment figure might correspond with a secure attachment relationship to one parent but compensate for an insecure attachment relationship to the other parent. Thus, over the course of our lives, we also observe a hybrid pathway that consists of both correspondence and compensation properties. We must wait on research to help us understand how and under which conditions such hybrid pathways operate.

Earned Security

The therapeutic process can help a patient to achieve "earned security" (Hesse, 2018, p. 570; Main & Goldwyn, 1989) in the patient's attachment relationships to the caregivers during childhood through emotionally corrective experiences with an emotionally responsive therapist and then generalize these experiences to establish a secure attachment relationship to a Higher Power (Granqvist, 2020). This process can also work in reverse: the patient can achieve earned security in their experiences with an attachment relationship to a Higher Power through a process of generalizing from their experiences with secure attachment relationships to their parents during childhood or to an emotionally responsive therapist. To underscore this point, patients do not achieve earned security exclusively by experiencing a secure attachment to a Higher Power: a secure attachment to an emotionally responsive romantic partner or therapist can also produce an earned secure state of mind with respect to attachment. To achieve earned security, the person's internal working model of attachment relationships changes from insecure to secure, thus overcoming the preferred secondary attachment strategy developed to defend against the caregivers' inconsistent responsiveness or consistent unresponsiveness during childhood.

If a patient is using their attachment relationship to a Higher Power to compensate for insecure attachment relationships to the caregivers during childhood, then the therapist can harness this attachment security to the Higher Power to assist the patient to begin to trust in these insecure attachment relationships, or at least to develop compassion for these caregivers. Through painstaking work in therapy, the patient can begin to embrace the spiritual truth, "everything is as it should be" and its corollary, "everything was as it should have been." The patient can eventually work toward forgiving the caregivers for their emotional unresponsiveness (both past and present) and, if necessary, detach from them. Having a secure attachment relationship to a Higher Power can facilitate this process because the patient can trust in God as a secure base to whom the patient can return throughout this painful process, regardless of whether it ends in reconciliation or detachment. A patient's reliance on a Higher Power as a surrogate attachment figure can be the therapist's chief ally in the reparation process.

The therapeutic challenge of assisting a patient in shifting from an insecure to a secure internal working model (thereby achieving earned security) consists of gently challenging their preferred secondary (defensive) attachment strategy, while remaining always emotionally responsive and accepting of their entire self—the needy and self-sufficient parts, the loving and hating parts, the committed and resistant parts. As discussed in Chapter 3, both negative major life events and psychosocial stressors as well as the brittleness of the patient's insecure attachment subclassification can influence the patient's journey to earned security. For example, a patient who is not in an acute crisis and who has a robust insecure attachment subclassification is going to be less motivated to shift their internal working model from insecure to secure. The stakes are just not high enough to risk all to entrust oneself to the care of a stronger and wiser attachment figure such as a Higher Power or a therapist. The urgency to grab the life preserver has not materialized because one is still able to tread water in the open sea. The danger is not yet imminent. Understanding these factors can help a therapist adjust their expectations for the patient's therapeutic trajectory. The psychoanalyst Bion (1967) recommended that a therapist should approach each therapy session without memory or desire. This stance guarantees that the therapist's expectations do not interfere with the patient's journey toward earned security. Regardless of whether the therapist approaches the session knowing about the patient's crisis level and secondary attachment strategy brittleness or instead prefers to empty themselves of all memory of the patient's predispositions, the therapeutic goal is nothing less than total acceptance.

Essential Elements of Attachment-Informed Psychotherapy

Attachment-Informed Psychotherapy (AIP) consists of understanding the quality of the internal working model of the attachment relationships of both patient and therapist and using this information to formulate an intervention plan that maximizes the opportunity for the patient to shift from an insecure to a secure internal working model of attachment relationships (known as "earned security"). Based on observations of narrative and interpersonal markers of attachment patterns (Daniel, 2015) within the first few sessions, the therapist can develop a working hypothesis regarding the patient's quality of attachment relationships to the caregivers during childhood as well as the quality of attachment relationship to a Higher Power (and other persons of emotional significance, such as romantic partners). Presumably, through their own experiences in psychotherapy, the therapist also has a working hypothesis regarding the quality of their own attachment relationships. After the understanding phase of treatment, in which the therapist develops a therapeutic alliance with the patient through empathy and validation, the explanatory phase follows, in which the therapist provides interpersonal and intrapersonal interpretations to explain the patient's emotional distress (Kohut, 1984; see Chapter 5). The therapeutic purpose of these interpretations is not to help the patient intellectualize their experience but rather to deepen the empathic connection and provide the patient with a corrective emotional experience (Alexander & French, 1946). Understanding how the therapist's and patient's internal working models of attachment relationships work together during this explanatory phase of treatment is vital to the treatment's success.

As discussed in Chapter 3, attachment patterns come in four types: secure, anxious-avoidant (i.e., dismissing), anxious-resistant (i.e., preoccupied), and disorganized/disoriented (unresolved). The therapist's and patient's internal working models fit together in four different configurations (discussed in Chapter 6). Even securely attached therapists have secondary (defensive) attachment strategies at their disposal for protection against the potential for attachment wounds. Therapists need to be aware of their own preferred secondary attachment strategy in their interactions with patients because this awareness is necessary for producing the "gentle challenge" (Dozier, 2003, p. 254) required to shift a patient from an insecure to a secure internal working model of attachment relationships.

Four Interaction Structures

These four different configurations are known as "interaction structures," or patterns of reciprocal interaction between therapist and patient, of which both partners are often unaware. In Chapter 6, I argued that two of these interaction structures stand a good chance of producing positive therapeutic results, which I am defining as achieving earned security in the patient's internal working model of attachment relationships. The other two interaction structures do not stand a good chance of producing positive therapeutic results. I labeled these four interaction structures "sterile," "chaotic," "expressive," and "containing." A sterile interaction structure, which is not likely to produce positive therapeutic results, consists of an anxious-avoidant patient paired with a therapist who has a complementary secondary attachment strategy of anxious-avoidance. Both partners rely on strategies to deactivate emotional arousal, resulting in their avoidance of intense emotions and deeply conflictual issues. An outside observer might characterize a typical session as boring and somnolent—nothing is going on. When nothing goes on, nothing changes.

A chaotic interaction structure, which is also not likely to produce positive therapeutic results, consists of an anxious-resistant patient paired with a therapist who has a complementary secondary attachment strategy of anxious-resistance. Both partners rely on strategies to hyperactivate emotional arousal, resulting in their escalation of intense emotions and deeply conflictual issues. An outside observer might characterize a typical session as chaotic and entangled—both partners are relying on each other for support in an intensely emotional climate. The therapist does not create the psychic space required for mentalizing feelings and intentions, so nothing changes.

An expressive interaction structure, which is more likely to produce positive therapeutic results, consists of an anxious-avoidant patient paired with a therapist who is using a noncomplementary secondary attachment strategy of anxious-resistance. The therapist uses a hyperactivating attachment strategy in their emotion regulation and mode of relatedness to provide a gentle challenge to the patient's deactivating attachment strategy. This intervention strategy serves the purpose of loosening the patient's overcontrolled emotions, which they can generalize to other emotionally significant relationships. An outside observer might characterize a typical session as vulnerability-enhancing and revitalizing—the therapist gives permission for the expression of vulnerable attachment needs. The patient's internal working model gradually shifts from anxious-avoidant to secure, one validating intervention at a time.

A containing interaction structure, which is also more likely to produce positive therapeutic results, consists of an anxious-resistant patient paired with a therapist who is using a noncomplementary secondary attachment strategy of anxious-avoidance. The therapist uses a deactivating attachment strategy in their emotion regulation and mode of relatedness to provide a gentle challenge to the patient's hyperactivating attachment strategy. This intervention strategy serves the purpose of regulating the patient's dysregulated emotions, which they can generalize to other emotionally significant relationships. An outside observer might characterize a typical session as firmly boundaried and emotionally regulated—the therapist creates the psychic space required for mentalizing feelings and intentions. The patient's internal working model gradually shifts from anxious-resistant to secure, one mentalizing intervention at a time.

Trusting the Spirit

In the context of whatever interaction structure the therapist and patient co-create, the therapist has broad latitude to intervene in their moment-to-moment interactions. The therapist must follow their spiritual intuition in both listening and responding to the patient's verbal and nonverbal communications, especially their emotional expressions. Just as the best jazz musicians follow wherever the Spirit leads them, so too do the best spiritually informed therapists rely on their spiritual intuition to intervene based on the moment-to-moment feelings experienced by the patient (see Chapter 5). The prophet Elijah waited to hear God's "gentle whisper" (I Kings 19:12; NIV, 1978). Did the whisper come from without or within? No one knows. Regardless of the location, the best spiritually informed therapists follow this gentle whisper—their spiritual intuition—in response to the patient's emotional expressions.

The goal of AIP is to produce a transformation of the internal working model of attachment relationships from insecurity to earned security. Only by trusting the therapeutic process will the therapist know when and how to provide a gentle challenge to the patient's secondary (defensive) attachment strategy to regulate the patient's emotions and experiment with a different mode of relatedness that might inch them closer to vulnerability and trust in someone outside themselves. The therapist becomes a new, unfamiliar caregiver who provides an environment of vulnerability, safety, and acceptance rather than the old, familiar caregiver who provided an environment of inconsistent emotional responsiveness, consistent emotional unresponsiveness, or frightening or frightened responsiveness (see Chapter 5).

The therapist can apply deactivating and hyperactivating attachment strategies equally to clinical material related to the attachment relationships to the caregivers during childhood as well as clinical material related to the attachment relationship to a Higher Power. Assisting the patient in shifting from using a secondary attachment strategy with respect to the caregivers during childhood to using the primary attachment strategy of proximity-seeking, openness, and balanced emotion regulation can generalize to the patient's attachment relationship to a Higher Power and vice versa. The patient's gradual shift from an insecure to a secure attachment relationship to a Higher Power can also generalize to the attachment relationships to the caregivers during childhood as well as to other emotionally significant relationships. Thus, no matter where the conversation about attachment relationships begins (i.e., caregivers, Higher Power, or even therapist), earned security in one attachment relationship can extend to the patient's other attachment relationships. Healing in these attachment relationships represents the royal road to emotional and spiritual well-being.

References

Ainsworth, M. D. S., Blehar, M. C., Waters, E., & Wall, S. (1978). *Patterns of attachment: A psychological study of the strange situation.* Erlbaum.

Alexander, F., & French, T. M. (1946). *Psychoanalytic therapy: Principles and application.* Ronald.

Barrett, J. L. (2012). *Born believers: The science of children's religious belief.* Free Press.

Bion, W. R. (1967). Notes on memory and desire. In J. Aguayo and B. Malin (Eds.), *Wilfred Bion: Los Angeles seminars and supervision* (pp. 136–138). Karnac Books.

Bowlby, J. (1980). *Attachment and loss*: Vol. 3. Loss, sadness and depression. Basic Books.

Daniel, S. I. F. (2015). *Adult attachment patterns in a treatment context: Relationship and narrative.* Routledge.

Dozier, M. (2003). Attachment-based treatment for vulnerable children. *Attachment and Human Development, 5,* 253–257.

Dylan, B. (1975). Shelter from the storm. In *Blood on the tracks.* Universal Music Publishing Group.

Feuerbach, L. (1841). *The essence of Christianity* (G. Eliot, Trans.). Cosimo Inc.

Freud, S. (1913). Totem and taboo: Some points of agreement between the mental lives of savages and neurotics (1913 [1912–13]). In J. Strachey (Ed. and Trans.), *The standard edition of the complete psychological works of Sigmund Freud.* (Vol. 13). Hogarth Press.

Goodman, G. (2025). *Practical applications of transforming the attachment relationship to God: Using attachment-informed psychotherapy.* Routledge.

Granqvist, P. (2020). *Attachment in religion and spirituality: A wider view.* Guilford Press.

Granqvist, P., & Kirkpatrick, L. A. (2018). Attachment and religious representations and behavior. In J. Cassidy & P. R. Shaver (Eds.), *Handbook of attachment: Theory, research, and clinical applications* (pp. 917–940). Guilford Press.

Hesse, E. (2018). The adult attachment interview: Protocol, method of analysis, and selected empirical studies, 1985–2015. In J. Cassidy & P. R. Shaver (Eds.), *Handbook of attachment: Theory, research, and clinical applications* (pp. 553–597). Guilford Press.

James, W. (1902). *The varieties of religious experience: A study in human nature.* Longmans, Green, and Co.

Kaswan, P., & Roy, A. (2024). Unearthing calf burials among Asian elephants Elephas maximus Linnaeus, 1758 (Mammalia: Proboscidea: Elephantidae) in northern Bengal, India. *Journal of Threatened Taxa, 16,* 24615–24818.

Kirkpatrick, L. A. (1998). God as a substitute AF: A longitudinal study of adult attachment style and religious change in college students. *Personality and Social Psychology Bulletin, 24,* 961–973.

Kirkpatrick, L. A. (2005). *Attachment, evolution, and the psychology of religion.* Guilford Press.

Kirkpatrick, L. A., & Shaver, P. R. (1990). Attachment theory and religion: Childhood attachments, religious beliefs, and conversion. *Journal for the Scientific Study of Religion, 29,* 315–334.

Kohut, H. (1984). *How does analysis cure?* University of Chicago Press.

Main, M., & Goldwyn, R. (1989). Adult attachment rating and classification system. Unpublished manuscript. Department of Psychology, University of California, Berkeley.

Main, M., & Solomon, J. (1990). Procedures for identifying infants as disorganized/disoriented during the Ainsworth Strange Situation. In M. T. Greenberg, D. Cicchetti, & E. M. Cummings (Eds.), *Attachment in the preschool years: Theory, research, and intervention* (pp. 121–160). University of Chicago Press.

NIV (New International Version). (1978). *The holy Bible.* Zondervan.

Rizzuto, A.-M. (1979). *The birth of the living God: A psychoanalytic study.* University of Chicago Press.

Rohr, R. (2016). *The divine dance: The trinity and your transformation.* Whitaker House.

Slade, A. (1999). Attachment theory and research: Implications for the theory and practice of individual psychotherapy with adults. In J. Cassidy & P. R. Shaver (Eds.), *Handbook of attachment: Theory, research, and clinical applications* (pp. 575–594). Guilford Press.

Author Index

Blehar, M. C. 3, 14, 27, **28**, 29, 31, 34, 41, 44, 159
Bluemke, M. 57
Bodhi, B. 6
Bordin, E. S. 89, 101, 105
Borman-Spurrell, E. 38
Borowitz, K. C. 39
Botein, S. 30
Bowlby, J. 3, 4, 7, 14, 23–7, 29, 44, 58, 61, 72, 75, 87–8, 91–2, 98, 103, 117, 120, 159
Boyatzis, C. J. 3, 18
Bradley, R. 42, 62–5, 89, 101, 103
Bradley, S. 38
Brand, B. L. 109
Braunwald, K. G. 30
Brennan, K. A. 41, 43
Bresgi, I. 39
Bretherton, I. 29, 31–4, 39
Bretscher, J. P. 61
Briggs, R. 99
Britner, P. A. 39
Britton, R. 133
Broberg, A. G. 73
Bronfman, E. 30
Brooks-Gunn, J. 31, 34
Brown, L. G. 118
Bruschweiler-Stern, N. 93–4, 135–7
Bryant, A. N. 8
Buchsbaum, H. K. 34
Burke, L. A. 9
Burker, E. J. 8
Burns, P. 88
Butler, S. F. 128

Cameron, J. 8
Carlson, E. A. 30, 38
Carlson, V. 30
Carr, A. C. 26
Carter, J. D. 3–4
Casement, P. J. 130, 138, 152
Cassibba, R. 70
Cassidy, J. 1, 14, 27, **28**, 29–34, 37, 38, 44, 61, 92, 117
Castle, D. 38
Castonguay, L. G. 155
Charone, J. K. 118
Chefetz, R. 109
Christie, J. 8
Chung, H. 91
Cibelli, C. D. 30
Cicchetti, D. 30, 34

Clark, A. 129
Clark, C. L. 41, 43
Clarke, A. 11, 41
Clarkin, J. 41, 87
Clarkin, J. F. 29, 38, 78, 87, 101, 103, 104, 118, 119, 121, 123, 133, 136, 144
Clausell, E. 11, 41
Clyman, R. B. 34
Coble, H. M. 87
Cohen, C. 68
Cohen, L. 39
Cohn, J. 5
Cole, B. S. 10
Cole, H. E. 38, 119, 120, 144, 145, 153
Cole-Detke, H. 38
Collins, N. L. 41
Connell, D. B. 30
Coolbear, J. 40, 41
Cooper, G. 117, 120, 150, 151
Costantini, A. 70
Cox, M. J. 39
Cox, S. M. 42
Crago, M. 118
Cramer, B. 39
Crastnopol, M. 118
Crittenden, P. M. 101, 122, 128
Crnic, K. 39
Crook, R. E. 103
Crowell, J. A. 10, 29, 41, 61, 103
Cue, K. L. 118, 119, 121, 130, 131, 144, 147, 153
Culp, A. M. 34

Dabriwal, V. 85
Daniel, S. I. F. 14, 30, 61–6, 73, 163, 165
D'Arcis, U. 39
Datta, A. 35
Davis, J. A. 8
Davis, M. K. 89
de Haas, M. A. 41
De Jong, A. **28**, 29, 31, 34
De Muralt, M. 39
de Wolff, M. 29, 117
Dean, T. 3, 10
Deane, K. E. 34
DeSear, P. 39
Dharma, K. 6
Diamond, D. 41, 87, 101, 119, 121, 144
Dozier, M. 9, 11, 38, 42, 67, 76, 86, 87, 93, 99, 101, 118–22, 124, 126, 129–31, 144, 147, 150, 153, 166
Dylan, B. 159

Subject Index

For Product Safety Concerns and Information please contact our EU
representative GPSR@taylorandfrancis.com
Taylor & Francis Verlag GmbH, Kaufingerstraße 24, 80331 München, Germany

www.ingramcontent.com/pod-product-compliance
Lightning Source LLC
Chambersburg PA
CBHW070337270326
41926CB00017B/3900

9 781032 913704